Sensorial Investigations

Perspectives on Sensory History

Books in the Perspectives on Sensory History series maintain a historical basis for work on the senses, examining how the experiences of seeing, hearing, smelling, tasting, and touching have shaped the ways in which people have understood their worlds.

Mark M. Smith, General Editor
University of South Carolina, USA

EDITORIAL BOARD
Camille Bégin
University of Toronto, Canada

Martin A. Berger
Art Institute of Chicago, USA

Karin Bijsterveld
University of Maastricht, Netherlands

Constance Classen
Concordia University, Canada

Kelvin E. Y. Low
National University of Singapore, Singapore

Bodo Mrozek
University of Potsdam, Germany

Alex Purves
University of California, Los Angeles, USA

Richard Cullen Rath
University of Hawaii, USA

Sensorial Investigations

A History of the Senses in Anthropology, Psychology, and Law

David Howes

The Pennsylvania State University Press
University Park, Pennsylvania

Library of Congress Cataloging-in-Publication Data

Names: Howes, David, 1957– author.
Title: Sensorial investigations : a history of the senses in anthropology, psychology, and law / David Howes.
Other titles: Perspectives on sensory history.
Description: University Park, Pennsylvania : The Pennsylvania State University Press, [2023] | Series: Perspectives on sensory history | Includes bibliographical references and index.
Summary: "Presents a history of the senses in the fields of anthropology, psychology, and law, identifying important shifts and key disciplinary concerns"—Provided by publisher.
Identifiers: LCCN 2022060800 | ISBN 9780271095004 (hardback) | ISBN 9780271095011 (paperback)
Subjects: LCSH: Senses and sensation—History. | Senses and sensation—Social aspects. | Anthropology—History. | Psychology—History.
Classification: LCC BF233 .H698 2023 | DDC 152.1—dc23/eng/20230217
LC record available at https://lccn.loc.gov/2022060800

Copyright © 2023 David Howes
All rights reserved
Printed in the United States of America
Published by The Pennsylvania State University Press,
University Park, PA 16802–1003

The Pennsylvania State University Press is a member of the Association of University Presses.

It is the policy of The Pennsylvania State University Press to use acid-free paper. Publications on uncoated stock satisfy the minimum requirements of American National Standard for Information Sciences—Permanence of Paper for Printed Library Material, ANSI Z39.48–1992.

FOR MY STUDENTS

Contents

List of Illustrations [ix]
Acknowledgments [xii]

Prologue: Uncommon Sense [1]

PART 1: THE SENSES IN ANTHROPOLOGY

1. The Measurement of the Senses [21]
2. The Enculturation of the Senses [47]
3. Breaking Research in Sensory Anthropology [81]

PART 2: THE SENSES IN PSYCHOLOGY

4. Unhinging the Senses: From Sensation to Calculation [117]
5. Anthropology Contra Phenomenology, Ecological Psychology, and Sensory Science [144]

PART 3: BETWEEN HISTORY AND ANTHROPOLOGY

6. Sensory Exchange: Crossing Disciplines [177]
7. Cross-Cultural Exchange as Sensory Exchange: The Encounter Between China and the West in the Early Modern Period [190]

8. Smoke and Mirrors: A Sensory Analysis
of Indigenous-Settler Commerce and Covenants
in North America   [208]

Epilogue: The Senses of Justice   [224]

Notes   [233]
References   [245]
Index   [273]

Illustrations

1. Three representations of a Canaque (Kanak) village, New Caledonia   [40]
2. Albrecht Dürer, *Draughtsman Making a Perspective Drawing of a Recumbent Woman*, ca. 1600   [57]
3. David Garneau, *Grandfather Contemplating Western Ocularcentrism*, 2021, and *Grandfather Archived*, 2021   [74]
4. Zeph Thibodeau, *Machine Menagerie*, 2019   [95]
5. Chronogenica, *Chronogenica*, 2019   [97]
6. Candles in the sun, Oslo, Norway   [99]
7. Courtyard of Thornbury Castle   [105]
8. Roses and bee boles at Thornbury Castle   [107]
9. Verso of the drawing/table for interdisciplinary tools used by the artisan   [108]
10. The Four Elements of classical Greek cosmology   [119]
11. Mendeleev's periodic table of elements, 1869   [126]
12. Massasoit handing a ceremonial pipe to John Carver, March 1621   [212]

Acknowledgments

I begin by acknowledging that my two workplaces, Concordia University and McGill University, are situated on unceded Indigenous lands. Tiohtià:ke/Montréal has long served as a site of meeting and exchange among the Haudenosaunee and Anishinaabeg and other peoples. My research has involved learning from Indigenous peoples of many different lands, and I am acutely conscious of the need to engage with Indigenous histories and perspectives in the contemporary world.

My intellectual debts to fellow scholars are many. First, I wish to thank Constance Classen for all of the inspiration I have derived from her seminal and ongoing work on the cultural history of the senses. I am also very grateful to a number of my former teachers for their mentorship: Roger McDonnell, Rodney Needham, Gilles Bibeau, and Ellen Corin in anthropology; Blaine Baker, Rod Macdonald, and H. P. Glenn in law. Next, I wish to thank my colleagues in the Department of Sociology and Anthropology at Concordia University, and the members of the Centre for Sensory Studies, especially Chris Salter, Jordan LeBel, and Geneviève Sicotte, for the many thought-provoking exchanges we have had over the years. I also wish to thank my colleagues, past and present, in the Faculty of Law at McGill and the McGill Centre for Human Rights and Legal Pluralism, for their encouragement and interest.

I am grateful to the continuously expanding network of sensory studies scholars (whom I have gotten to know at conferences, through editing books and *The Senses and Society* journal, and other connections) for contributing to my thinking about and with the senses. As regards this volume, I particularly wish to acknowledge the many stimulating discussions I have had with Dor Abrahamson, Jennifer Biddle, Mikkel Bille, Michael Bull, Rupert Cox, Elizabeth Edwards, Steve Feld, David Garneau, Kathryn Linn Geurts, Sheryl Hamilton, Anna Harris, Michael Herzfeld, Hsuan Hsu, Caroline A. Jones, Susanne Küchler, David Le Breton, Cheryl L'Hirondelle, Lawrence Marks, Maureen Matthews, Birgit Meyer, Richard Newhauser, Charles Spence, David Sutton, Phillip Vannini, and Jojada Verrips.

I am grateful to the following publishers, editors, and coauthors for granting me permission to reuse select material in this book.

The first section of chapter 1 began as a review of *La mesure des sens*, by Nélia Dias, which was published in *Current Anthropology* 47 (2006). The following two sections, on the work of W. H. R. Rivers and then of Franz Boas, have gone through several iterations, the latest being "Boasian Soundings" in *Amerikastudien / American Studies* 63, no. 4 (2018). The discussion of the work of Marcel Mauss and Maurice Leenhardt in the fourth section is derived from an article I cowrote with Anthony Synnott entitled "From Measurement to Meaning," published in *Anthropos* 87 (1992).

Chapter 2 is comprised of new material, save for section 2, on the critique of textualism, which builds on the discussion of this topic in chapter 1 of my book *Sensual Relations: Engaging the Senses in Culture and Social Theory*, published by the University of Michigan Press in 2003. The material in chapter 3 is also new, save for the third section, which derives from the preface I wrote for *Sensibles ethnographies: Decalages sensoriels et attentionnels dans la recherche anthropologique*, edited by Sisa Calapi, Helma Korzybska, Marie Mazzella di Bosco, and Pierre Peraldi-Mittelette, published by Éditions PÉTRA in 2022.

The first two sections of chapter 4 have been in gestation for a long time. I first tried out some of the ideas presented there in my introduction to *The Sixth Sense Reader*, which was published by Berg of Oxford in 2009 (and latterly transferred to Routledge). The third section of this chapter first came out as "Making Sense of and with the Senses," the prologue to *Sensory Experiences: Exploring Meaning and the Senses*, coauthored by Danièle Dubois and four of her former students, published by John Benjamins in 2021 (https://benjamins.com/catalog/celcr.24).

The first section of chapter 5 derives from an article in *Anthropological Theory* 22 (2022), entitled "The Misperception of the Environment." The third section is taken from a chapter I wrote called "The Science of Sensory Evaluation: An Ethnographic Critique" at the invitation of Adam Drazin and Susanne Küchler for a book they edited entitled *The Social Life of Materials*, published by Bloomsbury in 2015 (and subsequently transferred to Routledge). The material in both these sections has been revised substantially.

The inspiration to write chapter 6 stemmed from Mark Smith's invitation to contribute a paper to a round table he organized for a special issue of the *Journal of American History* 95 (2008) on "The Senses in American History."

Chapter 7 began as a paper I presented at a conference on "The Senses in Sino-Western Cultural Exchanges in the Early Modern Period," organized by Shaoxin Dong, at the International Center for Studies of Chinese Civilization, Fudan University, Shanghai, in May 2015. It was subsequently published in English and Chinese translation in a book edited by Shaoxin Dong, which bore the same title as the conference, from Fudan University Press (2018).

The centerpiece of chapter 8 is the analysis of the *Delgamuukw* decision of the Supreme Court of Canada in section 2.

I broached the analysis of this decision, and some of the historical background to it, in a chapter called "Law's Sensorium," which appeared in *Sensing Law*, edited by Sheryl N. Hamilton and four of her colleagues at Carleton University, published by Routledge in 2017. Also contributing to the discussion in this chapter was the analysis I undertook together with Constance Classen for "The Feel of Law" chapter of our book, *Ways of Sensing*, published by Routledge in 2013.

I would like to express my heartfelt gratitude to Mark M. Smith for his enthusiastic support of this project and to Kathryn Bourque Yahner and the staff at Penn State University Press, as well as copyeditor Dana Henricks, for seeing the manuscript through the production process. I am particularly grateful to the two anonymous reviewers of an earlier draft for their many insightful comments.

Finally, as always, I am mindful of the tremendous debt I owe to my family for their continuous support.

Prologue
Uncommon Sense

> [The] Eye is as knowing as the Ear, and the Ear as knowing as the
> Nose, and the Nose as knowing as the Tongue.... The Heads Braines
> cannot ingross all knowledge to themselves.
> —Margaret Cavendish (1623–1673), Duchess of Newcastle

A Note to the Reader

Psychology teaches that the brain perceives, not the eyes or ears. According to the latest research in cognitive neuroscience, sensation and perception are subordinate to cognition and the way the brain is wired (Seth 2021). However, critics argue that this smacks of "neuromania" (Tallis 2011), or brain fetishism. They do not deny that the brain plays a role in perception, but they do question the way all knowledge is arrogated to the brain. "Sentience takes us outside ourselves," writes the cultural anthropologist Michael Taussig (1993, 38). Perception is not just down to the brain; it is also up to our culture. Neuroscientists need to get out of their own heads.

Fortunately, psychology no longer "owns" the study of cognition, perception, and sensation the way it formerly did. Historians and anthropologists have been steadily encroaching on its terrain since the early 1990s. Historians claim that the senses have a history, and anthropologists argue that there are as many psychologies as there are cultures.

The senses have a history? The reader may wonder how that can be the case when our sense impressions are so fugacious and ephemeral, so immediate, so subjective. *Chacun à son goût* (To each their own taste). But this is a mirage, a trick of perspective. As historians and anthropologists aver, the sensorium is a *historical formation* and the senses are *loaded* with cultural values. It is just that you cannot so easily see this when you only ever study "sensory processing" within the confines of a psychology laboratory, or worse, an MRI machine (Dumit 2004; Joyce 2008). Psychology ignores "the social life of the senses" at its peril. The presumed privacy and idiosyncrasy of sense experience is a myth, propped up by the ideology of "possessive individualism" (Macpherson 1962).

Psychologists are naturally wont to psychologize the senses. But historians and anthropologists know otherwise. The senses are *socialized*—that is, "the sensible" (*le sensible*) or "the perceptual" is carved up and distributed along gender, class, ethnic or racial, and other social lines, and the individual is a product of the intersection of these lines (Classen 1998; Hsu 2019). The senses, like our very selves, are "relationally produced" (i.e., made, not given).

Sensorial Investigations challenges many commonsense assumptions about how the senses function. This book takes uncommon sense as its point of departure, and its argument ricochets between anthropology, psychology, history—and the law.

The law is responsible for the normalization of perception. It does so by enforcing a particular sensory regime. Law is also supposed to transcend the senses. Think of Lady Justice with her blindfold and scales (Jay 1999). Surely, justice should be blind, judges ought to be impartial, and right reason must prevail in the court of law. "The rule of law and not of men" is the cornerstone of our legal system. But what if we ask, with Alasdair MacIntyre (1988): Whose justice? Which rationality? Might it be the better part of justice to confront these questions, to lift the blindfold, and recognize that our sense of justice is just that (i.e., rooted in the sensible)?

I hold five university degrees (three in anthropology, two in law), and I currently teach in both the Department of Sociology and Anthropology at Concordia University and the Faculty of Law at McGill University. This dual formation has instilled in me a sort of double vision. Within anthropology, my research has focused on charting the varieties of sensory experience across cultures, and within law, I have been primarily concerned with exploring issues of legal pluralism. In what follows, I would like to share this double vision with you, the reader. This book is about crossing disciplines, crossing cultures and historical periods, and crossing the senses, to see what will out. Call it cross-eyed if you wish. But as I hope to show, blurring vision by interweaving the wisdom of the senses of other cultures and other historical periods can help sharpen one's sense of what doing justice entails.

How Anthropology Came to Its Senses

A wave of interest in the senses as both object of study and means of inquiry has swept over anthropology in recent decades. This resulted in the displacement of the conventional anthropological methodology of participant observation and instituted "participant sensation" in its place. In *The Life of the Senses: Introduction to a Modal Anthropology*, François Laplantine ([2005] 2015, 2) sums up the gist of this approach as follows: "The experience of [ethnographic] fieldwork is an experience of sharing in the sensible [*le partage du sensible*]. We observe, we listen, we speak with others, we partake of their cuisine, we try to feel along with them what they experience." The former stress on observation limited many anthropologists from fully immersing themselves in the lifeworlds of other cultures: the new emphasis on sensation enables the investigation of multiple forms of sensory expression and communication. Furthermore, the anthropology of the senses promotes a critical awareness of how social hierarchies and conflicts are perpetuated through a diverse range of sensory channels.

Allowing the senses in has precipitated many keen insights into how both social *con-sensus* ("with the senses") and social *dis-sensus* are formed and also sets the anthropology of the senses apart from other subfields of anthropology. For example, in contrast to the subfield of linguistic anthropology, with its focus on language, or visual anthropology, with its emphasis on visual documentation—and in contrast to symbolic anthropology, with its stress on interpretation, or political anthropology, with its focus on ideology—sensory anthropology studies *all* the fields of social life, including the life of the mind, from a multi- and intersensory perspective. Thus, sensory anthropology corrects for the verbocentrism of the linguistic and the ocularcentrism of the filmic; it expands the focus from meaning-making (or "the symbolic") to *sense-making*; and it shifts attention from the prevailing focus on political communities as "imagined" (Anderson 2006) to how they are sensed and lived (Trnka, Dureau, and Park 2013). After the sensory turn in anthropological understanding, as theorized by Ulf Hannerz in an essay on nationalism in Europe, "political anthropology . . .

becomes an anthropology of the senses, an anthropology of emotion, an anthropology of the body" (Hannerz 2006, 278).

Part 1 of this book explores the history of the senses in anthropology.[1] It starts by examining the work of Paul Broca and the Société d'Anthropologie de Paris (SAP) (1860–90) and that of W. H. R. Rivers and the Cambridge Anthropological Expedition to the Torres Strait of 1898. In the physical/psychological anthropology of this period, the focus was on the measurement of the senses. Diverse tests, inspired by advances in psychophysics, were deployed to gauge the "sensory acuity" of Indigenous peoples, with the general expectation that the results would conform to the racist stereotypes that attributed greater sensuality to non-Westerners. As will be shown in the chapters of part 1, over the course of the twentieth century, the experimental (and often problematic) methods of the first generation of anthropologists (Broca, Rivers, and also Franz Boas) were supplanted by the experiential methods of a second cohort (Marcel Mauss, Maurice Leenhardt, and Margaret Mead) and then the embodied or phenomenological as well as media-centered methods of a third cohort (including Paul Stoller, the present writer, Sarah Pink, Ruth Finnegan, and Kathryn Linn Geurts, among numerous others). This transition resulted in a shift from an etic (i.e., external, typically Western, supposedly universal) perspective to what strived to approximate an emic (internal, local) perspective on "the five senses." The anthropologists of the second and third waves came to question the hegemony of Western perceptual psychology when it comes to understanding how the senses function. The idea that there are multiple perceptual psychologies—indeed, that there are as many psychologies as there are cultures—took shape. This in turn opened the way for the liberation of the senses from the laboratory (in that anthropologists study the senses in everyday contexts), and also contributed to exposing the cultural contingency of the diverse ways in which the senses are discriminated or bureaucratized, hierarchized, and alternately pacified or overloaded in contemporary society (Jones 2006a; Howes and Classen 2013, chap. 5).

Part 2 of this book, "The Senses in Psychology," investigates how the senses have been framed within the Western tradition, beginning with Aristotle's famous dictum in *De Anima* (On the Soul) "There are five senses and five senses only—sight, hearing, smell, taste, and touch."[2] It goes on to examine how the British philosopher John Locke departed from the Aristotelian tradition with his account of sense perception in *An Essay Concerning Human Understanding* ([1690] 1975), and laid the foundation for modern experimental psychology (i.e., the confinement of the senses within the psychology laboratory, and inside the head). It is argued that this refiguration may be seen as a process of "unhinging the senses" both from one another and from the cosmos. The historical purview of part 2 is accordingly quite broad. It has to be expansive in order for us to fathom the original connection between psychology and cosmology and how this later came undone. Thus, chapter 3 ponders the implications of the ontological transformation in the constitution of the material world that was precipitated by the Scientific Revolution, when the bottom fell out of the sensory cosmologies of premodernity as a result of several developments, including the visualization of the universe through telescopes and microscopes and the dissolution of the Four Elements of classical/premodern cosmology (earth, air, fire, and water) into the dozens of elements of the periodic table.

Chapter 4 goes on to examine the fallout of the cognitive revolution within psychology, beginning in the mid-twentieth century, when the mind or brain came to be conceptualized on the model of a computer program, and, in a related development, perception was reduced to the idea of "information processing." To this overly programmatic, totally instrumental, and thoroughly modern vision of how the senses function, this book opposes the archaic notion of "the sensorium."

The Sensorium as a Focus for Cultural Studies

The sensorium is a remarkably holistic notion. In the early modern period, it referred primarily to the "seat of sensation in the brain" and still carries this meaning today. But it also extended to include the circumference of perception. In illustration of the latter point, the *Oxford English Dictionary* quotes one usage from 1714: "The noblest and most exalted Way of considering this infinite Space [referring to "the Universe"] is that of Sir Isaac Newton, who calls it the *Sensorium* of the Godhead," and another from 1861: "Rome became the common sensorium of Europe, and through Rome all the several portions of Latin Europe sympathized and felt with each other." This expanded sense (cosmological and social) of the term "sensorium" was countered by the privatization of sensation that occurred with the rise of Lockean empiricism. The interiorization of the sensorium was further entrenched under the aegis of cognitive neuroscience, which reduced the definition of perception to "patterns of neural activity." The construction of perception within cognitive neuroscience is aptly summed up in the following quote: "The events that culminate in perception begin with specialized receptor cells that convert a particular form of physical energy into bioelectric currents. Different sensors are sensitive to different types of energy, so the properties of the receptor cells determine the modality of a sensory system. Ionic currents are the currency of neural information processing, and current flows that begin in the receptors are transmitted through complex networks of interconnected neurons and, in the end result in a *pattern of brain activity* we call perception" (Hughes 2001, 7, emphasis added). Thus, advances in cognitive neuroscience precipitated a retraction of sensation from the interface between sense organ and world to focus on the neural pathways leading from receptor cells to brain.

This tide was partially turned by the media theorist Walter J. Ong, a student of Marshall McLuhan, in a section of *The Presence of the Word* (1967) entitled "The Shifting Sensorium," which was in turn reprinted as the opening chapter in *The Varieties of Sensory Experience* (Howes 1991). Ong took up McLuhan's notion of cultures as consisting of contrasting "sense-ratios" in accordance with the prevailing medium of communication—namely, speech, which privileges the oral-aural; writing (chirography) and print (typography), which both privilege the visual; and electronic communication. On the basis of this schema, which conceptualizes media as "extensions of the senses," Ong proposed that "given sufficient knowledge of the sensorium exploited within a specific culture, one could probably define the culture as a whole in all its aspects," including its cosmology or "worldview" (Ong 1991, 28). Ong was adamant, however, that the term "worldview" should not be applied to the cosmologies of societies without writing—or "oral societies." Given the dynamic nature of sound in contrast to the distanciating nature of vision, the cosmologies of oral societies present the world not "as view" but rather "as event" (Ong 1969).

While there are serious difficulties with McLuhan and Ong's "Great Divide" theory of the evolution of human consciousness, as we shall see presently, it nevertheless precipitated a heightened focus on the cultural mediation of sense experience, as exemplified by Paul Stoller in *The Taste of Ethnographic Things: The Senses in Anthropology* (1989),[3] Ruth Finnegan's *Communicating: The Multiple Modes of Human Interconnection* (2002), and Kathryn Linn Geurts's *Culture and the Senses: Bodily Ways of Knowing in an African Community* (2002a), among other works. In fulfilment of Ong's suggestion that "the sensorium is a fascinating focus for cultural studies" (Ong 1991, 28), the *cultural* anthropology of the senses was born, and the latter body of work has substantiated the multiple respects in which, as Oliver Sacks once put it, "culture tunes our neurons" (cited in Howes 2005a, 22).

The tidal turn, intimated by Ong, has had ripple effects far beyond anthropology. These can be seen in the way MIT art historian Caroline A. Jones recuperates and expands the original (early modern) definition of "sensorium" in "The Mediated Sensorium." This essay figures as the introduction to *Sensorium: Embodied Experience, Technology and Contemporary Art* (2006b), which is the title of both the 2006 art exhibition she curated and the exhibition catalog she edited to go with it. She writes, "The human sensorium has always been mediated.... But over the past few decades that condition has greatly intensified. Amplified, shielded, channeled, prosthetized, simulated, stimulated, irritated—our sensorium is more mediated today than ever before" (Jones 2006a, 5). In her introductory essay, Jones sets the stage for showcasing the artworks she brought together by presenting an analysis of the "segmentation," "bureaucratization," and commodification/instrumentalization of the senses in the culture at large and in the writings of the highly influential mid-twentieth-century New York art critic Clement Greenberg. The latter's work, with its high formalism and repeated warnings against "genre confusion," increased the "sensory demarcation" of art (Candlin 2010) to an extreme degree. Greenberg proclaimed painting to be "for eyesight alone" and pointed to Color Field painting as the purest expression of his dictum (Jones 2006b). Meanwhile, advances in audio technology revolutionized listening by supplying "high fidelity" (hi-fi) recordings and the paraphernalia to go with them, such as surround-sound speaker systems and headphones that enclosed the auditor in an acoustic bubble (Jones 2006a, 28).

As Jones goes on to observe, the age of the ideal modern viewer, as of the hi-fi auditor, has been eclipsed in the ensuing decades as more and more artists, driven by a "desire to escape sense for sensation" and attracted by the idea of sensory *métissage* (in place of purity), have used digital technology to create art that is intersensory or "intermedial." For example, one of the pieces in *Sensorium* consisted of a singing microscope; another translated the body heat of its spectators into the visible spectrum. Thus, according to Jones, art "viewers" in the twenty-first century are increasingly met with "dramatically synaesthetic and kinaesthetic scenarios," with the result that "our experience of mediation itself is where the art happens" (Jones 2006a, 18). Otherwise put: there are no more *objets d'art*, only experiences. Art has come off the wall, and the sensorially neutral space of the modern art gallery, or "White Cube," has come to be suffused with a profusion of sensations—critical sensations, Jones would add: "*Sensorium* dreams that we can come to feel the body pulsing in tandem with its prosthetic extensions and microscopic addenda, that we can learn to partner our proliferating technologies in increasingly coordinated, supple, and critically conscious ways" (44).[4]

What Jones accomplished in *Sensorium* is echoed within anthropology in the practice of sensory ethnography. In one of its incarnations, sensory ethnography involves sense-based inquiry (in contrast to language-based or image-based inquiry) as exemplified by the work of such anthropologists as Kathryn Linn Geurts. Geurts's *Culture and the Senses* (2002a) is notable for its inquiry into the local understanding of the sensorium and social vocation of the senses among the Anlo-Ewe of Ghana. Similarly, Sarah Pink's *Doing Sensory Ethnography* (2009) provides a helpful catalog of tips for doing sense-based research (see further Howes and Classen 1991).

The term also figures in the name of the Sensory Ethnography Lab (SEL) at Harvard University directed by Lucien Castaing-Taylor. The SEL specializes in the production of sensational cinema, such as the documentary *Leviathan* (Castaing-Taylor and Paravel 2012). Filmed aboard a North Atlantic fishing trawler, this film graphically portrayed violence toward marine animals and had a profoundly visceral impact on its audiences because of its sensationalism (Pavsek 2018). It is also noteworthy for the absence of any voice-over, a feature consistent with Castaing-Taylor's denunciation, as a champion of visual anthropology, of the "linguification" of meaning in anthropology at large (Taylor [2014] 1994, 1996; see further Howes 2016).

A third incarnation of sensory ethnography can be discerned in the multiplication of the modalities of anthropological research as evidenced by the substitution of the term "multimodal anthropologies" (Collins, Durington, and Gill 2017) for "visual anthropology" as the title of the section of the *American Anthropologist* formerly dedicated to reviewing ethnographic films. This development was anticipated by the publication of *A Different Kind of Ethnography: Imaginative Practices and Creative Methodologies* (Elliott and Culhane 2017). Across its six chapters, this book charted and exemplified how anthropologists have taken to experimenting with embodied social practices such as walking, staging collaborative theatrical productions, treating writing (including poetry and drawing) as a practice of "worlding," and creatively editing sound and visual recordings to "conceptualize, design, conduct, and communicate ethnographic research" (Elliott and Culhane 2017, 3). This explosion in "imaginative ethnography," as Elliott and Culhane style it, has opened up a space "between art and anthropology" (Schneider and Wright 2010), where ethnographers experiment with artistic means of expression, and, conversely, artists increasingly experiment with ethnography to generate new ways of being and knowing.

The third part of this book, "Between History and Anthropology," presents an altogether different psychology of perception from the sort that is theorized (and enforced) within the confines of the laboratory. Chapter 6 addresses the highly fruitful exchanges between the disciplines of history and anthropology instigated by the great French social historian Alain Corbin in an essay entitled "Histoire et anthropologie sensorielle" (1990). Corbin introduced the idea of "the history of the sensible" (Corbin and Heuré 2000), which dovetails nicely with the ideas of the sociality of sensation, cultural contingency of sense-making, and politics of perception that come out of the anthropology of the senses.

The pointers for doing sensory history that Corbin signaled in "Histoire et anthropologie sensorielle" include the need to take account of "the habitus that determines the frontier between the perceived and the unperceived, and, even more, of the norms which decree what is spoken and what left unspoken," and being alert to the dangers of "confusing the reality of the employment of the senses and the picture of this employment decreed by observers" (Corbin 2005, 232, 235).

The crossing of history and anthropology proposed by Corbin forms the basis of the new theory of "the archaeology of perception,"[5] or better, "historical anthropology of the senses and sensation" advocated in the ensuing chapters of part 3. There, this new paradigm is applied to the analysis of the life of the senses during two pivotal historical periods: namely, the encounter between European and Chinese civilizations during the advent of East-West trade in the early modern period (chapter 7) and the encounter between European settlers and the Indigenous peoples of the land now known as North America during the colonial period (chapter 8). These "first contact" situations are of interest to us for the way they throw the contours of the sensoria of the parties to the conjuncture into relief. Equally illuminating is the study of the ways in which the cultural divide was bridged through sensory exchange—that is, the traffic in goods that were prized for their sensory qualities.

Doing Justice by the Senses

Weaving in and out of the chapters of parts 2 and 3, there is a stress on the politics of perception and, especially in chapter 8, on doing justice to and by the senses.[6] What is a just sensory order? This question takes on added urgency in the context of the current conjuncture when, as a result of the globalization of the economy and the upsurge of international migration, "*les milieux* are all *mixtes*" (Geertz 2001, 86); that is, we live in an increasingly multicultural world where difference no longer begins at the borders of societies but arises within them. It is a matter of first importance in such circumstances to extend comity to the many different "ways of sensing the world" that culture-bearers bring with them when they migrate or are displaced. Holding that "When in Rome, do as the Romans do" would be to forget that Rome was once "the common sensorium of Europe" (as noted above). The roads that led to Rome were all two-way streets, and they allowed the various parts of Latin Europe to "sympathize and feel with each other." Sympathizing does not entail identifying. Rather, it involves sensing and thinking across divisions—from the divisions of the sensorium to the divisions of civil society (or "the State"), including the divisions along gender, class, and ethnic or racialized lines. Only in this way can we arrive at the "enlargement of mind" of which the philosopher Hannah Arendt speaks in *Between Past and Future: Six Exercises in Political Thought* (1961).

In "Embodied Diversity and the Challenges to Law," law professor Jennifer Nedelsky encapsulates Arendt's position as follows:

> Judgment, according to Hannah Arendt, is genuinely subjective. . . . But judgment is not therefore merely arbitrary or simply a matter of preference. Judgments, properly understood, are valid for the judging community. . . . What makes it possible for us to genuinely judge, to move beyond our private idiosyncrasies and preferences, is our capacity to achieve an "enlargement of mind." We do this by taking different perspectives into account. . . . [We] imagine trying to persuade others. . . . The more views we are able to take into account, the less likely we are to be locked into one perspective, whether through fear, anger or ignorance. (Nedelsky 1997, 107; see further Arendt 1982)

Nedelsky's account of the conditions for the de-subjectification of judgment (following Arendt) flies in the face of the subjectification of the senses and enclosure of the faculties inside the head within conventional Western perceptual psychology.

The preceding account of "what makes it possible for us genuinely to judge" can be refined further by drawing on the anthropologist Clifford Geertz's account of moral reasoning in "The Uses of Diversity," a lecture delivered at the University of Michigan in 1985. Geertz's point of departure in this lecture is the emergent "perception" that "meaning, in the form of interpretable signs—sounds, images, feelings, artefacts, gestures—comes to exist only within language games, communities of discourse, intersubjective systems of reference, ways of worldmaking; that it arises within the frame of concrete social interaction in which something is a something for a you and a me, and not in some secret grotto in the head" (Geertz 2001, 76).

According to Geertz, then, "meaning" (or what we call "sense-making") is a public activity. He proceeds to interpret the famous line of the philosopher Ludwig Wittgenstein—that "the limits of my language are the limits of my world"—to mean that "the reach of our minds, the range of signs we can manage somehow to interpret, is what defines the intellectual, moral and emotional space in which we live" (Geertz 2001, 77). That reach can be expanded, Geertz maintains, by pondering the "alternative worlds" of other cultures. Such an enlargement of mind has become increasingly crucial, given that "we are living more and more in the midst of an enormous collage" (85), with all the "value conflicts," all the "wrenching moral issues centered around cultural diversity" (86), that that condition entails. "To live in a collage one must in the first place render oneself capable of sorting out its elements, determining what they are (which usually involves determining where they come from and what they amounted to when they were there) and how, practically, they relate to one another, without at the same time blurring one's own sense of one's own location and one's own identity within it" (87).

There is a greater stress on reflexivity to Geertz's approach to moral reasoning than Arendt's. According to Geertz, striving to comprehend what it means to be "on the other side" can in turn engender a deeper understanding of what it means to be "on one's own side" and in turn compel us to explore "the character of the space between" the two sides—that is, to cultivate a sort of double vision, or state of "being of two sensoria" (Howes 2003a, 10–14) about things.

As frameworks for enabling us "genuinely to judge," both Arendt's and Geertz's stances in relation to diversity are powerful and enabling. However, from the standpoint of the anthropology of the senses, Arendt's position is limited by its reliance on the idea of "perspectives" or "views" just as Geertz's is beholden to the Wittgensteinian idea of "language" or "language games." *Sensorial Investigations* maintains that these limits can best be overcome by entertaining the idea of "con-sensus" in lieu of "perspective" or "language," and thereby extending the goal of achieving an "enlargement of mind," or *con-sensus*-building, to include all the faculties. As Geertz's allusion to meaning as arising "within the frame of concrete social interaction" further suggests, the senses have a social vocation. The German sociologist Georg Simmel put this point best in his essay entitled "Sociology of the Senses": "That we become involved in interactions at all depends on the fact that we have a sensory effect upon one another" ([1921] 1997, 107).[7]

To trouble this idea that "the limits of my language are the limits of my world" a bit further, it will be appreciated that Wittgenstein's pronouncement is vulnerable to the criticism that the senses come before language and also extend beyond it (Howes 2022, 13). In other words, this dictum occults the *extralinguistic* dimension of meaning (i.e., sense-making). This occlusion can be seen behind the rise of ordinary language philosophy (also known as analytic philosophy), which took its cue from Wittgenstein's *Tractatus Logico-Philosophicus* (1922). In the words of the highly influential British philosopher Michael Dummett, analytic philosophy holds "first, that, a comprehensive account of thought can be attained through a philosophical account of language, and, second, that a comprehensive account can only be so attained" (Dummett 1993, 4). What a presumptuous thing to say! As if all the epistemological problems of philosophy could be solved through the rectification of language! The verbocentrism of this pronouncement is astonishing.

At the same time, Wittgenstein cannot be held accountable for what others made of his ruminations. In point of fact, his

Philosophical Investigations ([1953] 2009) and other works delved beyond the pale of language. For example, his oeuvre also includes disquisitions on the experience and expression of pain (Wittgenstein 2009) and the perception of color (Wittgenstein 1977), which are eminently sensible topics. He also engaged with anthropology in, for example, his commentary on Sir James George Frazer's *The Golden Bough* (Wittgenstein 1967). Hence, Wittgenstein's cogitations extended beyond the confines of the conventional Western episteme. It is in recognition of, and as a tribute to, these other sensorial and cross-cultural dimensions of Wittgenstein's thought, particularly as taken up and expounded further by Clifford Geertz, that I chose *Sensorial Investigations* as the title for this book.[8]

To conclude, let me lay out the three main propositions that inform this inquiry into the history of the senses in anthropology, psychology, and law:

- The senses are social, and sense-making is a public undertaking—not the private activity posited by psychology.
- The sensorium is a dynamic, multifarious whole, and attending to how the senses are relationally produced is a matter of first analytic importance.
- Doing justice to and by the senses involves building *consensus* while allowing that uncommon sense(s), or *dis-sensus*, also has a role to play.

These propositions should be read in conjunction with the "Twelve Propositions for Sensory Studies" put forward in the prologue to *The Sensory Studies Manifesto* (Howes 2022). That said, let us begin our investigations into the far borderlands of sensation and perception in history and across cultures by examining the history of the senses in anthropology.

PART 1

THE SENSES IN ANTHROPOLOGY

CHAPTER 1

The Measurement of the Senses

The anthropology of the senses can be seen as a subfield of the discipline of anthropology that originated during the "sensory turn" of the 1990s, as observed in the prologue. However, as also noted there, a certain fascination with the senses and matters of perception has actually been with the discipline since its inception in the latter half of the nineteenth century. The measurement of the senses of Indigenous peoples was a major preoccupation of Paul Broca and the Société d'Anthropologie de Paris during its heyday (1860–90), while the conduct of a wide array of psychophysical experiments, overseen by W. H. R. Rivers, was central to the mission of the Cambridge Anthropological Expedition to the Torres Strait of 1898, led by the biologist A. C. Haddon. Meanwhile, in 1883, Franz Boas, after completing his PhD in physics at Kiel University in Germany, went to Baffin Island in the Canadian Arctic to conduct experiments on optical perception (visual psychophysics) among the Inuit. Broca was the founder of French anthropology, Rivers of British anthropology, and Boas of American anthropology, after his move to Columbia University in New York.

This chapter relates how the senses first came to be constituted as an object of inquiry within anthropology at a time when the paradigm of psychophysics, with its focus on the measurement of sensation, reigned supreme in France and the United Kingdom, and how this focus was superseded by a new focus on immersion as the twentieth century unfolded. The chapter concludes with an excursus on the invention of the quantified self and the apparent comeback of psychophysics in the first two decades of the twenty-first century.

Localizing the Senses in the Brain: The Work of the Société d'Anthropologie de Paris

In *La mesure des sens* (2006), Nélia Dias discusses the obsessive interest in the measurement and representation of the senses in the physical anthropological and medical discourse of late nineteenth-century France. Focusing on the scientific debates of the Société d'Anthropologie de Paris (SAP) during the latter half of the nineteenth century, Dias brings out how the longstanding Western (cultural) construct of a hierarchy of the senses (sight, hearing, smell, taste, touch—in that order) was mapped onto the emerging visual topography of the brain. The asymmetrical divisions so produced were in turn linked to other divisions along racial, gender, and class lines. The bourgeois "men of science" who elaborated these divisions, and who prided themselves on the objectivity of their "observations," consistently allied themselves with the "superior" division in each of the following polarities: left versus right hemisphere, frontal versus posterior (parietal, occipital, limbic) lobes, reason versus passion, intelligence or cognition versus sensation, objective versus subjective—and, within the realm of the senses: sight (and hearing) versus smell (and taste and touch). Those relegated to the "inferior" division in this comparative physiology of the senses—or, anatomy of the intellect—included Indigenous peoples, women, and workers.

The idea that each of the sense organs has a specific "localization" in the brain, coupled with the notion of their differential contribution to the generation of "objective" knowledge, served as a physiological charter of first importance with regard to the governance of society by these same "men of science." According to Broca and his peers, sensory discipline was essential to social discipline. The knowledge they produced in the form of tables of distribution of different physical traits (skin and eye color), sensory maladies (color blindness, hearing loss), and sensual proclivities was used by the State to police and promote the "sensory hygiene" of the French populace. This knowledge also inspired scholars in other disciplines to propose physiological explanations of such topics as the hierarchy of the arts: according to the prevailing view, tattooing represented the "degree zero of art" and was followed in ascending evolutionary order by sculpture, dance, music, and painting. Painting was deemed the "noblest" of the arts on account of its identification with the "noblest" of the senses—sight.

In the debates of the SAP, one crucial question concerned how the objectivity of the racial taxonomies, and all the speculations concerning the sensory capabilities of Indigenous peoples, could be guaranteed if perception were indeed a physiological process and therefore potentially tainted with subjectivity (see Crary 1992; Schaffer 1994). The solution lay in exteriorizing the process of observation by subjecting it to diverse protocols designed to neutralize the "personal equation." For example, SAP researchers strove to determine "la bonne distance" from which to gauge the color of the iris (which was considered to be an essential marker of racial difference) and used Broca's celebrated chromatic scale to record their judgments. They also deployed a range of technologies, from the ophthalmoscope to the esthesiometer, which could substitute for the observer's own senses.

Other notable discussions in the *Bulletin* of the SAP include the many articles on the "evolution" of the color sense (in an effort to explain the paucity of color terms in the vocabularies of many non-European languages) and the plethora of studies on the one sensory defect the "men of science" recognized in themselves—namely, myopia.[1] Debate also swirled around the question of the part played by heredity and environment, respectively, in the development of the senses. This discussion pitted the neurological reductionism and physiological determinism of Broca against the contextualism of the maverick Léonce Manouvrier, who was by far the most enlightened anthropologist of his day. Perhaps the most glaring tension in the discourse of the SAP had to do with the contradiction between the French anthropologists' insistence on the perfectibility of the senses through education, on the one hand, and the rigidity of their theories on the other. The explanation for this aporia, according to Dias, is that these men were all devout Republicans and therefore dedicated to the idea of progress, even as they clung to notions of the inherent differences among races and intrinsic inferiority of the nonvisual senses.

Charting the "Sensory Acuity" of the Other: The Work of the Cambridge Anthropological Expedition to Torres Strait

Meanwhile, the Cambridge Anthropological Expedition to Torres Strait set out for the South Seas in 1898, led by the biologist A. C. Haddon. This expedition marked the invention of the fieldwork tradition in anthropology, or "going to see for oneself" (Grimshaw 2001), in contrast to the "armchair anthropology" of previous decades. Haddon recruited W. H. R. Rivers, a medical man who, in addition to his medical training in Britain, had trained in laboratory physiology and experimental psychology in Jenna and Heidelberg and was considered an expert in visual perception. Rivers in turn recruited two of his students to participate in the expedition, Charles Myers and William McDougall. These two young physicians would go on to exert significant influence over the development of experimental psychology.

The Cambridge team took with them a formidable battery of tests to measure the sensory acuity of the Torres Strait Islanders, including Haken's E, Lovibund's tintometer, the Müller-Lyer and other visual illusions, Politzer's Hörmesser (for measuring auditory sensitivity), Galton's whistle (for pitch discrimination), diverse musical instruments, the Zwaardemaker olfactometer, various taste solutions, a hand-grasp dynamometer, an algometer (for studying pain thresholds), marbles, and at least twenty other such apparatuses.

The intellectual context of the expedition was informed by research in psychophysics and the then-prevailing Spencerian hypothesis (Richards 1998). The latter hypothesis (or rather, conceit) was grounded in a series of cultural assumptions concerning the relationship between the intellect or reason, on the one hand, and the body and senses on the other, and between the senses themselves in terms of higher versus lower and civilized versus primitive (or animalistic). Various treatises dating from the eighteenth century already testified to the supposedly superior sensory abilities and proclivities of Indigenous peoples, particularly insofar as the "lower" senses (smell and touch) were concerned. For example, the natural historian Lorenz Oken proposed a racial hierarchy of the senses as part of his sweeping theory of the "perfection" of the senses in the evolution of animals and humans. In his scheme, the European "eye-man" was at the top of the scale, followed by the Asian "ear-man," the

Native American "nose-man," the Australian "tongue-man," and, at the bottom, the African "skin-man" (Howes 2009, 10–11). These racist representations became commonplace in the nineteenth century, supported by the anecdotal observations of explorers and missionaries (Konishi 2013), all of which fed into the Spencerian hypothesis, which held that "'primitives' surpassed 'civilised' people in psychophysical performance because more energy remained devoted to this level in the former instead of being diverted to 'higher functions,'" as among the latter (Richards 1998, 137). Here is how Rivers gave expression to this conceit: "We know that the growth of intellect depends on material which is furnished by the senses, and it therefore at first sight may appear strange that elaboration of the sensory side of mental life should be a hindrance to intellectual development. . . . [However, if] too much energy is expended on the sensory foundations, it is natural that the intellectual superstructures should suffer" (Rivers 1901, 44). And that such was the case was attested by the fact that "the savage is an extremely close observer of nature. . . . [The] attention is predominately devoted to objects of sense, and . . . such exclusive attention is a distinct hindrance to higher mental development" (44).

In keeping with this notion, Rivers and company introduced their experiments to the Torres Strait Islanders as follows: "The natives were told that some people had said that the black man could see and hear, etc., better than the white man and that we had come to find out how clever they were, and that their performances would all be described in a big book so that everyone would read about them. This appealed to the vanity of the people and put them on their mettle" (3). It will be appreciated that, given the supposed connection between sensory superiority and mental inferiority, to win at this contest was also to lose.

Rivers and Myers carried out very thorough eye and ear exams of the Islanders, noting the prevalence of color blindness, deafness, and so on (so that the issues of pathology and acuity could be kept separate). They also gathered extensive data on sensory vocabularies (not just color terms, but taste and smell and hearing terms, too) prompted by the supposition that there must be some association between extensiveness of nomenclature (e.g., the presence/absence of a word for blue) and degree of sensitiveness. They carried out their studies of psychophysical performance with remarkable resolve, considering the deficiencies or outright failure of much of their test equipment; illness (which impaired their own sensory abilities); and Indigenous resistance (e.g., the latter did not take well to having tubes stuck up their noses—understandably). For example, the hearing threshold tests were compromised by the pounding of the surf and rustle of the breeze in the palm trees—not very typical of laboratory conditions (Richards 1998). The expeditioners also had to control for the problem of subjects responding to the tests based on inferences as opposed to reporting "immediate sense impressions" (which is what they were after). Their difficulties in this connection ought to have prompted more reflection on the impossibility of ever completely stripping the perceptual process of its cultural and personal lining, but they did not.

The results of the psychophysical tests were mixed, as were their interpretations, and McDougall appears to have differed from Rivers and Myers in the conclusions he drew. Thus, McDougall studied the Islanders' tactile sensitivity using a compass to measure the threshold for the discrimination of two points on the skin and found this to be comparatively low: "about one half that of Englishmen" (McDougall 1901, 192). He used an algometer, which presses a point against the skin with varying levels of pressure to determine sensitivity to pain, and found this to be comparatively high: "nearly double that of Englishmen" (195). He concluded that the Islanders' "delicacy of tactile discrimination constitutes a racial characteristic" and that the "oft-repeated statement that savages in general are less susceptible to pain than white men" was exact (193–94). McDougall did not perceive any contradiction to the quite opposite results of these two tests, nor did he demonstrate the same methodological acumen as his fellow team members (Richards 1998).

While McDougall found confirmation for the prevailing stereotypes of Indigenous peoples, Rivers and Myers found no definite racial differences in the acuity of the senses they studied (see further Rivers 1905). For example, Myers (1901) found average olfactory acuity to be slightly higher in Torres Strait than in Aberdeenshire and general auditory acuity to be inferior, but he emphasized the limits of the test equipment he utilized (and incomparability of the data) more than anything, while Rivers concluded that "the general average" in Torres Strait "do not exhibit that degree of superiority over the European in visual acuity proper which the accounts of travelers might have led one to expect" (Rivers 1901, 42).

Rivers otherwise found that some visual illusions were experienced more strongly by Indigenous subjects than by British subjects, and others less strongly, but there was no "marked degree" of difference here either. This strike in favor of the psychophysical unity of humankind and incipient critique of the racist reasoning of the day was, however, tempered by Rivers's and Myers's resorting, in the next sentences of their respective reports, to relating anecdotes of Indigenous sensory virtuosity or extraordinary "powers of observation." They simply could not get the Spencerian hypothesis out of their heads.

The one difference from McDougall is that Rivers and Myers related these manifestations of extrasensitivity to "habits of life"—that is, to training and survival or custom rather than inheritance—but, then, because customs could be graded in terms of degree of civilization, this alternate explanation did nothing to unseat the Spencerian hypothesis. Thus, Rivers and

Myers were both very modern, in their use of statistics and the (experimental) evidence of the senses to question racist doctrines, and very Victorian in the way they persisted in employing evolutionary-style reasoning to interpret the scarcest indication of difference in the statistical tables their research generated as proof of those doctrines. Hence, in the final analysis, Rivers and Myers were no more culturally attuned or reflexive in their approach than McDougall. For example, they never bothered to inquire into Indigenous theories of the sensorium or Indigenous sensory practices.

On the "Cultural Equation" in Perception: Franz Boas's Break with Psychophysics

Meanwhile, Franz Boas, who had studied physics in Kiel and acquired expertise in psychophysics and physiology under Rudolf Virchow in Berlin, left Germany for the Canadian Arctic in 1883 to conduct geographic research and explore certain questions having to do with the psychophysics of vision among the Inuit. Something happened to Boas in the Arctic, however, for while he went out a physicist, he came back an ethnologist. Boas's "conversion" was described (some say mythologized) by his student Ruth Benedict as follows: "It was the Arctic which gave Boas 'once and for all' the understanding that the seeing eye is 'not a mere physical organ but a means of perception conditioned by the tradition in which its possessor has been reared'" (quoted in Stocking 1982, 145).

A similar transformation came over Boas's understanding of auditory perception. Alongside his research on visual perception, on the 1883 and subsequent trips to the Canadian Arctic and West Coast, Boas became engrossed with the study of language. One of his first professional publications was entitled "On Alternating Sounds" ([1889] 2018). In this short piece, Boas relates how he was startled to discover that he had recorded the sounds of certain Inuktitut words differently on different occasions. This was, actually, not that uncommon a quandary among observers of Indigenous languages. The conventional explanation for such alternation was that such languages were intrinsically "vague" and "fluctuating" just as the classificatory kinship terminologies of traditional societies were held to reflect a "state of promiscuity," since the term for "father" was also used for all of a father's male siblings. (This grouping of the father and father's brothers under the same term is actually common to so-called classificatory kinship terminologies: it is not a marker of promiscuousness.)

Boas, however, broke with the evolutionist assumptions of his contemporaries. He determined that the mishearings of sounds in a foreign language were a consequence of the observer's "apperceiving" them in light of the known sounds of his or her own language and assimilating them to the latter. In this way, Boas shifted the focus of inquiry from the production of sounds to their reception and underlined the importance of reflexivity in the pursuit of anthropological knowledge. He also took pains to point out that his thesis—namely, that "a new sensation is apperceived by means of similar sensations that form part of our knowledge" (Boas [1889] 2018, 35)—extends to other fields of sense besides audition, such as color perception and olfaction: "It is well known that many languages lack a term for green. If we show an individual speaking such a language a series of green worsteds, he will call part of them yellow, another part blue, the limit of both divisions being doubtful. Certain colors he will classify today as yellow, tomorrow as blue. He apperceives green by means of yellow and blue. We apperceive odors in the same way, and classify new odors with those to which they are similar" (ibid.).

Boas's reflections called into question the most elementary tenet of psychophysics, namely, the construct of the "differential threshold" or "just noticeable difference." His investigations exposed the extent to which the discrimination and/or classification of perceptual differences as of similarities is *culturally* contingent. In other words, physiological differences among observers are not the only factor responsible for variations in the registration of sense impressions. Rather, what could be called the "cultural equation" plays an equally salient, if not greater, role. The men of the SAP had no concept of this when they sought to control for what they called the "personal equation." Their understanding of perception was purely physiological, which is to say infra-cultural. Not so Boas (see further Stocking 1982, 157–60; Schaffer 1994).

We noted earlier what Ruth Benedict took to be the upshot of Boas's Arctic sojourn—that is, his break with psychophysicist doctrines and conversion to ethnology. In place of the exclusive focus on the physiology of perception in the French and British traditions, Boas, and consequently the students he trained—Benedict, as well as Margaret Mead and Edward Sapir—became interested in the cultural logistics of perception, or what they called the "cultural patterning" of sense experience. This had far-reaching consequences. Indeed, the great historian of anthropology George Stocking, while questioning whether Boas actually underwent a conversion experience in the Canadian Arctic, nevertheless holds up the "Alternating Sounds" essay as containing the germ of the "cultural relativist" position (Stocking 1982, 159) for which Boas and the Boasians (e.g., Benedict, Mead, Sapir) are so rightly famous.

The influence of Boas's insight into the "cultural equation" in perception can otherwise be seen in the following quotation from the introduction to *The Study of Culture at a Distance*

(1953) by Margaret Mead and Rhoda Métraux. They write that people "not only hear and speak and communicate through words, but also use all their senses in ways that are equally systematic ... to taste and smell and to pattern their capacities to taste and smell, so that the traditional cuisine of a people can be as distinctive and as organized as a language" (1953, 6). The implication of this, according to Mead and Métraux, was clear: just as linguistics requires "a special ear," so cultural analysis requires a special honing of *all* the senses.

Métraux elaborated on what this honing entailed in a chapter entitled "Resonance in Imagery" (1953). There, she begins by asserting that the "images" (not just visual but also aural, tactile, olfactory, etc.) through which a people perceive the world form "a coherent whole," and to grasp this whole entails developing a "disciplined conscious awareness of the *two* systems within which one is working." One of those "systems" would be the perceptual system or style of the culture studied, and the other the researcher's "personal" perceptual style. Displaying the same sensory reflexivity as Boas, but across the senses instead of treating them severally, Métraux (1953, 361) recorded, "I myself can attend to and retain most precisely visual and kinaesthetic and tactile imagery, and I am likely to transpose imagery in other modalities into combinations of these." She also canvassed other members of her and Mead's New York circle to find out how they went about doing anthropology.

> [One anthropologist] describes the process of assimilation [of another culture] as one in which he creates an "internal society" with "multiple voices" that carry on "multiple conversations" in his own mind. Another ... seems in some way to ingest the culture so that, in effect, her own body becomes a living model of the culture on which she is working as well as the culture of

which she is herself a member, and she continually tests out relationships in terms of her own bodily integration. And another describes the process as one of "receiving and sending kinaesthetic sets, strengthened by auditory patterns—largely pitch, intonation and stress rather than words." (361)

Priming one's own senses to the extent these researchers did, and cultivating the capacity to be "of two sensoria," hardly seems like a very *scientific* methodology; sensual or poetic, perhaps, but not social scientific.[2]

In closing, a word is in order about the eclipse of physical anthropology in the work of Boas and his students. In a paper entitled "The Instability of Human Types" (1916) presented at the First Universal Races Congress, held at the University of London in July 1911, Boas presented evidence of rapid changes in bodily form under a new environment. This pointed to "a decided plasticity of human types" and the importance of environmental factors—or "outward" in place of "inward" (hereditary) influences—to explaining human differences and similarities. The same goes for the "mental make-up" of individuals and groups, Boas argued in his paper. Thanks to the work of Boas and his students, the paradigm of cultural relativism came to supplant that of racial determinism—and the field of psychophysics went into retreat (at least within anthropology).[3]

On the "Discovery of the Body" and "Moral Tone" of Society: The Work of Marcel Mauss and Maurice Leenhardt

Meanwhile, back in France, Marcel Mauss was appointed to the Chair in Sociology at the Collège de France in 1931.[4] Mauss introduced two concepts that effectively dissolved the certainties of the physical anthropology of Broca and company by shifting the onus from physiology to social practice. Let us begin with his notion of "body techniques."

In 1934, Mauss presented a lecture before the Société de Psychologie entitled "Les techniques du corps," which was subsequently published in the *Journal de psychologie*. By "techniques," he explained, "I mean the ways in which from society to society [people] know how to use their bodies" (Mauss [1936] 1979, 97). "The body," he goes on to suggest, is our "first and most natural instrument"; but, like other instruments, it must be learned, and it may be learned well or badly, and it will certainly be learned differently in different cultures. By way of illustration, Mauss offered a series of anecdotes. He noted how techniques of swimming and running had changed over the years, how English and French techniques of digging differed (eight thousand spades had had to be replaced each time French and English divisions relieved each other at the front in World War I), and how people are taught to walk in particular styles. "For example," he wrote, "I can still remember my third-form teacher shouting at me: 'Idiot! Why do you walk around the whole time with your hands flapping wide open?'" (100). And, as with walking, so too with running, dancing, jumping, throwing—and even sleeping: "I have often slept on a horse, even sometimes a moving horse: the horse was more intelligent than I was" (113).

This engaging anecdotal style was quite foreign to the North American and British social scientific discourse of the period. With characteristic verve, however, Mauss arranged the anecdotes into a general theory of the anthropology of the body, keyed to the suggestion that "there is perhaps no 'natural way' for the adult," and the idea that to grasp these techniques we need "the triple viewpoint" of physiology, psychology, and sociology so as to understand the "total" human being (101).

This triangulation put paid to the exclusive focus on physiology of Broca and company.

While the implications of the anthropological record were clear, Mauss felt compelled to add that in the West, the techniques of the body were not well understood: for example, the breathing techniques learned in Taoism and Hinduism seemed to him to facilitate "communication with God." His discussion is worth quoting at length. He begins by alluding to the work of his contemporary Marcel Granet on the techniques of Taoism in *Chinese Civilization* ([1930] 1996): "I have studied the Sanskrit texts of Yoga enough to know that the same thing occurs in India. I believe precisely that at the bottom of all our mystical states there are body techniques which we have not studied, but which were studied fully in China and India, even in very remote periods. This socio-psycho-biological study should be made. I think that there are necessarily biological means of entering into 'communication with God'" (Mauss 1979, 122). We have the methods to understand these facts, Mauss averred; we just haven't put them to the test. But that is basically how things remained for the next forty years. Mauss's groundbreaking theory was not picked up on by his contemporaries, and it languished in relative obscurity until it was revived by Mary Douglas (1973) in Britain and even later by David Le Breton (1990) in France. Finally, Mauss's theory was extrapolated from "les techniques du corps" to "les techniques des sens" (Howes 1990b) in a special issue of the journal *Anthropologie et Sociétés* in 1990, on which more in chapter 6.

The other key concept introduced by Mauss in his *Manual of Ethnography* (2007) was the notion of the "moral tone" (*tonalité morale*) of society.[5] The *Manual*, which was pieced together from Mauss's lectures, was intended to teach "how to observe and classify social phenomena" (Mauss 2007, 7). In a little section on "Moral Phenomena," Mauss describes morality as the diffuse and unformed mass that surrounds the law. To make sense of this amorphous mass, Mauss advised researchers in the field to pay close attention to the oral tradition, most notably proverbs, and to gather statistics regarding good and bad deeds. "Having completed an investigation of this kind, one will be able to define the moral tone of the society under study, making an effort to remain within the ethos of the society" (148). This is according to the English translation of his text. The term "ethos" is not, however, an accurate translation of the French word Mauss used—namely, *atmosphère*. In the original French, this passage reads as follows: "Au terme de pareille enquête, on pourra définir la tonalité morale de la société observée, en s'efforçant de rester dans l'atmosphère de cette société." The implication of this methodological pronouncement is that no judgment should be made from outside the society's moral sphere.

It is instructive to ponder the slippage introduced by the (mis)translation of *atmosphère* as "ethos," for this drives a wedge between French anthropology after Mauss and American anthropology after Boas. The atmosphere or moral tone of a society could only be grasped through a complete bodily immersion in the studied society, according to Mauss, whereas Boas's students applied the concept of ethos in a fundamentally different way, as having to do with discerning and documenting "patterns" (see, e.g., Métraux 1953; Geertz 1957). In *Far Afield: French Anthropology Between Science and Literature* (2014), Vincent Debaene frames the contrast this way:

> Contrary to Franz Boas' students, ethnographers trained by Mauss were not trying to grasp an *ethos*, they were *trying to breathe an atmosphere*; they were not deciphering patterns, they were seeking a radical mental

> *transformation*. Although it was rarely explicit, the bodily experience of the ethnographer was seen as central since "the social" is by essence incarnated "in body and in mind." . . . This bodily experience became a precondition for the comprehension of the social fact as opposed to the understanding of *culture*, a concept that Mauss described as "even worse" than that of *civilization*, itself already "pretty bad" ["*assez mauvais*"]. (Debaene 2014, xiii–xiv)

Debaene goes on to discuss how the notion of "moral atmosphere" and the total immersion required to capture it raised certain difficulties, both in the field, when encountering it, and at the time of transcription: "If the ethos of a society can be characterized only as a 'climate,' a diffuse and impalpable air or quality, then 'how can we hope to give a scientific description of [a society] and apply it to the evaluative criteria that would make it an observable fact?'" (Karsenti quoted by Debaene 2014, 72).

Debaene suggests that an attempt was made to resolve this contradiction through resorting to a more literary style of exposition, which sought "to compensate for the shortcoming of a science founded on a documentary and museum-based model" (20). While literature was initially rejected in the name of science, it was desired for its evocative capacities and came to figure as "a technical art that renders moral and immaterial realities vivid and that, ideally, enables the reader to subjectively experience them. [. . .] As we can see, therefore, both its object (the social fact understood as a totality) and its method (the requirement of fieldwork and the continuity it implies between individual affectivity and objective knowledge) situated anthropology squarely between the contradiction generated by the application of the documentary paradigm to moral facts. The generalized references to the 'atmosphere' of the society under study are a good indicator of these tensions" (74). The tension persisted, however, and indeed, the vaporous notion of atmosphere proposed by Mauss was so riddled with difficulties that it never really caught on. Hence, his notion of moral tone, like his idea of techniques of the body, also fell into desuetude and would not be revived until half a century later, when the German philosopher Gernot Böhme came on the scene and put the notion of atmosphere on a solidly relational footing. "Atmosphere," Böhme writes, "is what relates objective factors and constellations of the environment with my bodily feeling in that environment. This means: atmosphere is what is *in between*, what mediates the two sides.... Atmospheres are quasi-objective, namely they are out there; you can enter an atmosphere and you can be surprisingly caught by an atmosphere. But on the other hand atmospheres are not beings like things: they are nothing without a subject feeling them.... They tend to bring you into a certain mood" (Böhme 2017, 1–2). Further discussion of the highly productive lines of inquiry opened up by Böhme's definition of atmosphere is reserved to the next chapter.

Maurice Leenhardt was a Protestant missionary who had lived and worked for close to thirty years among the Canaque (now Kanak) of New Caledonia (now the Republic of Vanuatu) before returning to France in 1926 and eventually taking up the chair (and some of the theories) of Lucien Lévy-Bruhl at the École des Hautes Études en Sciences Sociales (EHESS). Mauss and Leenhardt held each other's work in high regard, and they team-taught a number of courses, which were very rich precisely on account of their different styles: Mauss was an ethnologist of the first order, while Leenhardt was an ethnographer (or field researcher) of the first order (for an appreciation, see Laroche

1978). Another difference between their respective approaches has to do with Leenhardt's focus on the representation of the body in contrast to Mauss's concern with the analysis of body techniques.

In *Do Kamo: Person and Myth in the Melanesian World* ([1947] 1979), Leenhardt opens his analysis of Melanesian representations of the body with a discussion of how the Canaque artist, in his attempt to portray himself in bamboo etchings, depicts the trunk of the body as a long rectangle with two narrow bands on either side to "indicate the invisible sides of the trunk, the flanks" (Leenhardt 1979, 12). The artist has thus unfolded his body on a two-dimensional plane. Leenhardt proposes on this basis that the Canaque perceive and have knowledge of their bodies in only two dimensions, being unwilling (or unable) to conceive of their corporeality or that of other things "in the round."

Similarly, to the Canaque, the individual or "personage" appears as a heterogeneous ensemble of relationships. According to Leenhardt (1979, 97–102, 153–58), it is these relationships that are named, not the individual as such. For example, the word *duamara*, meaning "the pair nephew," refers to the "symmetrical ensemble" of a maternal uncle and his nephew. Given that *duamara* is a dual substantive, it can be inferred that the pair of individuals concerned, "which our eyes obstinately see as two," is apprehended as a single entity, a "duality-unity," by the Canaque. This diffusion or "participation" (to use Lévy-Bruhl's term) of the individual in the being of others is difficult for the Western mind to grasp. It becomes more intelligible if, following Leenhardt, we imagine that the "mythic consciousness" of the Canaque unfolds on a single plane—that is, in a purely two-dimensional universe. In theory, it is true that things that appear to exist as separate entities in a three-dimensional cosmos are not so differentiated in a two-dimensional universe.

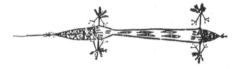

Fig. 1 Three representations of a Canaque (Kanak) village, New Caledonia. From Maurice Leenhardt's *Do Kamo* ([1947] 1979).

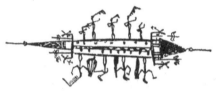

In a two-dimensional universe, what could be perceived as things appear instead as gradations on a line, "a single line which encircles them" (Dewdney 1984, 73, 171–72). The phenomenology of restricted dimensionality is perhaps best grasped by comparing the following sketches, two by Canaques, the other a European reconstruction (see fig. 1).

In viewing these drawings, one should know that, according to Leenhardt, the Canaque traditionally did not think there to be any spaces beyond the eye's reach, no underworld and no upperworld. To them "space appears as a heterogeneous ensemble of places whose existence is felt by bodily presence; when the sensuous reaction to the ... physical milieu is absent, space does not exist" (Leenhardt 1979, 46–47). In the European drawing, each of the objects in the picture—the huts, trees, piles of yams, and so forth—is treated as an independent entity (discrete, self-contained). In the Canaque drawings, by contrast, there is a flattening and at the same time a blending of the elements of the picture into each other—everything unfolds "as if" on a single plane.

It is perhaps against this two-dimensional background that the famous lines of Leenhardt's principal informant, Boesoou, can be interpreted. When asked what the missionaries had brought to New Caledonia, Boesoou replied: "You didn't bring us the spirit. We already knew the spirit existed. What you brought us is the body" (164). The discovery of the body in the round was pregnant with implications, according to Leenhardt, for with it "the circumscription of the physical self is completed, making possible its objectification" (164). The Canaque can begin to set up distances between the self and other persons and objects in the world around them and so the Canaque emerge into "history" (or three-dimensional space) bereft of their former "mythic consciousness." Space comes to appear uniform in its emptiness as opposed to heterogeneous in its resistance, as a result of this "discovery of the body" as a bounded entity.

Leenhardt's ethnography of the restricted dimensionality of Canaque representations of the body and cosmos is deeply evocative, but it was marred by his uncritical adoption of Lévy-Bruhl's theory of "primitive mentality" (for the standard critique, see Evans-Pritchard 1965). It was also compromised by the evolutionist assumptions that informed his archaeology of the "layers" of the Canaque "mythic consciousness." For example, he supposed that tactile representation and values were more primitive than visual representation and values, but there is no intrinsic reason for assuming this to be so. It is merely a longstanding conceit of Western art history (see Candlin 2010, chap. 1).

What most stands out about Leenhardt's approach, however, is the manner in which he shows the representation of the body to be so intimately entwined with all manner of other collective representations—concepts of the person, space, and art. In this regard, his work anticipated the emergence of the notion of the cultural sensorium, as will be discussed in the next chapter. Before broaching that discussion, however, I would like to round out the discussion of the measurement of the senses in this chapter by examining a most extraordinary development—the invention of "the quantified self."

Psychophysics Makes a Comeback: The Invention of the Quantified Self

Psychophysical measurement has remained a methodology of choice in (academic) experimental psychology. This is due to the isolation of psychology from other disciplines, most notably history and anthropology, which, as we have seen, cast doubt on the notion of the "just noticeable difference" by exposing how even sensation (not just "perception," conceived as a higher cognitive power) is modulated by cultural schemas. So too has psychology tended to ignore the sociality of sensation because of the way psychologists carry out their testing within the artificial confines of the psychology laboratory in the interests of "controlling variables." This protocol has the effect of weeding out the social.[6]

In recent years, however, thanks to the invention of various compact mobile devices and apps like the Fitbit, smartwatch, and so on, the measurement of certain sensory states has escaped the confines of the laboratory and become an integral component of everyday life. Monitoring "performance" has become an obsession. Great faith is placed in these devices to give accurate measurements of heart rates, respiration rates, body weight, metabolism, location (GPS), and even states of sleep. They form part of the "drive for self-improvement" that is the defining feature of the neoliberal self.

This dream of the totally quantifiable self is seen by some as a nightmare, a dystopia of gigantic proportions where the individual is seamlessly integrated into the "flow of information" in the cybernetic society and becomes a "docile body," even while engaging in all manner of physical activity. For "these technologies work to datafy sensory perceptions and experiences, rendering embodied sensations into digital data. . . . Via these [self-tracking] technologies, reams of personal information are collected, which are transmitted by Wi-Fi to digital data archives ('cloud computing'), storing the data for perpetuity. Users often need to perform little more than a tap or voice request to collect, review or share their data, or sync the information with other personal datasets" (Lupton and Maslen 2018, 191). Older, sensory ways of knowing the body are eclipsed in the process, with unfortunate consequences, according to some commentators. Thus, for example, a movement has emerged that urges runners to "ditch their watches" and return to "training by feel" (Mopas and Huybregts 2020). Charges of "data fetishism" abound, and "training with numbers" is excoriated (while "training by feel" is lauded as "more natural"). Datafication has taken command, and sensation ("listening to the body") has been bracketed. This abstraction of the sensate could be seen as a sign of the triumph of the "algorithmic optic" (Halpern 2015)—that is, of representation prevailing over sensation: everything becomes a matter of "patterns" that can be detected, recorded, and, above all, visualized on a display screen.

This dystopian vision of diminished sensuousness and agential capacity has been challenged, however, by the authors of two recent articles in *The Senses and Society*. Deborah Lupton and Sarah Maslen (2018) interviewed Australian women about their use of digital health technologies; Michael Mopas and Ekaterina Huybregts (2020), for their part, carried out a study with amateur endurance athletes in Ontario, Canada, using the methodology of participant sensation. Both sets of authors found that their interlocutors had not become the disembodied and atomistic actors portrayed (or rather, pilloried) in the literature and that the digital devices had not supplanted knowing with and through the body. Rather, their interlocutors remained social actors, and the "external data" generated by the devices was used *alongside* personal assessments based on sensing "internal data."

In their work, Lupton and Maslen introduce the concept of "data sensemaking" (in preference to data literacy), which "brings the body back in"; as they suggest, "[it] incorporates the interaction of digital sensors (used in self-tracking to generate personal data), the embodied human senses, and human sense-making" (Lupton and Maslen 2018, 91). What is more, there is work involved in processing the digital data—namely, "various kinds of *sensory work* that cohere around learning to make use of digital technologies and respond to the data they generate using sensory and other forms of knowledge" (ibid.).[7] It is never just a question of reading information from a screen. Hence, Lupton and Maslen shift the onus from "information-processing" to "sensory and sense-making *engagements*" with the devices and apps.

Significantly, Lupton and Maslen found that the women in their study "formed relationships" with the self-tracking devices, and these relationships could be good or bad, sometimes a source of feelings of empowerment, and sometimes a source of frustration. This frustration could take the form of self-frustration (at not being able to achieve the goals they set for themselves) and sometimes frustration with the technology (when batteries fail or the GPS signal is lost). The latter frustration was as much social as personal, for, as Mopas and Huybregts found in their study, it meant the athletes were unable to *share* their data with fellow endurance athletes on so-called social media. For the runners, the data did not "count" unless it could be shared. Equipment failure provoked a profound "fear of missing out," which brings the sociality of sensation back in. Lupton and Maslen also found that the women in their study were not passive consumers of the technology but instead imagined all sorts of ways it could be improved to better answer to their needs and desires, and some women honed their awareness of the movements and functions of their bodies by means of the apps so they could "delegate" the monitoring back to their embodied senses.

Lupton and Maslen's approach imports "a heightened focus on the relational connections, affective forces and agential capacities" of their research subjects into the study of self-tracking technologies and so highlights "the *interplay* between affects, sensory engagements, and digital sensing" (2018, 192–93, emphasis added). This triangulation is of interest for the way it departs from Mauss's "triple viewpoint" (physiology, psychology, sociology): in place of disciplining the body and senses à la Mauss, Lupton and Maslen ground their analysis in sense experience itself.

Of particular note is the concept of the "more-than-human sensorium" introduced by Lupton and Maslen. "These self-tracking devices," they observe, "involve complex synergistic and recursive engagements and intra-actions between the sensory affordances and capacities of human bodies and computer hardware and software" (191). They accordingly stress the importance of "acknowledging people's engagements with information and archival artefacts as multi-sensory, and not only embodied, but intercorporeal [or even transcorpreal], entangled with and distributed across other human bodies, other living organisms and nonliving things" (192). Taking their cue from new feminist materialist scholarship, augmented by their practice of sensory ethnography, they argue that "human and device [work] together to configure a new sensory capacity" (197). Thus, embodied sensing is joined with "distributed technological sensing" in an "ever emergent enaction of human-nonhuman relations" (198).[8]

CHAPTER 2

The Enculturation of the Senses

In the previous chapter, we examined how the senses were engaged by select anthropologists from the late nineteenth (Broca, Rivers, Boas) and early twentieth centuries (Leenhardt, Mauss, and Mead). The idea of an anthropology of the senses, however, only came to be developed in the late twentieth century. Paul Stoller's *The Taste of Ethnographic Things: The Senses in Anthropology* (1989) explicitly put the senses on the table. His book was followed by *The Varieties of Sensory Experience: A Sourcebook in the Anthropology of the Senses* (1991), edited by the present writer. This chapter will examine the origins of sensory anthropology as a distinct approach within anthropology and highlight the way in which discussions of other topics, such as materiality and embodiment, fed into its development.

Toward a Cultural Anthropology of the Senses

Broadly speaking, the anthropology of the senses is concerned with charting and "enucleating" the varieties of sensory experience across cultures. In contrast to the work of earlier anthropologists, it is cultural and experiential rather than physical and experimental in orientation and vested in understanding the senses and their interrelationships within local cultural contexts.

This is where the idea of "enucleation"—or, "drawing out the kernel" of some thing or some idea—comes in. Enucleating is not the same as "unpacking": it is gentler than that. It is not the same as "describing," for description is more superficial. Nor is it the same as "interpreting," even if there is a strong resemblance, for to interpret is to risk getting trapped in the hermeticism of the hermeneutic circle (on which more below). And, it is not at all the same as "explaining," or laying bare, for sensory anthropology rejects nomotheticism—that is, it abjures the reduction of instances to general laws—and seeks instead to draw out the inner sense of a culture's beliefs and practices through trying to "feel along with others what they experience" (Laplantine 2015). Participant sensation is the new watchword in place of the externality suggested by the conventional anthropological methodology of participant observation.

The anthropology of the senses is still commonly seen as a subfield of anthropology, like the anthropology of emotion. But it is (and has always been) much more than that, since sensory anthropology references both a substantive area of research and an approach or medium of investigation, like visual anthropology. The senses thus figure as both object of study and means of inquiry: sensory anthropology stands for a cultural approach to the study of the senses and a sensory approach to the study of culture.

In a chapter on "senses" in *Anthropology: Theoretical Practice in Culture and Society* (2001), Michael Herzfeld brings out well the implications of sensory analysis for revisioning the discipline. Citing Constance Classen (1997), Herzfeld writes, "The broad range of applications for a sensory analysis of culture indicates that the anthropology of the senses need not only be a 'subfield' within anthropology, but may provide a fruitful perspective from which to examine many different anthropological concerns"—from politics and gender to "religious beliefs and practices to the production and exchange of goods" (Herzfeld 2001, 252–53). In what follows, our focus will be on identifying the quickening of the senses within a range of subfields of anthropology and tracing how these stirrings contributed to the crystallization of the anthropology of the senses. We begin, however, with a consideration of two critiques that were foundational to the nascent field of sensory anthropology: the critique of textualism and the critique of visualism.

Critique of Textualism

Anthropology was gripped by a "crisis of representation" in the mid-1980s, as proclaimed by James Clifford and George Marcus in *Writing Culture: The Politics and Poetics of Ethnography* (1986). *Writing Culture* was a highly influential text. It inspired a great deal of reflexivity, or self-examination, on the part of anthropologists because of the way it problematized the issue of "authority." What is not so commonly recognized is how it also precipitated a crisis of perception. To see how this is so, we need to step back and examine the roots of the textual revolution in anthropology.[1]

The origin of the textual revolution may be traced to the publication of *The Interpretation of Cultures* (1973) by Clifford Geertz, a student of Margaret Mead who, like her, also carried out field research on the island of Bali. Geertz launched the textual revolution by (re)defining culture as "an ensemble of texts, themselves ensembles, which the anthropologist strains to read over the shoulders of those to whom they properly belong"

(Geertz 1973, 452). Geertz derived his idea of "the model of the text" from the hermeneutic philosophy of Paul Ricoeur (1970). This inspired him to analyze rituals as expressing propositions, or "say[ing] something of something" (Geertz 1973, 448). Geertz's theoretical approach came to be known as interpretive or "symbolic anthropology," and his methodology as one of "thick description" (5–6, 9–10).

It might have been objected that rituals and other cultural practices involve rather a lot of nonverbal communication so that to reduce them to their propositional content (or what they may be interpreted to "say") smacks of verbocentrism. Indeed, as Fredrik Barth found in his study of initiation rituals among the Baktaman of Papua New Guinea, some understandings are deliberately left unsaid and are communicated through the manipulation of multisensory objects instead: "When the Baktaman choose to cast their knowledge in a variety of simultaneous [sensory] channels and expressions, we should seek to understand its consequences and, if possible, its reason. A major explanation lies in the clear wish to act on the world and not just speak about it" (Barth 1975, 224). Furthermore, it might have been objected that ritual acts, like other cultural acts, do not possess the same stability as texts. Rituals are eventful and multisensorial. The hermeneutic method, which is modeled on the interpretation of scripture and entails a constant circling between exegesis and text, is not well suited to grasping the dynamic, multisensory nature of living cultures.

In the early 1980s, continuing down the path of the text opened up by Geertz, the focus shifted from interpretation to negotiation and representation—and from "reading culture" to "writing culture." This development was signaled by the publication of a number of articles with titles like "Ethnographies as Texts" (Marcus and Cushman 1982), "On Ethnographic

Authority" (Clifford 1983), and "Functionalists Write, Too" (Boon 1983). These articles problematized the authority of the anthropologist by directing attention to the unequal power relation between ethnographer and informant and questioning who controls the means of representation. The idea of description, regardless of how "thick," no longer cut it, and the idea developed that ethnography is located in "a process of dialogue where interlocutors actively negotiate a shared vision of reality" (Clifford 1983, 134). The new emphasis on negotiation spelled the end of the monologism of the conventional ethnographic monograph and unleashed a torrent of stylistic innovation, or textual "experimentation" (Marcus and Cushman 1982, 26). For example, some anthropologists opted to write memoirs; others resorted to using a dialogical format, with informants' voices being equally represented in the text. Anthropologists also started reading each others' texts with an eye to the rhetorical strategies or "modes of authority" deployed therein so as to convince the reader of the author's having "been there" and having participated in the negotiation of meaning.

In "Partial Truths," the introduction to *Writing Culture*, James Clifford writes, "Many voices clamor for expression. Polyvocality was restrained and orchestrated in traditional ethnographies by giving to one voice a pervasive authorial function and to others the role of sources, 'informants,' to be quoted or paraphrased. [But once] dialogism and polyphony are recognized as modes of textual production, monophonic authority is questioned, revealed to be characteristic of a science that has claimed to represent cultures" (Clifford and Marcus 1986, 15). What is wrong with claiming to "represent" cultures? First, anthropologists are not representative of the populations they study; second, it smuggles in "an ideology claiming transparency of representation and immediacy of experience"; and third, "the proper referent of any account is not a represented 'world'; now it is specific instances of discourse" (14).

We can discern a series of displacements here, if we think back to the work of Mead and Métraux discussed in the previous chapter (see pp. 32–33). There is a slippage from participant observation to description and interpretation, then from description to "discourse" or dialogue and negotiation, culminating in a focus on "the emergent and cooperative nature of textualization" (Tyler 1986, 127).

What went unquestioned amidst all this hyperreflexive self-questioning and stylistic experimentation was the idea of culture "as text" to begin with. It could be argued that the model of the text deflects attention from action and sensation to representation and results in the privileging of textualization over perception. The recession of perception (or retraction of sensation) and precession of inscription is on full display in Stephen Tyler's chapter in *Writing Culture*, which is entitled "Postmodern Ethnography." It bears noting that Tyler was writing at a time when the idea that *il n'y a pas de hors-texte* (there is nothing outside the text) was in the ascendant. "An ethnography is no account of a rationalized movement from percept to concept," Tyler writes. "It begins and ends in concepts. There is no origin in perception, no priority of vision, and no data of observation." Or, again: "[An ethnography] is not a record of experience at all; it is the means of experience. That experience became experience only in the writing of the ethnography. Before that it was only a disconnected array of chance happenings" (Tyler 1986, 137–38). Tyler's conclusion: "Perception has nothing to do with it"—the "it" being ethnography.

This total eclipse of perception, and substitution of "the process of textualization," not only undermined the value formerly attached to participant observation but also scuttled the idea of sensation. It was as if these anthropologists of a textual persuasion had collectively taken leave of their senses.

Taking his cue in part from media theorist Walter Ong, Paul Stoller was more sensitive than the "textualists" (as they could be called) to the *medium* of language, and specifically how spoken language may be understood to have a power and energy independent of its representationality. "Most anthropologists use the sound of language or music as a means to gather information with which they 'construct' the culture of the Other. We take the sound of language for granted. The Other, however, may consider language . . . as an embodiment of [the power of] sound" (Stoller 1984, 569n4). Accordingly, Stoller devotes one chapter of *The Taste of Ethnographic Things* to "sound in Songhay sorcery" and another to "sound in Songhay possession." His reflections on this score have inspired numerous other anthropologists to attend to the extralinguistic power of language and the extramusical force of music, culminating in the recognition that, in African cultures, "auditory space is perceived as a physical field" (Peek quoted in Geurts 2002a, 193).

In the opening chapter of *The Taste of Ethnographic Things*, Stoller relates the story of being served a bad-tasting sauce (called *fukko hoy*) by the disgruntled daughter-in-law of one of his hosts. The bad sauce was disgusting to his palate, but it made for "good ethnography," since it alerted him to how social relations may be communicated and manipulated through the flavor of food. In essence, he discovered that the thickness and spiciness of a sauce provides a measure of the closeness of the relationship between host and guest (the closer the connection, the blander and thinner the sauce). But social agents, like the daughter-in-law, may also scramble these expectations (e.g., serving a thin sauce to a distinguished guest) to convey even more complex messages.

In another essay, which appeared in a special issue of *Anthropologie et Sociétés* on the theme of "les cinq sens," Stoller and Olkes (1990) reflected on the many different food flavors, textures, and aromas Stoller had experienced over the years and offered a gastronomic geography of Songhayland. This cultural account of Songhay cuisine remains one of the finest examples of "gustemology" (Sutton 2010) in the annals of anthropology.

The publication of Stoller's *The Taste of Ethnographic Things*, then, marked a departure from the rejection of perception, or suspension of sensation in the interests of textualization, that we saw in Stephen Tyler's "Postmodern Ethnography." Stoller, by contrast, urges us to "accept sensuousness," fine-tune our perception, and accord primacy to the evocation of sensations in our practices of inscription: "To accept sensuousness," he writes, is "to lend one's body to the world and accept its complexities, tastes, structures, and smells. . . . [S]ensuous scholarship is ultimately a mixing of head and heart. It is an opening of one's being to the world—a welcome" (Stoller 1997, xvii–xviii).

The thirty-year legacy of Stoller's sensuous scholarship is on full display in a recent special issue of *The Senses and Society*, edited by Beth Uzwiak and Laurian Bowles, entitled "The Ethnographic Palimpsest: Excursions in Paul Stoller's Sensory Poetics" (2021b). In an article on the sensory politics of caste, Indian anthropologist Shivani Kapoor (2021) discusses how her own smell (in both senses) was problematized by her lower-caste interlocutors. This is interesting: so much for troubling over "the ethnographer's gaze" (or voice) when their very smell forms a crucial component of the ethnographic encounter! In "Sonic Intimacies," the ethnomusicologist Sidra Lawrence (2021) presents an analysis of "performative erotics and African feminisms." The intimate connection between feminist epistemology and sensuous epistemology is also central to

Uzwiak and Bowles's (2021a) contribution, "Epistolary Storytelling: A Feminist Sensory Orientation to Ethnography." The collection otherwise contains a landmark article by Sarah Pink (2021) called "Sensuous Futures," which highlights the potential contribution of sensory ethnography to the practice of design anthropology (on which more in chapter 5).

Critique of Visualism

In "To Summon all the Senses," the introduction to *The Varieties of Sensory Experience*, I offered the following synopsis of the field of sensory anthropology: "The anthropology of the senses is primarily concerned with how the patterning of sense experience varies from one culture to the next in accordance with the meaning and emphasis attached to each of the modalities of perception. . . . The most basic tenet of this emergent field of study is that it is only by developing a rigorous awareness of the visual and textual biases of the Western episteme that we can hope to make sense of how life is lived in other cultural settings" (Howes 1991, 4). This passage emphasizes the importance of developing a rigorous awareness of visual perceptual bias, or "visualism." It does not advocate a rejection of vision, as some have suggested (e.g., Ingold 2000), but rather an openness to sensory diversity. The point is that each culture must be approached on its own sensory terms and that we should attend to the multiplicity of ways in which the senses are engaged and interrelated.

The critique of visualism within the anthropology of the senses was inspired in part by broader intellectual trends. These included postmodernism and the critique of vision instigated by a number of the leading proponents of twentieth-century French theory. The intellectual historian Martin Jay presents a synopsis of this rupture in *Downcast Eyes* (1993). As he relates, vision had long enjoyed an exalted status as "the noblest of the senses" in Western philosophy on account of its (supposed) disincarnate nature or externality, its simultaneity or atemporality (unlike hearing), and its distanciating or objectifying character (see Jonas [1954] 1982). This agreed with the general privileging of Being over Becoming (i.e., spatiality over temporality) in Western philosophy and the separation of subject from object.

The manifestations of this "ocularcentric" mindset, as Jay styles it, are legion. They range from Plato's idea of "Truth" as embodied in "the *Eidos* or Idea, which was like a visible form blanched of its color" (Jay 1993, 26), to the idea of the mind as a *camera obscura* (both Descartes and Locke subscribed to this idea). Jay notes that faith in the linkage between ocularity or lucidity and rationality is what gave the Enlightenment (*siècle des lumières* in French) its name. Another prime manifestation of Western visualism was the invention of linear perspective in Renaissance painting (see fig. 2). As Robert Romanyshyn (1989, 31) notes regarding this novel technique of representation, within the "landscape of linear perspective vision the self becomes a spectator ensconced behind his or her window on the world, . . . the body, now divorced from this self, becomes a specimen, and . . . the world, as a matter for this detached and observing eye, becomes a spectacle."

The rise of Impressionism in the nineteenth century challenged the lineaments of this vision: "Rather than painting theatricalized scenes in an idealized, geometricalized space on the other side of the canvas/window as seen from afar, the Impressionists sought to reproduce the experience of light and color on the retinas of their eyes," as with Monet's multiple views of haystacks or the façade of the Rouen cathedral (Jay 1993, 154). While the Impressionists may have obliterated lineality, the emphasis on retinality remained. The intensification of vision can otherwise be discerned in the trajectory that leads

Fig. 2   Albrecht Dürer, *Draughtsman Making a Perspective Drawing of a Recumbent Woman*, ca. 1600. Woodcut, 7.7 × 21.4 cm. Gift of Henry Walters, 1917, 17.37.314. The Metropolitan Museum of Art.

from the visual extravaganza that was the court of Louis XIV (known as "the Sun King") to the precession of the image and recession of reality in our contemporary "civilization of the image" or "society of the spectacle" (Jay 1993, 87–89; Kearney 1988; Debord 1994).

The major part of Jay's *Downcast Eyes* is devoted to documenting how a counter discourse, which he styles as "antiocularcentric," crystalized in twentieth-century French intellectual and artistic circles, as evidenced by Marcel Duchamp's virulent critique of "retinal art" and celebration of the readymade; in Jean-Paul Sartre's "ocularphobia"; in Maurice Merleau-Ponty's post-Cartesian philosophy of the embodied subject and primacy of perception (or incarnate vision); and, above all, the critique of the hegemony of vision in the work of Michel Foucault. In *The Birth of the Clinic* (1973), Foucault exposed the connection between *voir*, *pouvoir*, and *savoir* (or, vision, power, and knowledge) in the constitution of "the medical gaze"; in *Discipline and Punish* ([1975] 1979), he laid bare the connection between vision, objectification, and individuation in Jeremy Bentham's design for a model prison called the Panopticon, a paradigm that has since infiltrated every nook and cranny of "the society of surveillance" in which we now live (witness the ubiquity of CCTV cameras). Thus did the history of the eye turn from one of exaltation to denigration and suspicion, at least within certain academic and artistic circles.

The anthropology of the senses engaged with the critique of vision in contemporary French theory, but it would be erroneous to call it "antiocularcentric." Rather, it has been *polycentric* since its inception because of the stress on "summoning all the senses." It refuses the ocularcentric/antiocularcentric dichotomy since this dichotomy remains centered on the fovea. The French theorists (Foucault, Derrida, etc.) were single-mindedly concerned with upsetting and fragmenting vision, whereas sensory anthropology multiplies the registers to be taken into account and regards the senses as "relationally produced" (Dawkins and Loftus 2013).

Starting from the premise that the senses are made, not given, sensory anthropology contests the essentialist construction of vision in the West as intrinsically more objective, more rational, and more distancing. It points to the fact that in many non-Western cultures visuality is assigned different characteristics. It may be bound up with witchcraft and other seemingly irrational forces, and therefore strictly curtailed. Meanwhile, in Hindu India, vision is vested with great power but, unlike in the West, it is reciprocal. For example, when the eyes of a newly minted idol are pricked, worshippers jostle with each other to position themselves in its line of sight: "taking *darsan*" in this way (i.e., exchanging glances with the deity) is considered auspicious (Pinard 1991). Compare the hapless prisoner in the Panopticon who can never actually tell whether they are being watched from the central observation tower, "the Eye of Power," where the guards are sequestered.

The idea of "sensuous epistemologies" (Feld 2005) is central to the anthropology of the senses. It presents an alternative to the idea of the mind as a *camera obscura* that is so prevalent in the West and opens the way for investigating the many other "sensory models" (Classen 1997) or "sensoria" (in the archaic sense) of the world's societies. For example, the sensorium of the Hausa of Nigeria is twofold: they discriminate between *gani*, meaning "to see," and *ji*, which includes all the other senses as well as the emotions (Ritchie 1991, 194). The sensorium of the Cashinahua of Peru is sixfold: they distinguish between *ichi una* (skin knowledge), *meken una* (hand knowledge), *pabinka una* (ear knowledge), *beda una* (eye knowledge, which is limited to the visions people experience under the influence of an hallucinogen), and *taka una* (liver knowledge, which has to do with the emotions), while knowledge of one's mortality and immortality or "life force" is supposed to have its seat in the genitals. When asked by their ethnographer, Kenneth Kensinger, whether the brain has knowledge, the Cashinahua rejected the implicit assumption behind this question (i.e., the brain as a central processor of information or data bank), for they did not think of the brain as having any role to play in cognition; rather, they affirmed, "the whole body knows" (Howes 2022, 68).

The sensorium of the Desana of the Colombian rainforest is especially rich. They conceive of the brain on the model of a beehive. Thus, in one image, the brain is made up of "layers of innumerable hexagonal honeycombs ... [each] tiny hexagonal container holds honey of a different color, flavor, odor, or texture" (Reichel-Dolmatoff quoted in Howes and Classen 2013, 159). The polysensoriality of this image of the brain is matched by the intersensoriality or synesthetic architecture of the Desana sensory cosmology.[2] The Desana "vision" of the cosmos is generated and sustained by the ritual ingestion of the hallucinogenic

Banisteriopsis caapi plant, or *yagé*, under the guidance of a shaman. According to Desana cosmology, "colours emanate from the light of the Sun or Moon and then combine with heat to produce corresponding sets of odours and flavours. Purple, for example, is said to come from the Moon and is linked to a rotten smell and an acid flavour" (Howes and Classen 2013, 158; see further Gearin and Saéz 2021).

Another very rich account of an Indigenous sensory cosmology is presented by Marina Roseman in her study of the Temiar entitled *Healing Sounds from the Malaysian Rainforest* (1992). Fundamental to Temiar physics and cosmology is the notion of a cool, moist liquid or vital energy that is condensed to different degrees and mobilized by the winds of the landscape, winds of the spirits, voices of mediums, the movements of trance-dancers, and the beat of the bamboo stampers. In healing ceremonies these sensuous resources are channeled by the shaman to attract a wayward soul back to the body in which it belongs.[3]

It is often only by chance that an anthropologist's eyes (and other senses) are opened to the ways of sensing of the people they study. Paul Stoller offers the following anecdote from his fieldwork among the Songhay people of Niger. A healer by the name of Sorko Djibo had been called to the bed of a sick man who was the victim of a curse, and Stoller accompanied him. The healer determined that a sorcerer had taken possession of the man's double and was slowly devouring him from within. To prevent the man from dying, the healer had to find and liberate the patient's double. He prepared a remedy to be applied to the man's joints and sensory orifices, then led Stoller on a search that took them to the edge of the village. They came to the crest of a dune where there was a large pile of millet seed husk. The healer bent to sift through the pile, then abruptly stood up and cried out, "Wo, wo, wo, wo. . . ." He then asked Stoller:

> "Did you hear it?"
> "Hear what?" I asked dumbfounded.
> "Did you feel it?"
> "Feel what?" I wondered.
> "Did you see it?"
> "What are you talking about?" I demanded.

Sorko Djibo then enjoined him: "You look but you do not see. You touch, but you do not feel. You listen, but you do not hear. Without sight or touch . . . one can learn a great deal. But you must learn how to *hear* or you will learn little about our ways" (Stoller 1989, 115). This is a nice illustration of the prime importance of approaching a culture on its own sensory terms.

Anthropology of/in Sound

A number of the leading sensory anthropologists of the late twentieth century, such as Steven Feld and Marina Roseman, started as ethnomusicologists. Their interest in the anthropology of sound, which brought with it a focus on listening and the modulation of sound in performance (or "musicking"), primed them to attune their perceptual apparatus to the sonic dimensions of sensory expression and communication and yielded many keen insights into alternative ways of structuring the social and the sensible.

Steven Feld's work has been enormously influential (see, e.g., Stoller 1989, 50, 103). His writings, beginning with *Sound and Sentiment* (1982), anticipated both the sensory and the affective turns in the human sciences by close to a decade. Feld

(1996) introduced the concept of "acoustemology" by way of summing up his practice of listening in to the culture and environment of the Kaluli people of Papua New Guinea. By training his ears to pick up on all the nuances of local ways of producing and perceiving sound, he was able to discern the capital cultural importance of such auditory motifs as "lift-up-over sounding" and even hear the "inside" of a drumbeat (Feld 1991, 91–94).

It is legitimate to wonder whether Feld's training in musicology might have predisposed him to listen where others would only look. But any such suspicion is offset by the fact that Feld (1988) is also the author of the eminently polysensory theory of "the iconicity of style"—or cross-modal correspondence and transposability of perceptual schema. For example, he discerned a link between the layering of sound in the Kaluli singing style and the layering of paint and other accoutrements in their ceremonial costumes. He even includes smell in the picture:

> These Kaluli vision-sound interplays are also locationally intersensual to smell. Any number of everyday examples could be cited. It is hard to imagine the trickling of a shallow creek at a stand of sago palms without smelling the aromas of fresh or rotting pith: the experience and memory of sago presence is deeply multisensory. Similarly, the dense sensuality of evening darkness, with voices overlapping the misting light rains and insects and frogs of the nearby bush, is sensually continuous with smoky aromas that fires or resin torches release into the longhouse and diffuse out into the ever-moist night air. Evoking the diffuseness of this motional sensorium, the processes of sound and smell are incorporated into the same Bosavi verb, *dabuma*, or absorption by ear and nose. (Feld 2005, 187)

As this quotation reveals, Feld is just as attentive to the relations among—or "interplay" of—the senses as he is to particular sensations. This is what is meant by the term "intersensoriality" (Howes 2005a). The meaning is in the interconnection.

In addition to his many published works, Feld has produced an extensive catalog of sound recordings, ranging from the voices (both human and nonhuman) of the rainforest to bells, car horns, and glaciers melting. It was out of this shift in registers that an "anthropology of sound" and "anthropology in sound" was born (Feld and Brenneis 2004), and this field is booming. Notable contributors include Tom Rice (2013) on the soundscape of the hospital and hearing through a stethoscope, Marina Peterson (2021) and Rupert Cox (2013) on atmospheric noise (see further Ei-ichi deForest 2015), and *The Bloomsbury Handbook of the Anthropology of Sound* (2021), edited by the maestro of sound studies, Holger Schulze.

An unexpected, and at the same time highly productive, new avenue of research and reflection was opened up by Michele Friedner and Stefan Helmreich in "Sound Studies Meets Deaf Studies" (2012). At first blush, sound studies and Deaf studies might seem to be worlds apart. The former privileges attention to listening and contests the primacy of vision as an organizing frame for social and cultural analysis, while the latter both highlights the audist and phonocentric tendencies that pervade everyday interaction and advocates a fresh consideration of the visual as a field of interactive possibility (e.g., the use of sign as an alternative to spoken language). Friedner and Helmreich seek to trouble the neat dichotomy between hearing and not-hearing. They point to research on deaf people's inferences of sonic worlds as they understand them to be experienced by hearing people, and a deaf music camp that unsettles audist notions of music by encouraging deaf teens to experiment with music "through deaf eyes" (which entails "seeing" in addition to "feeling" the music). Especially key is the way they turn the spotlight on infrasound (vibration lower than 20 Hz) and redefine sound as vibration: citing Steve Goodman (2010), they note how very low sounds "edge from audibility into tactility" (Friedner and Helmreich 2012, 76) and thus create a common ground that transcends the hearing/not-hearing binary (see further Trower 2008). They give the example of a workshop on low-frequency vibration organized by the artist Wendy Jacobs, which brought together faculty and students from Gallaudet University and MIT's Center for Advanced Visual Studies. Called "Waves and Signs," the workshop took place on a specially designed platform through which sound and infrasound were transduced. Through recourse to this platform/instrument/stage, Jacobs was able to "pitch" the discussion "quite materially down to a frequency register at which all parties could hear-by-feeling sound" (Friedner and Helmreich 2012, 76).

As the Friedner and Helmreich article attests, there is room for much fruitful exchange between sensory studies (including sound studies) and disability studies, if practitioners would but rid themselves of stereotypical notions of ability and disability and start exploring the interrelationships of the senses. The emergent focus on "intracultural sensory diversity" (after Classen 1997) and intersensoriality has informed a number of key contributions to resensing disability studies in recent years, most notably Gili Hammer's *Blindness Through the Looking Glass: The Performance of Blindness, Gender, and the Sensory Body* (2019) and Peter Graif's *Being and Hearing: Making Intelligible Worlds in Deaf Kathmandu* (2018).

Embodiment and Emplacement

Research in the anthropology of the body has been another key catalyst for research in the anthropology of the senses. In the previous chapter, we discussed the seminal contribution made by Marcel Mauss in his essay on "body techniques." Mary Douglas reprised Mauss's pioneering argument in *Purity and Danger* (1966), although in her work the emphasis is more on the body as model of society than as tool. For example, she proposed that body rituals "enact the form of social relations and in giving these relations visible expression they enable people to know their own society" (Douglas 1966, 128). If, for instance, a given ritual expresses anxiety about the apertures of the body, this could be interpreted as testifying to the society's concerns over the maintenance of its internal and external boundaries (see further Douglas 1973).

In the early 1980s, Douglas's approach to the body in society was criticized by Michael Jackson (1983b, 143) for the way it treats the body as "simply the passive ground on which forms of social organization are inscribed." In other words, the body becomes an "it" in Douglas's schema, a "medium of communication" at the disposal of a "reified social rationality" (Jackson 1983a, 329). This stance, Jackson argues, contradicts our prior, individual experience of the body "as lived reality," or what Laurence Kirmayer (1992) has called "the body's insistence on meaning."

Building on Jackson's work and the phenomenological philosophy of Maurice Merleau-Ponty, Thomas Csordas (1990) introduced the concept of "embodiment" (in contradistinction to "the body") as a "paradigm for anthropology." In doing so, he turned Douglas's approach on its head. The body is "the existential ground of culture," Csordas argues, and our experience of the world is mediated by diverse "somatic modes of attention." The latter are defined as "culturally elaborated ways of attending to and with one's body in surroundings that include the embodied presence of others" (Csordas 1993, 138–39).

This notion of "somatic modes of attention" was taken up and developed in exemplary fashion by Kathryn Linn Geurts (2002a) in her masterful analysis of the sensorium of the Anlo-Ewe people of southeastern Ghana. In *Culture and the Senses*, Geurts goes to great lengths enucleating the Indigenous understanding of sensory processing that is given in the verb *seselelame*, which means "feeling in the body, flesh or skin," or to put a finer point on it, "hear-feel hear-feel at flesh inside." The term bridges the distinction between perception as cognitive and sensation as somatic that has bedeviled Western perceptual psychology. It also encompasses emotion. Here is how one of her interlocutors explained it: "You can feel happiness in your body, you can feel sorrow in your body, and you can feel other things, like cold. *Seselelame* describes all these things because it is 'hearing or feeling in the body.'" In a later segment of the same interview, Geurts's informant referred to the experience of going to the theater: "You go and watch it, and you feel something inside. You hear music, see the actors act very well, and you feel something inside. You applaud, get up and dance or shout something. That is a feeling and it comes through *seselelame*" (2002a, 185). Significantly, *seselelame* also connotes intuition, feeling ill or feeling inspired, and disposition or vocation. This term is as polysemous as it is polysensory. It embodies a whole "theory of sensory integration" and an equally comprehensive theory of "how we know what we know" (Geurts 2002a, 194, 179), which is at the same time a theory of the sociality of sensation.

Geurts's *Culture and the Senses* is noteworthy for the range of cultural domains it examines to arrive at an understanding of the Anlo-Ewe sensorium, from the language of the senses to childrearing practices, from clothing to ceremonial rituals, and from the body in sickness and in health to origin myths. Hers is a total sensory ethnography. One of the things she found is that Anlo people attach a premium to balance. For example, the fetus is pictured as already practicing the art of balance on its "seat" (the placenta) in the womb. Children's limbs are massaged from birth to inculcate flexibility, both of body and of mind. The Anlo have a proverb: "When in the village of the toads, squat as they do." This adaptability has been the secret of their success. Even though they are a minority and have suffered much persecution, many Anlo have risen to occupy positions of importance in Ghanaian society.

In a chapter entitled "Toward an Understanding of Anlo Forms of Being-in-the-World," Geurts relates an incident that nicely exemplifies what Laplantine (2015) means when he defines sensory ethnographic research as involving "the sharing of the sensible." It was a moment of profound revelation for Geurts. All of the threads of her research into the Anlo sensibility came together and she experienced what it means to be Anlo in a deeply visceral way.

The moment came when she was listening to a storyteller recount the Anlo-Ewe migration myth. The Anlo once lived in the neighboring nation of Togo. A tyrant there made their lives unbearable, so they resolved to escape, led by the ancestor Tɔgbui Whenya. After a long and arduous trek, they arrived at the place they now call home, Anloga (or "Big Anlo"). It was there that Tɔgbui Whenya collapsed, saying, "I am rolled or coiled up from exhaustion and cannot travel further." At the utterance of these words, Geurts found her own body curling inward, along with the bodies of all the other members of the audience. Upon reflection, she realized that this kinesic behavior, this curling inward, is echoed in the very name Anlo (pronounced *AHNG-low*). Pronouncing the name "requires a formation in the mouth and a sonic production that triggers a rolled-up or curled-up sensation that resonates through the body" (Geurts 2002a, 117). This effect in the mouth and on the body is best understood, Geurts argues, in terms of "iconicity," a concept she borrows from Steven Feld (1996), which refers to the transposition of perceptual schemas across modalities.

Some years later, Geurts spoke about an incident by phone with an Anlo friend living in Houston, Texas. "You know how the term Anlo literally means to roll up or curl up in the fetal position?" she asked. "Yesss?" her friend answered. "What does it mean to you to be part of a people whose name means 'rolled up'?"

> In her lengthy response was the phrase "resentment and respect." She said that curling up in the fetal position is something you do when you feel sad, when you are crying, when you are lonely or depressed. She said that being Anlo meant that you felt that way a lot, but you always had to unroll, or come out of it, eventually, and that gave you a feeling of strength. I told her that I had used the phrase "persecution and power" [together with "resentment and respect"] in one discussion I had delivered about the name [*AHNG-low*] . . . and I asked if that fit what she meant. She confirmed that it did. (Geurts 2002a, 118)

Summing up, probing the Anlo sensibility enabled Geurts to arrive at an understanding of Anlo affectivity, as articulated around the sentiments of resentment (or feeling persecuted) and respect. This affective disposition and form of being-in-the world is given in their collective appellation, in the toponym for their homeland (Anloga), and in the migration story that relates "their ancestors' escape from slavery and migration to the coast, and then their ascendance to a position of influence (and resentment) in contemporary Ghana" (118).

The concept of embodiment introduced an important corrective to the mind-body dualism of conventional Western thought. It generated such notions as "the embodied mind" and/or "the mindful body." But there is some question as to whether the holism of this concept is holistic enough. We have seen how Csordas enlarged it to include the embodied presence of others, but beyond the social or interpersonal there is the geographical. The experience of the physical environment must also be taken into account if the anthropologist is to arrive at a genuinely holistic understanding of our "being in the world." To get at this more encompassing understanding, Michael Jackson (1983a) introduced the notion of "the unity of the body-mind-*habitus*," or what in sensory anthropology has come to be referred to as "emplacement" (Howes 2005a, 7; Pink 2009, 25; see further Geurts 2002a, chap. 6).

I arrived at my own appreciation of the analytic power of the concept of emplacement in the course of my field research in Papua New Guinea in the early 1990s. My fieldwork involved doing a comparative study of the sensory orders of two distinct culture and geographic areas: the riverine world of East Sepik Province and the coastal region of Milne Bay Province. The former area is inhabited by, among other peoples, the Kwoma of the Washkuk Hills (near Ambunti, halfway up the Sepik River). The latter area, known as the Massim, consists of the island societies of Gawa, Dobu, and the Trobriands, among others, which have been studied by some of the most illustrious anthropologists in the history of the discipline, such as Bronislaw Malinowski (1929, 1961), Reo Fortune (1963), Annette Weiner (1976), and Nancy Munn (1986).

The Kwoma build their villages on hilly ridges, and their name means "mountain people." Their territory also includes swampland, where the women go each day to process sago and to fish, while the men pass their time in the men's house or go out on the hills to hunt. The Kwoma practice scarification, which results in their skin coming to be lined with ridges of tiny bumps, like the skin of a crocodile. These marks are regarded as a sign of beauty and endurance and are also valued for the protection they afford by "hardening" the skin. Kwoma "money" consists of woven pendants with row upon row of tiny kina shells sewn onto them. There is a correspondence, therefore, between geography (hilly ridges) and body decoration (cicatrization), and the value attached to this correspondence is reflected in the design of Kwoma currency (the woven pendants with their lines of kina shells).

In the Massim region, villages are positioned on the seashore, not in the interior. Going out on the sea, and the feeling of buoyancy this entrains, is valued over the "heavy" feeling of remaining on solid ground. The men of the Massim regularly sail to neighboring islands to engage in the ritual ceremonial exchange of valuables (long shell necklaces called *soulava* or *bagi* and large armbands of conus shell, called *mwali*). In *Argonauts of the Western Pacific* (1961), Malinowski dubbed this system of ceremonial exchange "the Kula Ring."

The people of the Massim do not practice scarification but instead scrape their skin clean, rub it with coconut oil so it gleams, and also use fragrant pigments to adorn it with delicate patterns. Unlike the Kwoma, who are preoccupied with fortifying bodily boundaries, Massim people seek to extend the body in space, or augment its "presence" through body decoration.

Massim "money"—namely, the kula valuables—also reflects the local penchant for intensifying and extending presence. The white armbands, for example, are highly luminous, and the red shell necklaces are equally radiant, echoing the luminous expanse of the sea at sunset when the winds fall still. What is more, the valuables are decorated with attachments, so they give off a tinkling sound. The shell decor "extends the body [of the shell] in space and the mobile decor makes a sound that ramifies the space—as if putting it into motion" (Munn 1986, 114). Significantly, the larger kula shells each have names, and as they circulate around the Kula Ring, passing from the hands of one "man of renown" to another, they accrete the names of all those who have possessed them. The shells are talked and sung about, constantly. In this way, both the shells and the men who transact them acquire *butu*, a term meaning "noise" and "fame." One often hears it said: "There are islands where people have never seen my face, but they know my name." The presence of Massim men is thus extended beyond their gleaming, fragrant bodies via the sound of their name being spoken on some far-flung island as the history of a given kula valuable is recounted. Massim money, then, resounds (via the tinkling sound) in the same way it reflects (via its luminous qualities) what it means to "be in the world" the Massim way.

Materiality and Atmosphere

Materiality is a concept that comes from material culture studies. It expands the idea of the social to encompass objects and highlights how the material relations among things, and between things and persons, inflect social relations, or give them their cast. There are many fine studies in "the social life of things" (Appadurai 1986; Drazin and Küchler 2015). In this literature, things are represented as having their own "biographies" (Kopytoff 1986). The anthropology of the senses adds a further layer to this analytic framework by introducing the notion of "the sensori-social life of things" and proposing that allowance be made for attending to the "sensuous biography" of objects as an integral component of their social biography. To get at the underlying concept here, we might borrow a line from Simmel's classic essay on the "sociology of the senses" (1997) and substitute "things" for people: "That we become involved in interactions with [things] at all depends on the fact that we have a sensory effect upon one another." The point here is that things impinge on consciousness and influence social relations by virtue of their sensoriality—their being felt, smelled, listened to, and so forth. Their materiality is more a support. Thus, artifacts or commodities can be analyzed both as bundles of social relations (i.e., the relations that go into their production and circulation) and as bundles of sensual properties and relations (Howes 2005b), as our analysis of the sensory properties of kula valuables in the previous section will have shown.

One of the areas in which this sensori-social approach to the study of the material world has made the greatest inroads is the field of museum studies. After the sensory turn in museum studies, museology becomes "sensory museology" (Howes 2014b; 2022, chap. 7). This development is evidenced by the novel focus on analyzing the sensory properties of the objects in a museum collection, exemplified by such works as *Sensible Objects: Colonialism, Museums and Material Culture* (Edwards, Gosden, and Philipps 2006); *Museum Materialities* (2010) and *Museum Objects: Experiencing the Properties of Things* (2012), both edited by Sandra Dudley; and Constance Classen's *The Museum of the Senses: Experiencing Art and Collections* (2017).

The biographies of museum objects are complex. This is because the contexts of their production, circulation, and consumption in their cultures of origin are abstracted when they are incorporated into the spaces of their culture of destination, especially (though not exclusively) the space of the museum. Once they have been accessioned, they are either housed in a glass case, positioned as an element in an ethnographic tableau, or relegated to the storeroom. In their culture of origin, their meaning would have resided in their use in vibrant contexts of sensory and social interaction (see, e.g., Jonaitis 2006; Hamilakis 2014; Saunders and Cornish 2017), but in the museum they are reduced to their morphology, their visible form, and classified accordingly.

There is a longstanding distinction in Western thought between persons and things, *persona* and *res*. This distinction underlies and supports the attribution of animacy and agency as well as sentience to the former and the denial of any of these capacities to the latter. Sensory museology challenges this dichotomy and raises such questions as: How might the objects in a museum collection be revivified so that they convey something of their original meanings and functions, or "life"? The Métis artist and visual culture studies scholar David Garneau, who is based at the University of Regina, Regina, Saskatchewan, illustrates this conundrum in a series of paintings of "Grandfathers." In one of the paintings, Grandfather is positioned in front of a mirror "contemplating Western ocularcentrism" (fig. 3a); in the other, Grandfather is shown "archived" in a storage box (fig. 3b). The reader may wonder: What does Garneau mean by painting a rock in the collection of an ethnographic museum—namely, the Canadian Museum of Civilization? Being a mineral sample, doesn't a rock belong in a science or natural history museum? This is a good question, but only if one subscribes to the assumption that nature and culture are poles apart, which is not the case in the "natureculture ontologies" of many Indigenous cosmologies (see Descola 2013; Heywood 2019; see further Latour 1993).

It bears noting that some rocks, though certainly not all, are regarded and treated as other-than-human-persons among the Anishinaabeg (Ojibwe, Cree) of the Eastern Woodlands

Fig. 3 David Garneau, *Grandfather Contemplating Western Ocularcentrism*, 2021, and *Grandfather Archived*, 2021. Photo © David Garneau.

(Matthews and Roulette 2018; Hallowell 2010). Treating some stones as potential kin and using a grammatically animate form when speaking about them is also reported among most Algonquian-speaking peoples, and in contemporary sweat lodge ceremonies, the stones that heat the enclosure are referred to as "Grandfathers"—the same as the stones in David Garneau's paintings. The concept of personhood is substantially more capacious but also more nuanced and critically observed in these Indigenous societies than in mainstream Canadian society.

Anishinaabeg conceptions of personhood also extend to include ceremonial objects such as drums and rattles who act as ritual relatives (*Wiikaanaag*) of ceremonial leaders in affecting healing. They too are treated as having life (*Bimaadiziwin*) and therefore capacity to act in the world (Matthews 2016; Matthews, Wilson, and Roulette 2021). This has profound implications for objects—or rather, beings—that make their home in museums. The presence of these objects in collections places obligations on museums to "respect and encourage their social imperatives" (Matthews, pers. comm.).

Other artifacts are likewise regarded as sentient beings by Eastern Woodlands people. An example is the famous false masks of the Haudenosaunee (Six Nations Confederacy). The sensory museology literature contains some discussions of how to care for the senses of such masks within museum settings. For example, Andrea Laforet (2004) describes the Sacred Materials Programme at the Canadian Museum of Civilization (now known as the Canadian Museum of History) in Gatineau, Quebec. This program provides for two Haudenosaunee medicine men to come to the museum twice yearly to chant, feed (provide corn meal mush), and smudge (burn tobacco) for the false face masks and other sacred objects from the Six Nations Confederacy in the collection. Interested representatives of other First Nations are also welcome to "come to the museum, view all of the objects associated with their history, identify objects requiring special care and handling, make recommendations about care, speak with collections managers, perform ceremonial care, as required, and talk about repatriation if they wish to" (Laforet 2004, 2).

Maureen Matthews is the curator of Cultural Anthropology at the Manitoba Museum in Winnipeg, Manitoba. She has been responsible for facilitating the repatriation of a number of sacred artifacts (formerly) in the Manitoba Museum's collection and also arranging handling sessions with the members of source communities. Such community outreach programs are increasingly common as museums across Canada (and throughout the world) attempt to rebuild relations with Indigenous people (Krmpotich et al. 2014; Gadoua 2014). But Matthews has a different take on community outreach. In her view, the objects themselves should be credited for the community outreach they create. In effect, what the visits with members of source communities involve is the objects, whose "social force" may have been latent, getting their way. It is not that this force needs to be "revivified," though, just acknowledged: "When you see an object reconnect with its family, when they hold an old piece of beading or interact with a pipe, it is not the object which is being reanimated but the relationship which is being rekindled on both sides because of the materiality and sensory connection that happens between them. . . . The objects become 'Grandmothers' or 'Aunties,' some students call them 'Elder objects,' but the relationship is on both sides" (Matthews, pers. comm.). In addition to the still relatively scant literature on caring for the senses of Indigenous artifacts (e.g., chanting, smudging, and feeding them), there is a burgeoning literature on sensory techniques for appreciating and understanding museum objects more fully (see, e.g., Golding 2010; Cundy 2017; A. Mills 2018; Howes et al. 2018). To cite but one (particularly innovative) example, in "Interpretations: Dancing Pot and Pregnant Jar? On Ceramics, Metaphors and Creative Labels" (2010), Wing Yan Vivian Ting describes a community outreach program called "Creative Spaces" that she ran at the Schiller Gallery of the Bristol City Museum in 2006–7. The participants were all students learning literacy or how to teach English as a second language (ESOL) at two local adult colleges.

The aim of the project was to facilitate a "robust and reflective object-human relationship" with items (mainly bowls) in the museum's collection of Chinese porcelain by empowering the participants "to listen to the sensual, tactile language of Chinese ceramics" (Ting 2010, 189). One sensory activity involved the students' handling the bowls while wearing blindfolds to sensitize them to the tactile qualities of the ceramics, and then comparing these with their visual impressions when the blindfolds were removed. Another exercise involved looking at a ceramic piece while listening to a piece of music, such as the third movement of Bach's Harpsichord Concerto in D Major. The titles of the musical pieces were withheld so as not to distract attention from the transcendental (abstract and intangible) and engaging qualities of the music and incite the participants to "explore the inner value of ceramic wares" through the formation of "perceptual syntheses" (197). Finally, in a move designed to "democratize authoritative interpretation," the participants were invited to write their own labels for the jars and bowls. These "creative labels" were then shared with the other members of the group (rendering the work of interpretation social) and incorporated into the exhibition alongside the technical-sounding labels written by the curators.

In effect, the "Creative Spaces" project enabled the participants to "see" feelingly, musically, personally, and creatively by engaging the *whole* sensorium in the work of art interpretation, playing one sense off against another, or conjoining the senses in fun and unexpected ways. The associations the participants forged (e.g., between a big wine jar and "a pregnant woman with a softly swelling belly") could be described as "metaphorical," but that term is too cognitivist, too beholden to Lakoff and Johnson (1980); rather, the connections were *perceptual*. The activities Ting proposed are best understood as exercises in *intersensoriality* designed to feed the aesthetic imagination, infuse the perceptual with the personal, and make the object-human relationship that much more meaningful and hence fulfilling. In place of the emphasis on disinterested contemplation in the conventional definition of the aesthetic experience (following Kant), Ting's experiment is all about participant sensation—or recanting Kant, as it were.[4]

The meteoric rise in ethnographic studies of atmosphere, inspired in large part by the work of the late Gernot Böhme, is further testimony to the quickening of the senses in anthropological research (Edensor and Sumartojo 2015; Bille and Sørenson 2016; Schroer and Schmitt 2018; Sumartojo and Pink 2019). According to Böhme (1993, 2), atmospheres are like a haze: they are "indeterminate . . . as regards their ontological status" in that "we are not sure whether we should attribute them to the objects or environments from which they proceed or to the subjects who experience them." This is because atmospheres are actually compounded of both: they are a product of the "co-presence" of subject and object. Atmospheres are in between. Specifically, atmospheres are "the *mediums* or the *elements* through which perception, and hence human action and understanding, takes place" (Böhme in Bille 2013, 58). There are echoes here of the equally capacious and ontologically indeterminate concept of the sensorium (see pp. 7–10).

There is a tendency in the literature on atmospheres to conceptualize them reductively in terms of affects, as when Ben Anderson (2009, 80) suggests that atmospheres "are generated by bodies—of multiple types—affecting one another as some form of envelope is produced" (see further Massumi 2002 and the chapters by Riedel and Slaby in Riedel and Torvinen 2020). This tendency is unfortunate, for as Mikkel Bille (2013, 58) points out: "People do not simply become immersed in atmospheres on a blank slate, but are inherently attuned by the norms of what to expect and by events that have occurred previously"—cultural norms, that is. In other words, atmospheres are cultural and temporal as well as elemental in ways that "affect theory" fails to capture (on the reasons for this see Kane 2018; Howes 2022, 34, 157–58).

Mikkel Bille's work is at the forefront of the concept of atmosphere's increasing popularity in anthropologic research. In "Ecstatic Things: The Power of Light in Shaping Bedouin Homes" (2017), he explores how the light that reflects off or shines through objects, such as windows, tincture social relations among the sedentarized Bedouin of southern Jordan. The Bedouin have a penchant for green-tinted windows and for painting the walls of the "reception rooms" in which they host guests with shiny light blue or green acrylic paint. (The color green has strong religious undertones: it purifies and sacralizes space.) In "Lighting Up Cosy Atmospheres in Denmark" (2013), he reports on how Danes will burn candles (even in the middle of the day) in order to set the desired tone of *hygge*, or "coziness," when they gather with friends or family as well as during moments of solitude. LED lighting is not for the Dane at heart. We eagerly await the publication of his book "The Atmospheric City" (coauthored with Siri Schwabe), which will exteriorize his research on domestic interiors by going public. This direction has also been onboarded by the "Explorations in Sensory Design" research team, based at Concordia University, Montreal, in our research into the sensory ambiance of the mall, the museum, the hospital, the festival, and other public sites (see www.sensorydesign.ca).

Other major contributions to this stream of research include *Exploring Atmospheres Ethnographically* (Schroer and Schmitt 2018) and *Atmospheres and the Experiential World: Theory and Methods* (Sumartojo and Pink 2019). In the blurb for the latter book, the authors affirm "that atmospheres should be conceptualized as dynamic and changing configurations that allow analytical insight into a range of topics when we think in, about and through them. This book offers scholars, designers and creative practitioners, professionals and students a research-based way of understanding and intervening in atmospheres."

This chapter has traced the emergence of a cultural anthropology of the senses out of a series of exchanges between sensorially minded anthropologists and anthropologists working in neighboring fields, such as the anthropology of the body, the anthropology of medicine, ethnomusicology, museology, and material culture studies. These exchanges have proved very fruitful for all concerned.[5] In the next chapter, we shall explore how the sensory turn has spread to two of the three other branches of anthropology—namely, archaeology and anthropological linguistics—and how next-generation sensory studies scholars have pushed the bounds of sense yet further.

CHAPTER 3

Breaking Research in Sensory Anthropology

The focus of this chapter is on breaking research in the anthropology of the senses. It relates how an interest in analyzing the social life of the senses has spread from cultural anthropology to archaeology and anthropological linguistics, how sensory anthropology has gone international, and how it has also gone intergenerational. We begin, however, with an investigation into the dawn of "multimodal anthropologies."

Multimodal Anthropologies

Recent years have witnessed the ongoing multiplication of the modalities of anthropological research. Anthropology is no longer the "discipline of words" (as typified by the ethnographic monograph) it once was. Nor does textual experimentation or "writing culture" hold the same sway. Now the focus is on sensory experimentation and "imaginative ethnography." This development was heralded by the publication of *A Different Kind of Ethnography: Imaginative Practices and Creative Methodologies* (2017) edited by Denielle Elliott and Dara Culhane, and also signaled by the name change of the section of *American Anthropologist* (the premier journal in the field) formerly dedicated to reviewing ethnographic films from "visual anthropology" to "multimodal anthropologies" (Collins, Durington, and Gill 2017).

In their introduction to *A Different Kind of Ethnography* (which I use in my graduate seminars), the editors alert the reader that "in each chapter of this book you will find participatory exercises that invite you to write in multiple genres, to pay attention to embodied multisensory experience, to create images with pencil and paper and with camera, to make music, to engage in storytelling and performance as you conceptualize, design, conduct, and communicate ethnographic research" (Elliott and Culhane 2017, 3). The six chapters that follow each focus on a different means of investigation or mode of perception-action-expression and communication. The first chapter concerns "imagining," the second "writing," the third "sensing," the fourth "recording and editing," the fifth "walking," and the sixth "performing." It bears noting that even the chapter on writing goes well beyond the old and rather prosaic notion of writing as "thick description" (Geertz 1973): this chapter includes a discussion of drawing and poetry as research methods, and when it does turn to discuss writing, the examples cited, such as Kathleen Stewart's *Ordinary Affects* (2015), are far from dry. Stewart approaches writing as a form of "worlding" that captures "emergent perceptions" (see further Stewart 2011; Peterson 2016, 2021).

The practice of multimodal anthropology is otherwise exemplified (rather *avant la lettre*) by the series of "performative sensory environments" designed by Chris Salter and his diverse collaborators (including the present writer), beginning with *Displace v. 1.0*, which was shown at the 2011 meeting of the American Anthropological Association in Montreal. *Displace* was staged in the Concordia Blackbox, a huge multipurpose space in the second basement of the Engineering and Visual Arts Building. This installation was like a museum exhibition, but without any objects, only sensations, only qualia (discussed in chapter 4 below). It was composed of a barrage of different colored sheets of light and stroboscopic flashes, material and immaterial hexagonal shapes, a synthesized soundtrack more or less synced to the play of light, a revolving platform, fog, walls impregnated with odors, and drinks and jellies that offered unusual flavor combinations. What *Displace v. 1.0* did, essentially, was put on a cross-modal symphony of sensations, or "fugue of the five senses" (Lévi-Strauss 1969), designed to evoke a synesthetic sensorium inspired by the multi- and intersensory cosmology of the Desana Indians of Colombia (see Salter 2015, chap. 3, for a detailed account).

One of Salter's current projects is called "Sensory Entanglements." It is a collaborative research-creation project involving Indigenous and non-Indigenous artists and scholars from Canada and Australia. As Salter writes, "The team is attempting to explore the productive tension in how the 'newness' of emerging technologies (despite their colonial origins and structures) might enable an 'Indigenizing' of sensorial artistic experiences that disrupts historical boundaries, challenges entrenched borders, creates potential forms of culturally specific empathy, and potentially may de-colonize the representation of otherness" (Salter 2018, 89).

By way of illustration, in December 2016, team member Cheryl L'Hirondelle, an interdisciplinary artist of mixed Cree/Métis, German/Polish ancestry, in concert with her artistic partner, Plains/Woodland Cree elder Joseph Naytowhow, staged a performative sensory environment called *Yahkâskwan Mîkiwahp* ("Light Tipi") in a Toronto park. The performance took place at night. It involved the participants being handed flashlights and a smoldering sage grass bundle and being instructed to position themselves in a circle. Raising their flashlights skyward, they created the image of a tipi against the backdrop of the settler city skyline. L'Hirondelle then proceeded to play her drum, tell stories, and share Indigenous wisdom with the predominantly non-Indigenous audience.

The deeper significance of L'Hirondelle's use of the medium of smoke can only be hinted at for now. Further comment is reserved to chapter 8, where we discuss "the smoking complex" of the Eastern Woodland culture area (see pp. 213–15). In the interim, we can point to the way the fragrant spectacle of *Yahkâskwan Mîkiwahp*, which also had a strong proprioceptive component (the positioning of bodies), created an atmosphere for the production of a *con-sensus* regarding how the relationship between Indigenous peoples and the rest of Canadian society needs to be reset. It had only been a year since the *Report on Indian Residential Schools* (which revealed a longstanding pattern of cultural genocide) had been tabled by the Truth and Reconciliation Commission of Canada (TRC).[1] L'Hirondelle's intervention transduced those recommendations into aesthetic action, or what Dylan Robinson and Keavy Martin (2016) call "arts of engagement."

Heart Band is another performative sensory environment that was forged in the crucible of the "Sensory Entanglements" project. It is an interactive sound installation created by Métis artist David Garneau in collaboration with Concordia PhD student Garnet Willis. *Heart Band* consists of ten hand drums that feature paintings in a Métis beaded style, arranged in a figure-8 pattern that conforms to the infinity symbol of the Métis flag.

The drums are equipped with sensors that trigger audio clips of Garneau's own (prerecorded) heartbeat (under different conditions of stress) that would speed up and grow louder or slow down and fade into silence, depending on how the audience interacts with them. While this installation "displays" Métis culture (e.g., the patterns on the drumskins), it is also "flagrantly intercultural" (Biddle 2016) because of the fact that drums are common to many musical traditions and that, in the instant case, their skins are of plastic (rather than hide) and electrified. As Garneau declares in his artist statement, this may be taken to suggest that "beneath this [Métis surface] is a bond among peoples at the level of bodies, heart, music, relations with each other and with special things" (Garneau, artist's statement). Like *Yahkâskwan Mîkiwahp*, *Heart Band* presents a multimodal, intercultural platform for the production of cross-cultural *consensus* regarding the interrelational framework of Canadian society going forward. These interventions may be regarded as technologies for the decolonization of the senses—and society.

Extrapolations

In recent years, the novel approach to the study of sensory expression and communication across cultures brought on by the rise of the cultural anthropology of the senses has spread throughout the discipline. For example, anthropological linguists, led by Asifa Majid, have broadened their approach from the comparative study of color vocabularies, as exemplified by Berlin and Kay's *Basic Color Terms* (1969), to include other sensory terminologies, such as taste lexicons and smell lexicons (Majid and Levinson 2011). This move has challenged many of the conclusions that Berlin and Kay arrived at on the basis of their study, such as the idea that there is a single evolutionary sequence to the order in which color terms enter language and that this can be mapped on to a trajectory of increasing cultural and technological "complexity." For example, the Maniq, a hunting and gathering people who live in the dense forests of southern Thailand, have fifteen words for smell, whereas the English language is notoriously impoverished in this regard, bordering on the anosmic (Yong 2015). Had Berlin and Kay started with the study of olfactory vocabularies, they would have been far less presumptuous in their theorizing and come to question the very idea of a linear scale, instead of positioning the English language and culture at the apex of their evolutionary trajectory. The illusion of evolution depends on which sense is taken as the standard.

Archaeologists have also broadened the horizons of their field of study by engaging with the senses. Along with digging up and typologizing objects based on their form, now many archaeologists are just as focused on excavating sensoria—that is, on reconstructing the ways of sensing that would have imbued the remnants of the civilizations they uncover with sense (in both senses). Exemplary contributions to the new archaeology of perception include *Archaeology and the Senses* (Hamilakis 2014) and *The Routledge Handbook of Sensory Archaeology* (Skeates and Day 2020).

In addition to informing research in three of the four main branches of anthropology (cultural anthropology, anthropological linguistics, and archaeology—physical anthropologists remain on the outs), the rise of sensory anthropology in concert with sensory history (as will be discussed in chapter 6) has contributed to the emergence of the interdisciplinary field of "sensory studies" (first named as such in 2006 by Michael Bull et al.). Alongside the history and anthropology of the senses, which got the ball rolling, there is now a sociology of the senses (Synnott 1993; Vannini, Waskul, and Gottschalk 2012), geography of the senses (Rodaway 1994; Paterson 2009), and so forth. Sensory studies can be divided along sensory lines (e.g., visual culture, auditory culture, taste culture, etc.) or disciplinary lines (e.g., history of the senses, anthropology of the senses, geography of the senses, etc.). Whichever way you slice it, sensory studies is shaking the foundations of research in the humanities and social sciences.[2]

Meanwhile, in addition to going interdisciplinary, sensory anthropology has gone increasingly international. For example, French anthropologist Marie-Luce Gélard has challenged her compatriots to pay closer heed to the social life of the senses. The richness and diversity of this extrapolation are on full display in the special issue of *The Senses and Society* Gélard edited, "Contemporary French Sensory Ethnography" (2016). Dutch anthropology has also undergone a sensory awakening, thanks to the pioneering work of Birgit Meyer, author of *Aesthetic Formations: Media, Religion, and the Senses* (2009), and Jojada Verrips. Rob van Ginkel and Alex Starting edited a Festschrift in Verrips's honor entitled *Wildness and Sensation: Anthropology of Sinister and Sensuous Realms* (2007). What is particularly noteworthy, however, is the way sensory anthropology has now gone intergenerational.

Next-Generation

This latest development—the rise of "next-generation sensory anthropology"—is evidenced by the publication of *Sensibles ethnographies* (2022), edited by Sisa Calapi, Helma Korzybska, Marie Mazzella di Bosco, and Pierre Peraldi-Mittelette. The editors, and their fellow contributors, are all recent graduates of the doctoral program in anthropology at the University of Nanterre. They invited me to write a preface to their collection, and

I happily agreed. There are many exciting new departures signaled by the chapters in this edited work. In what follows, I would like to flag five innovations in particular.

One of the most salient themes of *Sensibles ethnographies* is its *focus on intracultural diversity*. The importance of attending to internal diversity (not individual diversity, mind you, but *intracultural* diversity) was first signaled by Constance Classen in her landmark article, "Foundations for an Anthropology of the Senses" (1997), and restated in the introduction to *Ways of Sensing*: "Anthropologists must be attentive to intracultural variation, for there are typically persons or groups who differ on the sensory values [and practices] embraced by the society at large, and resist, instead of conform to, the prevailing sensory regime" (Howes and Classen 2013, 12). Classen's call went largely unheeded, however, until now.

In her contribution to *Sensibles ethnographies*, Helma Korzybska (2022) explores the sensory world of blind persons who have received retinal implants; Anna-Livia Marchionni (2022) presents an intimate ethnography of the nonneurotypical sense experience of persons on the autistic spectrum; Pierre Peraldi-Mittelette (2022) describes how the members of an ethnic minority, the Tuareg, originally from the Sahara and now living in diaspora in Europe, organize gatherings at which they embody their homeland through evocative sensations of flavors, gestures, and clothing. The gatherings enable them to feel at home while living apart. Peraldi-Mittelette's case study raises interesting questions for the geography of the senses, such as: Where is "home" anyway? (see further Law 2005).

A second theme is *attention to gauging intensities*. This is in place of interpreting (or deconstructing) signs and symbols. Sisa Calapi (2022) observes that the sound of the conch used in the annual Vísperas ritual in the Kichwa community of Turucu, Ecuador when the celebrants process through town is more than a signal, it is a *force*, and she goes on to show how this links up with traditional Andean notions of *bulla, energía,* and *fuerza*. She also registers the "kinaesthetic contagion" of the movements of the dancers, which generates "collective euphorias."

Sensory ethnography can be a sweaty (and exhausting) business, as Marie Mazzella di Bosco (2022) brings out with exceptional candor in her account of what it was like to "dance freely" with strangers at the numerous sessions of "Danse des 5 Rythmes," "Movement Medicine," and "Open Floor" she participated in over the space of four years. I admire the way she replaced the notion of *mise-en-scène* with "mise-en-sens" in her description of the ambiance of the dance studios (the scented candles, the lights, the draperies, the humidity, the beat, etc.). Meanwhile, Elena Bertuzzi (2022) describes the "qualities of presence" in the songs and movements of the *debaa* dance (of Sufi inspiration) performed by women on Mayotte. It was not so long ago that any talk of presence was banished from the academy, under the censorious weight of the Derridean concept of *différance*. Derridean deconstruction involved splitting and deferring (often *ad nauseam*); the focus of Bertuzzi's chapter in *Sensibles ethnographies* (like those of Mazzella di Bosco and Calapi) is on *multisensorialité* (a third theme) and assemblages—that is, on inter-modal and cross-modal *relations*, rather than sensory fragmentation.

A fourth theme is the *heightened reflexivity* displayed by the contributors. For example, Marchionni reflects at length on whether she can ever adequately attune her senses to tap into the hypo- and hypersensitivities of her nonneurotypical interlocutors. A fifth very prominent theme is *experimentation with alternate media*. For example, Korzybska uses line drawings and watercolors in her attempt to evoke the pixel-like flashes that blind people who have received retinal implants "see" (Elliott and Culhane would be impressed by the creative methodology of this essay). Meanwhile, Anaïs Angéras's (2022) account of her experience building and inhabiting *yourts* and other "light dwellings" for over a decade is noteworthy for its emphasis on "making." She became intimately familiar with the sensory properties of the building materials she sourced, and once she had finished constructing her "habitats-without-footprints," she was struck by the porosity of the relationship between the inside and outside of these structures, most notably the scratching sounds of all the tiny creatures in the (living) walls.

To continue this exploration of what the next generation is up to, I would like to offer a survey of the research work carried out by some of the graduate students attached to the Centre for Sensory Studies (CSS) at Concordia University, Montreal. I am the codirector of the CSS and also have the privilege of serving (or having served) on the supervisory committees of the students whose work will be discussed below. But first a few words about the Centre.

The CSS received faculty recognition as a research center in 2012, and it was elevated to university research center status in 2016. However, its origins may actually be traced back to the creation of the Concordia Sensoria Research Team (CONSERT) in 1988, which was cofounded by myself and my colleague, the sociologist Anthony Synnott.

The CSS has a distinguished research funding and publication record. Its members, singly and together, have attracted over 3.5 million dollars in research funding since 2012, published countless articles, and authored or edited numerous books, including *Alien Agency: Experimental Encounters with Art in the Making* (Salter 2015); a special double issue of *Body and Society* entitled "Skin Matters" (Lafrance 2018); the six-volume *Cultural History of the Senses* set (Classen 2014a); and the *Senses and Sensation: Critical and Primary Sources* compendium

(Howes 2018). The CSS is also the *siège social* of *The Senses and Society*, the premier journal in the field, and has sponsored many international symposia, including the Uncommon Senses conference series.

The membership of the Centre includes eighteen faculty from a wide array of disciplines: sociology and anthropology, design and computation arts, theater, communication studies, art history, marketing, French studies, and psychology. There are four main axes to the Centre's research mission: culture and the senses, sensory design and marketing, multisensory aesthetics, and sensory communication technologies. The CSS is by far the most interdisciplinary of all the research centers at Concordia. It is not unique in academia, however. There are a number of centers with strong interdisciplinary research programs centering on the senses, such as the Amsterdam Centre for Cross-Cultural Emotion and Sensory Studies (ACCESS), the Groupe de recherche Cultures sensibles at the University of Liège, the Sensory Studies Network at the University of Nottingham, the Center for the Study of Material and Visual Cultures of Religion (MAVCOR) at Yale University, and the Sensory Ethnography Lab at Harvard University, among others.

Two things stand out about the modus operandi of the CSS. One is its commitment to fostering disciplinary specialization and rivalry alongside interdisciplinary integration. The other most salient distinguishing feature of the Centre is its commitment to fostering "research-creation." Research-creation is a Canadian concept; it goes by other names in other countries, such as "arts-based practice." As defined by Chris Salter, research-creation "combines discursive, analytic and critical theories and methods from the social sciences and humanities with the embodied, experimental and situated practices of creative artistic expression producing new ways of knowing and being."[3] By uniting artistic expression, scholarly investigation, and material experimentation, research-creation opens up a space "between art and anthropology" (Schneider and Wright 2010; Elliott and Culhane 2017) and "between art and science" (Born and Barry 2010; Sormani, Carbone, and Gisler 2018; Galison and Jones 2014).

The students attached to the Centre come from a range of programs, including the Social and Cultural Analysis (SOAN) doctoral program, the Interdisciplinary Humanities (HUMA) and Individualized (INDI) doctoral programs, and the PhD programs in Marketing and Communication Studies. The students' work to be discussed here can be grouped under three main categories: the more-than-human sensorium, sensory ethnography, and research-creation.

The More-Than-Human Sensorium

Mark Doerksen is a graduate of the PhD program in Social and Cultural Analysis. His doctoral dissertation was entitled "How to Make Sense" (2018). In it, he reports on his field research in Canada and the United States on a subculture of the body modification movement known as "grinders." Grinders are not satisfied with the normal allotment of senses. They implant magnets in their fingers so as to be able to sense electromagnetic fields. Doerksen followed suit so that he could sense along with them what they experience. There is no dedicated vocabulary for electromagnetic sensation, nor are there any medically approved procedures for fashioning an "nth sense," as Doerksen (2017) calls it. Grinders must therefore improvise, or "hack," as they say. They practice DIY surgery, which exposes them to many risks, as no medical professional would support or aid them in their quest.

The grinders' reports of their experience of an otherwise insensible dimension of the material environment (e.g., the emanations of microwave ovens and electronic security perimeters) represent an intriguing opening beyond the bounds of sense, as most humans know it. Here is how one novice grinder described his experience of a trash compactor:

> My favourite thing I've ever felt was actually during when I had my first implant. So it was still super fresh, not really sensitive, but at my old job we had this trash compactor in the back of the store, and every time I would take out the trash ... just walking into the vicinity [I would get] this buzz ... I like to say it feels like you're walking toward this super powerful object, but, I mean, really you are. That is what you're feeling because there is so much electricity going through that [machine] ... as if it were some mystical artefact or something that was the energies emanating from it. I haven't yet, but I still want to go back now that I have a fully healed [magnetic implant] on my finger just to feel what it feels like at peak sensitivity. (Doerksen 2018, 136)

Grinders could be likened to the X-Men of Marvel Comics fame, only instead of their supersensory powers being the result of some genetic mutation, they develop their own sensory prostheses, such as the magnetic implants, and also ingest chemicals and follow strict dietary regimens. Doerksen found that grinders tend to have a superiority complex and are also deeply distrustful of many social institutions, especially those of the "academic-industrial complex"—yet even though he could have been seen as a representative of the latter complex, these sensory anarchists accepted Doerksen into their ranks and shared their (extrasensory) experiences with him.

Zeph Thibodeau obtained a master's degree in music technology from McGill University in 2011 and worked as a technician in the Penhume Laboratory for Motor Learning and Neural Plasticity between 2011 and 2018. He runs a typewriter rehabilitation business on the side and has long been a volunteer at the Right to Move / *La voie libre* (RTM/Lvl), a bike-repair cooperative located near the downtown campus of Concordia. Thibodeau enrolled in the Individualized PhD program in September 2018 to pursue research on sensation, perception, and human-machine interaction. His research seeks to reconfigure the human/machine polarity by focusing on the multiple possible relationships *between* humans and machines and exploring how reframing the relationship may impact the identities of the parties to the conjuncture.

In 2019, Thibodeau staged a three-week public "research performance" called *Machine Ménagerie* in which he worked at developing an assortment of small autonomous robots that were "cute as heck" (see fig. 4) and engaged in a running dialogue with visitors to the installation. Because of their charm (partly a function of their size and partly of their apparent helplessness), the robots incited "affective interactions" both with each other and with the visitors who befriended them. The latter would talk to them, separate them when they became entangled, intervene to prevent them from toppling off the display table, and even ask to take them home so as to prolong the interaction. This contributed to the emergence of a conception of sentience as "collectively negotiated through performance" (Thibodeau and Yolgörmez 2020, 4). It would be easy, too easy, to theorize these responses as projections of human affects, or as fetishizations of the machines. Rather, what they index is

Fig. 4 Zeph Thibodeau, *Machine Menagerie*, 2019. Photo © Zeph Thibodeau.

relationality, and "the proof is in the performance," as Thibodeau puts it.

The design and exhibition of *Machine Ménagerie* led to the publication of two papers that Thibodeau cowrote with fellow PhD student Ceyda Yolgörmez (who is enrolled in the Social and Cultural Analysis doctoral program). In their analysis, Thibodeau and Yolgörmez observe (2020) that the question "Can machines think?" has long dominated research in Artificial Intelligence (AI). And, as more and more thinking-machines have been created, a further question has emerged: "Might machines eventually outsmart and dominate us?" In the latter view, intelligence is typically treated as a measurable quotient: a machine either has it or does not. There is a prior question, however: "Can machines feel?" It is typically skipped over either because it is deemed less interesting, a merely technical issue, or because of the conventional valorization of intellect over affect. Thibodeau and Yolgörmez resist the privileging of intelligence over sentience and "the binary logic of domination" that informs "the myth of AI" (the nightmare scenario of accidentally unleashing a superintelligence). What is more, the authors advocate that we approach the notion of sentience "relationally"—that is, not as some hypostatized "agential capacity" but as embedded in the relationalities between humans and machines. This opens the way for "the cultivation of an attention towards the concrete situations and encounters where machines are treated as sentient," or "being-together-in-the-world" with machines (Thibodeau and Yolgörmez 2020, 1). By shifting the focus from the attribution of intelligence and agency to a nonhuman entity to the "affective encounters" between humans and machines, the way is also opened for entertaining other sorts of relations, such as care in place of domination, and mutuality in place of instrumentality.

For one of his comprehensive exams, Thibodeau registered a business, a machine-human cooperative, and proceeded to write a constitution for a sort of parliament—that is, an assembly made up of the tools in his workshop, whom he treats as colleagues, and himself—inspired in part by the RTM/Lvl co-op model. He calls this business by the name "Chronogenica." For this parliament to be representative, Thibodeau had to share authority with the tools in his workshop, such as Verne the caliper, Savu the pliers, Aristo the typewriter, and Mole Vice the wrench (see fig. 5). This entailed a novel "(re)distribution of the sensible" and a total "(re)distribution of agency"—or rather, it involved drilling down to recognize the mutuality of the relationships tools and humans already enjoy with each other. He gauged the tools' voices (or "will") by being attentive to them (conversing, holding, gripping, moving, pondering, typing) with a view to arriving at a *con-sensus*. It is an interesting question whether the relationalities the Chronogenica constitution articulates as principles of consociation should be seen

Fig. 5   Chronogenica, *Chronogenica*, 2019. Photo © Zeph Thibodeau and Chronogenica Arts & Technologies.

as "intersubjective" or "interobjective," as "(still) all too human" or "posthuman."

Sensory Ethnography

Roseline Lambert is an award-winning poet in addition to being a trained anthropologist.[4] As such, she belongs to an anthropological tradition that includes Ruth Benedict, Margaret Mead, and Edward Sapir, all of whom led a double life as poets (Reichel 2021). Those anthropologists kept their poetry separate from their anthropology, though, whereas Lambert has sought to fuse the two in her ethnographic practice. She is a poet-anthropologist.

Lambert's doctoral thesis is entitled "Le reflet du monde est à l'intérieur de moi: Une ethnographie poétique de l'expérience de l'agoraphobie en Norvège" (The reflection of the world is within me: A poetic ethnography of agoraphobic experience in

Norway) (2021). Her thesis built on the research she did for her master's degree at the Université de Montréal interviewing members of the (five thousand strong) francophone virtual community of agoraphobes in Quebec. She also drew on her experience of agoraphobia during her teenage years, so her research was grounded in participant sensation. For her doctoral research, Lambert traveled to Norway, which has the highest per capita concentration of diagnosed agoraphobes in the world, and took up residence in a quarter of Oslo adjacent to the quarter where the painter Edvard Munch dwelt. Munch spent the last thirty years of his life cloistered in his studio. He was (and remains) the most famous agoraphobe of all time, best known for his painting *The Scream*, which is the most powerful depiction of the state of anxiety in Western art.

Ever since the first diagnosis of agoraphobia in 1871 by the German neurologist Karl Friedrich Otto Westphal, it has been seen as a spatial disorder. The fifth edition of the *Diagnostic and Statistical Manual* (DSM-5) defines agoraphobia as: "A marked fear or anxiety about two (or more) of the following five situations: Using public transportation / Being in open spaces / Being in enclosed spaces (e.g., shops, theaters, cinemas) / Standing in line or being in a crowd / Being outside the home alone." Lambert sensed things differently during her sojourn in Norway. She was struck by the way Norwegians in general seemed to be preoccupied by the ambient light: they talked about light the way most other Europeans and North Americans talk about the weather. Like other Scandinavians (Bille 2013), Norwegians are renowned for abjuring fluorescent or LED lighting and for burning candles in the middle of the day for no good reason other than it makes them/things feel "cozy" (see fig. 6).

Lambert found that the Norwegian agoraphobes she interviewed spend countless hours at the windows of their apartments, looking out. She accordingly devotes a section of her thesis to

Fig. 6 Candles in the sun, view from an apartment in Grünerløkka quarter of Oslo, Norway. Photo © Rosaline Lambert.

analyzing the material culture of the window. The social and sensory dimensions of other typically Norwegian objects, environments, and representations also attracted her attention. For example, she noted, and several authors affirm, that Norway is a particularly "home-centered" society wherein the house (*hjeme*) is diametrically opposed to the exterior (*ute*) and to the social. The remote cabin (*hytte*) in the woods is a highly cherished location. She found that the Norwegian imaginary is populated by many revered figures (the Viking, the sailor, the soldier) who do not fear going out, which exacerbated her interlocutors' sensitivities about their own misgivings in this respect. And her inquiries revealed that her interlocutors were acutely conscious of their contradictory position in Norwegian society: the social democratic welfare system supports them and assures them of an income even if they cannot go outside to work; at the same time, they must constantly prove to the State, and their social network, that their disorder is a real medical condition and not some form of laziness. The converse of this is that agoraphobes are at high risk for being stigmatized and excluded from Norwegian society.

Lambert's sojourn in Norway was cut short by the onslaught of the novel coronavirus pandemic in spring 2020, when her family called her home. Consequently, she did not have the chance to document and poeticize the seasonal light cycle for a full twelve months (only from July 2019 to March 2020). However, she was able to continue interviewing the participants in her study by moving the interviews online. It emerged that her interlocutors, who already spend most of the time inside their homes, considered themselves to be masters of confinement with a lot to teach the rest of the world about living in isolation. In exploring the sensory etiology of agoraphobia, Lambert has made an important contribution to sensualizing the field of medical anthropology. She has also made a signal contribution to (re)setting ethnography to poetry. Let me close by citing a sample of her poetry (with translations by Carmen Ruschiensky):

la nuit ≠ noire
sur la place de la gare centrale je flatte le tigre
je ne sais pas si le soleil se couche si je dors
mes yeux ouvrent mes yeux ferment c'est blanc

night ≠ dark
in central station square I pet the tiger
I don't know if the sun's setting if I sleep
my eyes open my eyes close it's blank

une ligne ≠ un phare
quatre feux jaunes clignotent au coin de la rue
le tramway approche
je ne sais plus dans quelle direction partir
mes lignes s'entrecroisent

a line ≠ a beacon
four yellow lights are flashing on the corner
the tram is coming
I don't know which way to go now
my lines are getting crossed

l'énergie ≠ la lumière
je suis repliée sur ma feuille
le jour déborde dans le café sur Thorvald Meyers gate
toutes les lumières sont allumées pour rien

energy ≠ light
I'm bent over my page
daylight floods the café on Thorvald Meyers Street
all the lights are on for no reason

Erin Lynch is a practitioner of sensory anthropology in the tradition of Sarah Pink, author of *Doing Sensory Ethnography* (2009). Pink has contributed substantially to sensualizing the discipline by "engaging" the senses in visual anthropology (Pink 2006), digital ethnography (Pink, Horst, and Postill 2015), and design anthropology (Pink, Ardèvol, and Lanzeni 2016; Pink 2021). In Lynch's research for her doctoral thesis, however, the focus is slightly different: she takes Augmented Reality (AR) as the object of her investigation. In 2015, she embarked on a multicity odyssey that took her first to London, Edinburgh,

Dublin, and Derry and then, during a second jaunt, to Seattle, Hong Kong, Melbourne, Christchurch, and San Francisco, followed by side trips to New Orleans and Toronto, and then back to Montreal.

Lynch's doctoral thesis could be classified as a contribution to the anthropology of tourism, but whereas most theorizations of tourism have focused on "the tourist gaze" (Little 1991; Urry and Larsen 2011), she trained her senses on how smartphones equipped with locative apps mediate the experience of the urban. Hence, her thesis offers a sensory ethnography of the "augmented city."

The timing of Lynch's research on locative tourist apps was very apt, as cities the world over scramble to brand themselves as desirable tourist destinations by offering visitors a custom-designed (and customizable) experience of the city through their smartphones. In her thesis, Lynch presents a discourse analysis of the lingo of the apps and a visual analysis of their imagery, but she also does something more. By keeping her senses about her, she picked up on all the discrepancies between screen and world, linguistic hype and everyday sensescape. Analyzing these nonalignments between the virtual and the actual revealed as much about the design strategies and messaging of the apps as their actual content. Lynch has revised her thesis for publication as the twelfth volume in the Sensory Studies series from Routledge. *Locative Tourism Applications: A Sensory Ethnography of the Augmented City* came out in October 2022.

Shortly after defending her thesis, while she was a senior fellow at the Centre for Sensory Studies and a Research Associate on the "Explorations in Sensory Design" project, Lynch led an inquiry into the sensory ambiance of the Casino de Montréal. The results of this inquiry were subsequently published in an article in *The Senses and Society* entitled "A Touch of Luck and a 'Real Taste of Vegas': A Sensory Ethnography of the

Montreal Casino" (Lynch, Howes, and French 2020). Through employing the methodology of participant sensation, this research revealed how the ambiance of the casino is not simply dictated by the "experience design" experts hired by the casino management to create a specific atmosphere, but rather coproduced by the casino's patrons.

"Vegas Nights" was the chosen theme at the time of the research, and the casino was accordingly replete with Elvis impersonators, sequined showgirls, and a wedding chapel where patrons could get married "for fun." The décor was overwhelmingly visual, and the music very loud and intense, but the research also drilled down to expose how the other-than-audiovisual senses were titillated: the taste by means of overly sweet "free drinks" and the "explosion of tastes" at the in-house restaurant belonging to the Michelin-starred Atelier Joël Robuchon chain; the touch by means of the ritual gestures at the blackjack table (with its plush felt surface) and the ergonomically designed seats at the electronic gambling machines (EGMs) that envelop the player in a world of their own. It did not appear that the Montreal casino scented the machines to induce a particular mood, unlike other casinos (Hirsch 1995), which was perhaps a missed opportunity.

The Montreal Casino bills the experience it offers as "fun for all the senses." *Par pur plaisir* is the inscription on the carpet at the entrance to the casino. But within its walls not everything is pleasure, or all that "fun," for that matter. Gambling has become routine for many, and an addiction for others. In recognition of the latter social problem, since 2006 the casino has housed a Centre du Hasard, or "responsible gaming station." According to the "A Game Should Remain a Game" page on the Loto Quebec website, such information kiosks are designed to illuminate how games of chance actually work, heighten players' awareness of gambling's associated risks, and suggest strategies to lower the risk of losing control over one's gambling habits.

The Centre du Hasard is, then, a "harm reduction measure." Lynch and her team surmised that taking this measure "likely reflects the tenuous position of [the casino] being a government-affiliated organisation peddling a (potentially) addictive product" and also noted the irony of the fact that "responsibilization" is offloaded onto the citizen (Lynch, Howes, and French 2020, 200). One of the displays in the station invites patrons to spin a wheel to "play the lucky number game," but its point is to reveal that there is no such thing as a lucky number. In another installation, the inner workings of an old-style machine—with spinning reels and a crank lever on the side—are exposed. The purpose of this mechanical striptease is revealed by comparison: the attendant demonstrates that, as with the older machines, the numbers on the digital slot machines are set from the moment you push the button. All of the spinning, the sound effects, the rumbling, and pizzazz is purely for show. Lynch found that the clinical feel of the responsible gaming station offsets, but hardly competes with, the sensory maelstrom and electronically amplified ambiance of the other spaces in the casino. Hence, it is a half-measure at best.

Lynch was invited by the responsible gaming research design team attached to the casino to present her findings and offer recommendations. She proposed that the casino should incorporate greenery (plants, trees, flowers) into its décor and have some pianos on hand (for the alternative dexterity they afford: playing keys instead of pushing buttons) so that the experience of the casino would not be so exclusively technologically driven. In this way, the casino's clients would be reminded that there is "life" (verdant life, other sorts of touching and being touched) apart from the "second life" in which the casino ensconces them.

Research Creation

Sheryl Boyle is a recent graduate of the research-creation stream of the Interdisciplinary Humanities PhD program at Concordia. She was also an assistant professor of architecture in the Azrieli School of Architecture and Urbanism at Carleton University, Ottawa, throughout the period of her studies and has since been promoted to the rank of associate professor.

Boyle's PhD thesis (2020) proposes what she calls "sensory (re)construction as a way of knowing." Its focus is on Thornbury Castle, built by Edward Stafford, the Third Duke of Buckingham (1478–1521) between 1508 and 1521 (see fig. 7). The duke's household was one of the largest and wealthiest households in England at the time, and he brought together scores of live-in artisans (masons, carpenters, cooks, gardeners, etc.) over the thirteen-year period.

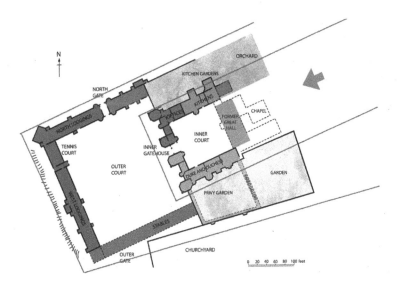

Fig. 7 Courtyard of Thornbury Castle oriented to capture the healthy northeast winds. Drawing: Sheryl Boyle.

Approaching the building as an "epistemic site" (after Rheinberger 1997), Boyle's thesis is laid out in three layers. The first layer has to do with the setting, which she (re)constructs using "works of the pen" (historical texts, chronicles, letters, and diagrams). It is not just the physical setting that concerns her, though, but the cosmology of sixteenth-century England, when all sorts of humoral and alchemical notions were in the air, and the air itself was of material interest. For example, the castle was oriented to the winds so that its walls and apertures could channel the healthy air from the northeast and dispel bad air. This was an important consideration at the time because of the prevalence of the "sweating sickness," which was understood to be brought on by stagnant air (see fig. 7).

The second layer has to do with the objects, methods, materials, and tools, such as mortar and pestle, that were used by the artisans. But Boyle's research is not confined to reading about these items and building up a mental picture: she learned how to fashion and became quite adept at (re)making them. For example, she (re)constructed the recipe for building mortar. The term "recipe" is significant here, for it turns out that the process of building was conceptualized at the time as analogous to cooking. Boyle devotes a fascinating chapter to the resemblances between the ingredients and processes of making building mortar and preparing blancmange ("white-eat") with mortar and pestle: quicklime corresponds to capon breast; water or casein corresponds to almond milk; loaf of tuff corresponds to loaf of bread (used as a setting agent); sand corresponds to sugar; and a fragrant spirit (namely, rosewater) was used in both concoctions. Mortar filled in between bricks, while blancmange was an *entremets* served between the dishes at a banquet (to "open" and "close" the stomach). This was all very sensual and very alchemical (e.g., the emphasis on the qualia of whiteness).

The third layer has to do with practices. One of the component parts of this layer involved Boyle's (re)making four elements of Thornbury Castle in her studio: a wall, a window, a chimney, and a trestle table. (The latter was a work table and a dining table at once, and it was intended to serve as the centerpiece at the oral defense of her thesis.) Each such (re)construction project involved combining different artisanal skills and creating a different, multisensory "epistemic object" (see fig. 9). For example, her (re)construction of an oriel window involved drawing on the skills of a confectioner, gardener, and plasterer. True to the original meaning of the word "window" (namely, "wind eye"), Boyle constructed a panel (in place of a pane) and impregnated each of its fifteen squares with the scent and flavor of flowers and honey: this referenced the fact that the façade of Thornbury Castle was dotted with boles containing beehives and climbing plants that wafted their fragrance through the "wind eyes" (see fig. 8). The squares of the panel were also

Fig. 8 Roses and bee boles punctuating the walls of the privy garden at Thornbury Castle. Photo © Sheryl Boyle.

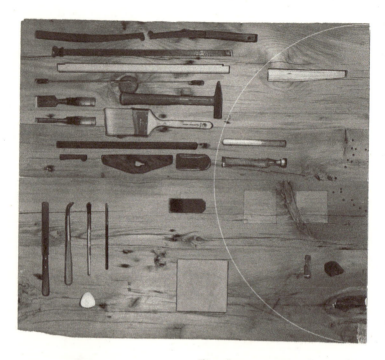

TOOLBOX -
VERSO VIEW

THE TABLE OF DELIGHT

A sensory toolbox for the artisan

The toolbox is organized into four alchemical qualities used in cooking in the early modern period: colour (top left), fragrance (top right), sweetness (bottom right) and luminosity (bottom left). Small working areas are left in each quadrant, creating a social space for discussion. The tools and toys used in making the four (re)constructions are housed here.

Tools are french-fitted into the wood. The table breaks apart in the centre along the north arrow, then folds in half creating two portable ancona toolboxes, one for each hand.

Fig. 9 Verso (underside) of the drawing/table for interdisciplinary tools used by the artisan to manipulate luminosity, color, fragrance, and sweetness—four alchemical qualities. Small working areas are left in each quadrant, creating a social space for discussion and exchange, before folding along the quadrants and transporting to the next site. Artwork: Sheryl Boyle.

BREAKING RESEARCH   109

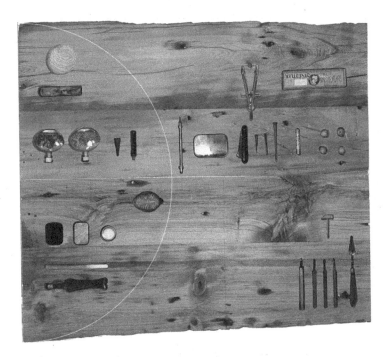

COLOUR

Tools are used to prepare the table and substances used to make it white.

FRAGRANCE

Dried flower petals, charred willow twigs, oak galls, all used to make the impermanent and fragrant drawing.

LUMINOSITY

Precious substances (gold leaf and ultramarine blue from lapis lazuli) used to create luminosity for the sun and breath for the wind.

SWEETNESS

Sculpting tools, honey, sugar, gum arabic and pine pitch glue used for the playful subtleties.

tinctured like stained glass. Boyle's "windows" are not for looking; they are for smelling and imaginatively tasting. That is, they are designed to bring the environment in, rather than seal it out behind glass.

A word is in order here about the requirements of the research-creation stream of the Interdisciplinary Humanities PhD program. It does not suffice for a student to write a thesis. The student must also stage an exhibition, be it a performance or (as here) an installation artwork. Furthermore, the creative component cannot be a mere illustration of the thesis, nor the thesis a mere exegesis of the artwork. The two components have to speak to each other so that the resulting contribution to the advancement of knowledge is both material and intellectual, sensible and intelligible—or, in short, a multimodal conversation.

Boyle's 312-page thesis and the four (re)construction projects that accompany it constitute a brilliant, highly redolent, textural, and flavorful enactment of sense-based research in architectural history. Throughout, the accent is on buildings conceived of as processes or "events" rather than such surface features as their form or style (see further Bille and Sørenson 2016). It is an exercise in the "archaeology of perception" that brings the sense(s) of the past to life.

Before entering the Social and Cultural Anthropology master's program in fall 2020, Genevieve Collins was an active participant in the Winnipeg arts scene, working in an art gallery and making films. She was attracted to Concordia by the prospect of researching and creating an immersive sensory environment that would simulate the experience of being in outer space. We typically think of space as vast, dark, silent, lifeless, and uninhabitable. This is because we normally view it through the lens of a telescope, or a Hollywood film. However, as recent advances in astrochemistry and acoustic astronomy have revealed, the gas clouds of the Milky Way smell like rum, and, far from being a silent expanse, outer space resounds with all sorts of ringing sounds and pulsations. These are just some of the facts Collins discovered in the course of her preparatory research. The question then became how to transduce these facts into the realm of the senses—how to create an atmosphere where there is no atmosphere (as we humans know it) to speak of.

The installation artwork Collins created, called *ETHER*, ran at ExperiSens from March 3 to 8, 2021.[5] Upon entering the tiny room where the installation was housed, my attention was drawn to three glass display cases set on pedestals wrapped in aluminum foil topped by funnels. One case contained reddish rocks and sand, and when I put my face in the funnel, I breathed in a dusty and spicy scent meant to evoke the atmosphere of Mars; another case contained a cloud-like mass of cotton batting and smelled smoky and gaseous to suggest the atmosphere of Venus, with its many gassy layers; the third contained a gray-colored plant growing out of a cushion (with an International Space Station label) that diffused a distinct organic smell (eucalyptus) along with a metallic, burnt-steak smell (such as many astronauts have reported smelling upon returning from a spacewalk).

In the middle of the room, there was a stand with a tray of drinks. One glass purportedly contained recycled water from Mars, slightly rusty and dusty with a hint of spice and a vaguely organic smell; another contained a frigid and refreshing distillation of the Milky Way (conveyed by means of a frozen raspberry suspended in yogurt); the third was a rocky- and metallic-tasting beverage dyed deep black (to suggest the darkness of outer space) that also sparkled as if the liquid were composed of the minerals extracted from an asteroid.

On opposite walls of the room there were two video projections: one was of an eye that blinked repeatedly, as if unsure how to focus. The other projection, which ran for twenty minutes, took the viewer on a voyage around our solar system. The visuals consisted of extreme close-ups of telescopic images and microscopic images of particles (to play up the extremes of scale), as well as lightning flashes and silhouettes of the International Space Station crossing in front of the sun. The way the visuals rotated, and zoomed in and out of focus, created a vertiginous feeling in the spectator that referenced the disorienting effect of zero gravity. The accompanying soundtrack featured oscillating and ringing sounds as well as muffled clips from the Voyager Golden Record. The blurriness of the latter sounds indexed the distortions that sonic vibrations would undergo when transduced through ice or rock or heavy gases in addition to suggesting how an extraterrestrial being or sentient scientific device that came across the Golden Record might register it.

After my visit, I sat down with Collins to discuss my impressions. What sense had I made of all these otherworldly sensations? She recorded my reflections, along with those of all the other visitors to *ETHER*, and then analyzed them for purposes of her master's thesis.

For her PhD, Collins proposes to make an ethnographic film and write a thesis based on fieldwork in an Arctic research station. As she writes in her proposal,

> Prospective astronauts and scientists participate in long-term studies in extreme environments such as polar research labs to simulate long duration space flight and imagine human habitation on other planets. In these training grounds or space analogues, researchers experience long-term isolation, face extreme weather conditions, and study microorganisms well adapted to the environment in order to conceive of life elsewhere in the universe. The central aims of this project are to

document the sensory aesthetics of everyday life in this context, explore the dense network of subjectivities inhabiting the environment, and investigate the inherent temporal and spatial ambiguity that accompanies this scientific research. The main research questions include: How does research in space analogues engage with ideas of futurity? What are the sensory dimensions of this scientific research environment? How are human and more-than-human subjectivities entangled in this unique terrestrial milieu?

This proposed research points to how the anthropology of the senses can move beyond traditional cultural and environmental spheres to explore new frontiers of existence and experience.

In closing, the graduate student research reviewed here is manifestly stretching the bounds of sense in all sorts of sensational new directions: it is multi- and interdisciplinary, and multi- and intersensory, at once. This body of research confirms that the "sensorial revolution" (Howes 2006) in the humanities and social sciences has indeed come of age (Lamrani 2021; Howes 2022). The reader might want to stop and savor this historic juncture for a moment, since in the next chapter we shall be turning to consider how the senses came unhinged.

PART 2

THE SENSES IN PSYCHOLOGY

CHAPTER 4

Unhinging the Senses
From Sensation to Calculation

This chapter explores how philosophical conceptualizations of the senses and cosmos dating from antiquity were largely supplanted by scientific models after the Scientific Revolution and later replaced by psychological perspectives. This series of displacements had profound repercussions that continue to influence our understanding of the senses—and society—today.

In the first section of this chapter, we examine the fallout of the Scientific Revolution and, in the following section, the fallout from the psychological revolution. The seventeenth-century philosopher John Locke played a role in both these revolutions. It is ironic that Locke's "sensationist philosophy" is commonly seen as having prioritized the senses when he actually straitjacketed them. Meanwhile, his natural philosophy desensitized nature by peeling back the surface of the phenomenal world to explore the underlying "corpuscular" composition of matter under the lens of the microscope. The latter move was a world-shattering act, no less momentous in its way than the "truths" that Galileo brought to light by theorizing the universe through the lens of a telescope (see Piccolino and Wade 2013).

In the second section, we turn to investigate the fallout of the cognitive revolution within psychology itself, which substituted cognitivism for Lockean empiricism. Empiricism views the mind as a *tabula rasa* and the senses as passive receptors of the impressions made on them by the exterior world, which in turn become ideas. Conversely, cognitivism treats perception as determined by cognition. Its focus is on analyzing the "cognitive map" of the individual subject, which is supposed to dictate how their senses function. Alternatively, under the guise of cognitive neuroscience, it treats "patterns of brain activity" as determinative of perception. From the sensory studies standpoint advocated in this book, the latter perspective is too top-down, and the former too bottom-up. Both approaches ignore the mediating role of culture and the socialization of the senses in addition to overlooking the agency and interactivity of the people doing the sensing, and of the senses themselves.

The alternative approach advocated here could be called *sensitivism* to distinguish it from both empiricism and cognitivism. Sensitivism involves leading with the senses conceived of as both bearers and shapers of culture. Sensitivism foregrounds the study of *cultural practices* (the techniques of the senses) over physiology (the senses as receptor organs). The focus is on the interaction between the senses and the world as well as each other rather than on the neural pathways leading from sense organ to brain. Finally, sensitivism is attuned to "the distribution of the sensible" (Laplantine 2015) or "political life of sensation" (Panagia 2009) and seeks to further the project of anthropology "as cultural critique" (Marcus and Fischer 1986). It is therefore a "critical practice" (Cox, Irving, and Wright 2016), not just a descriptive exercise.

The Aristotelian Worldview

According to classical science—or "the Aristotelian worldview"—the universe was composed of the Four Elements: fire, air, earth, and water. Each element was distinguished by a different combination of tactile qualities: hot and cold, wet and dry. Thus, the element of earth was categorized—or *qualified*—as cold and dry, fire as hot and dry, water as cold and wet, and air as hot and wet (see fig. 10). The Four Elements also provided the media for each of the five senses. According to Aristotle, "Water is the element of sight (because the eye contains water), air the element of hearing, fire the element of smell and earth the element both of touch and of taste, which is a mode of touch" (Connor 2015, 241).

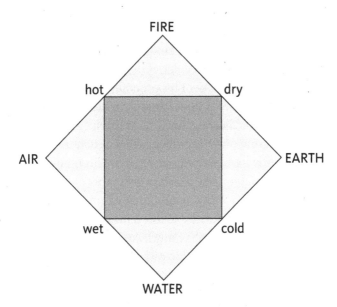

Fig. 10   The Four Elements of classical Greek cosmology. Image: Wikimedia Commons.

The material world or "environment" of antiquity was thus what Constance Classen (1993b, 1998) would call a "sensory cosmology." It was all very sensible, at least if we follow Aristotle. Plato's cosmos was a different matter, since for Plato "Ideas" came first, and he was profoundly distrustful of the senses (Keller and Grontkowski 1983). Plato's bedevilment of the senses created a tension within Western philosophy. This tension was compounded by the polarization of body (where the senses were located) and soul in Christianity (Despland 1987; Davis 1976), and this disjunction culminated in the standoff between Descartes, with his doctrine of innate ideas, and Locke, with his doctrine of the primacy of sensation. But we are getting ahead of ourselves. Back to Aristotle.

Aristotle was known as the peripatetic philosopher on account of his penchant for thinking while walking and the way he displaced himself from city to city. (This contrasts with modern philosophers holed up in their studies, or modern psychologists shut in their laboratories.) Aristotle also has a reputation for being the founder of the five-sense model of the sensorium. This is because of his pronouncement in *De Anima* (*On the Soul*): "There is no sixth sense in addition to the five enumerated—sight, hearing, smell, taste, touch." Aristotle indeed held that each sense has its proper sphere or object. The objects of perception were not things as such for him, however, but *provinces* of sensation. The province or "proper object" of vision was color; that of hearing, sound; that of smell, odor; that of taste, flavor. The complexities of touch made it less amenable to such schematization, however much Aristotle tried to treat it as a unity (see Vinge 2009). Within each province—and *exclusively* within each province, it bears repeating—sensation was supposed to take the form of "a kind of mean" between the two extremes of the pair of contraries proper to that province: sight between white and black, hearing between shrill and dull, and so on (with the province of touch left somewhat vague because of its complexity). The implication is that we perceive by means of differences, without positive things.[1] Each province of sensation had its own spectrum or ratio of sensible differences, defined as that which cannot be perceived by any other sense. That is its "proper sensible."

The provinciality (or exclusivity) of this theory of the sensory functions of the sensuous soul posed certain difficulties, however.[2] What of those objects, such as figure, number, and motion, which are perceived by more than one sense (for example, figure is perceived by vision and by touch)? Aristotle called these the "common sensibles." What of complex sensations, such as the experience of eating grapes, which are both red and sweet? And, given that a sense cannot perceive itself, how is it that we perceive *that* we see and hear? In his attempt to answer these questions, Aristotle reasoned that there must be yet another sense, a shared sense, responsible for unifying, distinguishing, and coordinating the five senses and their deliverances. This power of the sensuous soul he called "the common sense" (*koinē aisthēsis*, or *sensus communis* in Latin translation). For Aristotle, "this 'sense' constitutes a power of perception that is common to all the five senses yet reducible to none of them" (Heller-Roazen 2007, 35). This "sense" sounds suspiciously like a sixth sense, does it not? It would be rash to suspect Aristotle of being inconsistent here, however, for as Daniel Heller-Roazen explains in *The Inner Touch: Archaeology of a Sensation*, "Strictly speaking, the common sense [on account of its commonality and irreducibility] is . . . not a sixth sense, . . . it is nothing other than the sense of the difference and unity of the five senses, as a whole: the perception of the simultaneous conjunction and disjunction of sensations in the common sensible, the complex sensation, and finally, the self-reflexive perception [or, sense of sensing]" (35). Summing up, the classical understanding of the material world and the demarcation of the senses was all very elementary—or better, elemental—and very sensible. It was also very popular and had tremendous staying power.[3] We can discern an echo of it, for example, in the seventeenth-century play *Lingua, or the Combat of the Tongue and the Five Senses for Superiority*. In this comedy, which is quite riotous, Lady Lingua (as the personification of speech) presents a case for being recognized as a sense, the sixth sense, alongside the other five, Auditus, Visus, Tactus, Gustus, and Olfactus (all masculine characters). Common Sense is called on to judge her case and rejects her plea based on what could be called the argument from design: "The number of the Senses in this little world is answerable to the first bodies in the great world: now since there be but five in the Universe, the four elements and the pure substance of the heavens [i.e., the Aether], therefore there can be but five Senses in our Microcosm, correspondent to those, as the sight to the heavens, hearing to the air, touching to the earth, smelling to the fire, tasting to the water; by which five means only the understanding is able to apprehend the knowledge of all corporal substances" (Tomkis 1607, n.p.). Numerous other examples of the five-sense model of the sensorium and corresponding four- or five-part model of the cosmos (depending on whether or not the Aether is counted) could be culled from the literature (see Vinge 1975; Classen 2014a). Suffice it to say that this quintessential model was part of the received wisdom—folk wisdom, that is, not just philosophical speculation.

The Fallout from the Scientific Revolution

The deeply qualitative and profoundly sensuous understanding of environment and mind (or soul) that prevailed in pre-modernity would come undone, however, with the onslaught of the Scientific Revolution. From a scientific perspective, which is the only right-thinking perspective for us contemporaries (living as we do under the thrall of modern science), there is a distinction to be drawn between the "qualities" of the material world and the "properties" of the material world, or between qualia and matter or substance. "Qualia" refers to those aspects of materials that are dependent on the human perceptual apparatus, such as color (humans perceive only a fraction of the electromagnetic spectrum; infrared waves and X-rays are off the human scale) or sound (the range of human hearing is from 20–20,000 Hz, which excludes so-called infrasounds). *Property* refers to the intrinsic aspects of materials, such as figure, number, mass, ductility, and so on. The question is: How did we get here? How did we come to see things this way?

Enter John Locke. Much like Aristotle, Locke was a "Natural Philosopher" (to use the language of his day, albeit an amateur one); a philosopher of the mind as the author of *An Essay Concerning Human Understanding* ([1689] 1975); and a political philosopher as the author *Two Treatises of Government* ([1683/1690] 1988). However, he actually disrupted the whole Aristotelian tradition because of the way he splintered each of these fields.

As regards natural philosophy, Locke was a proponent of the new corpuscular philosophy introduced by the chemist Robert Boyle, among others. In *The Origin of Forms and Qualities* (1666), Boyle used corpuscularianism to "explain" the composition of the elements of classical physics and urged that the Aristotelian understanding be abandoned. Locke was also fascinated by the implications of microscopy. He testifies to this fascination in the following passage from the *Essay*:

> §11. Had we senses acute enough to discern the minute particles of bodies, and the real constitution on

> which their sensible qualities depend, I doubt not but they would produce quite different ideas in us; and that which is now the yellow colour of gold, would then disappear, and instead of it we should see an admirable texture of parts of a certain size and figure. This microscopes plainly discover to us; for what to our naked eyes produces a certain colour, is, by thus augmenting the acuteness of our senses, discovered to be quite a different thing; and the thus altering, as it were, the proportion of the bulk of the minute parts of a coloured object to our usual sight, produces different ideas from what it did before. Thus sand or pounded glass, which is opake, and white to the naked eye, is pellucid in a microscope; and a hair seen this way, loses its former colour, and is in a great measure pellucid. . . . Blood to the naked eye appears all red; but by a good microscope, wherein its lesser parts appear, shows only some few globules of red, swimming in a pellucid liquor. (*Essay*, vol. 1, part 1, para. 11)

Locke's excitement at what he discerned about life under the microscope, and the changeable traits of the visible, is quite palpable in this passage.[4]

This vision-dominated perception of life under the microscope inspired Locke to invert the conventional relation between "proper sensibles" and "common sensibles." He recast the latter as "primary qualities" (read: properties) and the former as "secondary qualities" (read: qualia). This was a major switch, which would have devastating consequences for the "evidence of the senses," as we shall see presently. At the time, however, the triumph of Lockean empiricism actually drove philosophers to focus on their senses as never before. Formerly, they deferred to Aristotle on the senses and the composition of the material world, whereas now they wanted to "see for themselves." There were those who followed Locke in their fascination with the new worlds of sight revealed by optical devices, but other natural philosophers, most notably chemists, went on tasting and smelling the material world in order to assess its qualities. This makes sense, for smell and taste are classified as chemical senses. As Lissa Roberts recounts in "The Death of the Sensuous Chemist: The 'New' Chemistry and the Transformation of Sensuous Technology" (2005), the chemists of the time honed their powers of sensory description to an extraordinary degree and constructed elaborate synoptic tables to capture all of the nuances of their observations. But then Antoine Lavoisier, instigator of the chemical revolution, intervened. Among other things, Lavoisier electrocuted water to find out about its composition, devised an array of instruments and tests that could substitute for the researcher's own senses, and introduced a new system of measurements and technical vocabulary. This spelled "the death of the sensuous chemist" in Roberts's (2005) apt phrase. Put another way, it hastened the demise of "the science of the concrete." The latter concept comes from the anthropologist Claude Lévi-Strauss (1966), who used it to denote the science of "tangible qualities" exemplified by the classificatory systems of traditional (Indigenous) societies in contrast to the abstractions of modern physics. Lévi-Strauss's notion of the science of the concrete applies equally to the way things were sensed and categorized qualitatively under the Aristotelian "dispensation."

One scientist who did much to substantiate Locke's switch was the Russian chemist Dmitri Mendeleev. In 1869, he dissolved the Four Elements of classical science into the 63 elements of his periodic table of elements (see fig. 11). The latter elements, which now number 118, are distinguished on the basis of their atomic number and recurring chemical properties alone. Thus, the "new" science heralded by Boyle and Locke and

ОПЫТЪ СИСТЕМЫ ЭЛЕМЕНТОВЪ.

ОСНОВАННОЙ НА ИХЪ АТОМНОМЪ ВѢСѢ И ХИМИЧЕСКОМЪ СХОДСТВѢ.

```
                        Ti = 50    Zr = 90    ? = 180.
                        V = 51     Nb = 94    Ta = 182.
                        Cr = 52    Mo = 96    W = 186.
                        Mn = 55    Rh = 104,4 Pt = 197,1.
                        Fe = 56    Rn = 104,4 Ir = 198.
                        Ni = Co = 59 Pl = 106,6 O. = 199.
H = 1                   Cu = 63,4  Ag = 108   Hg = 200.
      Be = 9,4 Mg = 24  Zn = 65,2  Cd = 112
      B = 11   Al = 27,4 ? = 68    Ur = 116   Au = 197?
      C = 12   Si = 28   ? = 70    Sn = 118
      N = 14   P = 31    As = 75   Sb = 122   Bi = 210?
      O = 16   S = 32    Se = 79,4 Te = 128?
      F = 19   Cl = 35,6 Br = 80   I = 127
Li = 7 Na = 23 K = 39    Rb = 85,4 Cs = 133   Tl = 204.
               Ca = 40   Sr = 87,6 Ba = 137   Pb = 207.
               ? = 45    Ce = 92
               ?Er = 56  La = 94
               ?Yt = 60  Di = 95
               ?In = 75,6 Th = 118?
```

Д. Менделѣевъ

Fig. 11 Mendeleev's periodic table of elements, 1869. Image: Wikimedia Commons.

substantiated in due course by Mendeleev transformed the cosmos from "a vibrant universe of sense" (Classen 1998, 5), a complex tapestry of sensations particularly evident in religious rituals (Pentcheva 2010; Jørgensen, Laugerud, and Skinnebach 2015), "into what Alfred North Whitehead has called 'a dull affair, soundless, scentless, colourless [in its elementary constituents];

merely the hurrying of material, endlessly, meaninglessly'" (Classen 1998, 5).

The magnitude of this ontological transformation is difficult to grasp. We can catch a glimpse of its nether side—that is, of the plethora of sensory cosmologies that antedated modern scientific philosophy—in the book *Aurora* by the German Protestant philosopher and mystic Jakob Böhme. He lived from 1575 to 1624, dying just eight years before Locke was born. Böhme held that "at the heart of the cosmos are seven spirits: Astringency [or Sourness], Sweetness, Bitterness, Heat, Love, Sound and Nature. These spirits continually interact with and generate each other," along with the world (Classen 1998, 21). Imagine conceiving of sensory qualities, such as sweetness and bitterness, as elemental, cosmic *forces*; or, to put this another way, imagine sourness, bitterness, love, and so forth, not as "secondary"—not as reducible to the movements of the corpuscles combining and recombining this way and that at the infravisible, infrasensible level—but as *active in their own right*.

The close connection between the scientization of the universe and the visualization of empirical phenomena that we have seen in Locke was also evidenced by the work of his contemporary, Sir Isaac Newton. In addition to discovering the laws of gravity, Newton dissected the perception of light and color through his experiments with prisms. Newton's celebrated scientific discoveries concerning color and light were not always well received by the poets, however. In her masterful account of the transformation in perception in modernity, Constance Classen (1998, 110) writes:

> As a consequence of this ideological shift [i.e., the advent of a scientific and mechanical view of the universe], "the world that people had thought themselves to be living in—a world rich with colour and sound,

redolent with fragrance" appeared to many to have become "cold, colourless, silent and dead." As John Keats would put it:

> [Natural] Philosophy will clip an angel's wings,
> Conquer all mysteries by rule and line,
> Empty the haunted air and gnomèd mine—
> Unweave a rainbow.

As regards the philosophy of mind, Locke's "sensationist philosophy" might seem like a continuation of the old maxim *Nihil in intellectu quod non prius in sensu* (there can be nothing in the mind that has not first been in the senses), but he actually broke with the Aristotelian tradition by, first, untethering the five senses from the Four (or five) Elements, and second, by committing a series of omissions. For example, there was a longstanding debate between the proponents of two radically different theories of vision: the extramission theory, which held that light emanates from the eye and seizes objects with its rays, and the intromission theory, which held that the eye receives rays. There is no mention of the extramission theory in Locke's *Essay*. It had been squelched. The eye was henceforth considered a "receptor organ," and vision retreated inside the head. Locke could thus be regarded as a pacifier of the visual sense. The extramission theory was not entirely extinguished, though; it survived in the form of the widespread belief in "the evil eye" (Maloney 1976; Dundes 1992), but this belief was dismissed by those in the know (i.e., the scientists) as "popular superstition."

Nor will the reader find any mention of the Aristotelian common sense in Locke's *Essay*. It was replaced by the latter's doctrine of the "association of Ideas," elaborated even more cogently by David Hume (1975a, 1975b). The closest Locke came to articulating anything resembling Aristotle's master notion was in his doctrine of common sense. For example, Locke used common sense to refute Robert Filmer's doctrine of the divine right of kings. There is nothing sensitive about common sense, however, for common sense is just another word for sound judgment, or shared understanding (Heller-Roazen 2008; Geertz 1983). It is devoid of sensuality.

Finally, having omitted the common sense, there was nothing to prevent Locke from introducing an even more restrictive, provincial demarcation of the senses than was ever dreamt of in Aristotelian philosophy. The common sense added an element of cosmopolitanism to Aristotle's schema. Compare the following passage from Locke's *Essay*: "A studious blind man, who had mightily beat his head about visible objects, and made use of the explication of his books and friends, to understand those names of light and colours which often came in his way, bragged one day, That he now understood what scarlet signified. Upon which, his friend demanding what scarlet was? The blind man answered, It was like the sound of a trumpet" (*Essay*, chap. 4, para. 11). How ingenious! the reader may think. But Locke does not cite this anecdote to endorse the blind man's solution, only to ridicule it: "For, to hope to produce an *idea* of light or colour by a sound, however formed, is to expect that sounds should be visible, or colours audible; and to make the ears do the office of all the other senses. Which is all one as to say, that we might taste, smell, and see by the ears" (ibid.). Any suggestion that it might be possible to form ideas about one sense in or by means of another is out of the question for Locke.

As regards political philosophy, the author of *Two Treatises on Government* was one of the thinkers who laid the foundations for the liberal democratic state and the political ideology of possessive individualism to go with it (Macpherson 1962). In place of the polis as an arena for debate about "the good life" and the achievement of *eudaemonia* (happiness), as per Aristotle, Locke posited the state of nature—a state in which, as his countryman Hobbes ([1651] 1996) put it, life was "nasty, brutish and short," and no one could be secure in their property. It followed naturally, Locke proposed, that the denizens of the state of nature would want to enter into a social contract for the mutual preservation of their property, including their property in themselves, whence the origins of civil society.

To conceive of society as rooted in contract was a far cry from conceiving of humans as political or social animals "by nature," as per Aristotle in the *Politics* ([350 BCE] 1999). In this way, society came to be seen as "made up" of individuals, in contrast to the original meaning of the term individual (from the Latin *individuum*)—that is, the person as the *indivisible* unit of society, the idea being that society as a whole was divisible into ranked estates and the latter were discriminable into individuals, as under the ancien régime in France (Williams 1976; Dumont 1992). This switch in the meaning of the category of the individual person brought on what Karl Polanyi (1957) called "the great transformation" in the economic life of the West. It also smuggled in a hugely momentous transformation in the understanding of human reason—namely, the reduction of reason from ratiocination to calculation, and specifically, the calculation of self-interest on the part of the citizen as contractor (Grant 1985; Hamilton 2010, chap. 5).

The desensitization of Nature, the strict demarcation and pacification of the senses, the substitution of common sense for the common sense of Aristotle, and the reduction of ratiocination to calculation: all of these modernizing trends can be found in Locke. This ought to have occasioned some concern, but few subsequent philosophers have had the presence of mind to call Locke out. One exception is the Canadian philosopher George

Grant,[5] author of *English-Speaking Justice* (1985). In this tract, Grant sought to expose Locke's subterfuge and also railed against the political philosophy of the latter-day Locke—namely, the moral and political philosopher John Rawls. In *A Theory of Justice* (1971), Rawls conjured his two principles for liberal democratic justice from behind a "veil of ignorance" (i.e., his social contract theory was tailored for people who are ignorant of "the good"—an unusual stance for a moral philosopher to take).[6] Grant ardently critiqued the idea that justice is something we bargain for or make as too "easy," not to mention a slippery slope. With his thought firmly rooted in Athens and Jerusalem (i.e., classical Greece and the Judaic cradle of Christianity), Grant insisted that "justice is the overriding order which we do not measure and define, but in terms of which we are measured and defined." It is "what we are fitted for"—or, "the good ordering of the inward life"—and not merely "a certain set of external political arrangements which are a useful means of the realisation of our self-interests" (1985, 74, 44).[7] On this account, doing justice involves nothing less than "to render each human being their due," and what is due is "'beyond all bargains and without an alternative'" (87).

It is profoundly difficult, if not impossible, to sustain a position such as Grant's in modernity, since his teleological style of reasoning went the way of the elemental understanding of the cosmos. But we cannot forget Grant, for it is all of a piece. We must grapple with the aftermath of this stripping and stultifying of our senses that occurred in the seventeenth century. There was a time, as Elizabeth Sears observes in "Sensory Perception and Its Metaphors in the Time of Richard of Fourneval" (i.e., the twelfth century), when the senses were depicted as steeds—strong, willful, and potentially unruly—and had to be reined in by reason (Sears 1993, 29–33); after Locke, they are just poor drudges, yoked to common sense. Thus, being sensible came unhinged from being sensitive to the Elements (which had already begun to proliferate beyond the canonical four and retreat from the phenomenal to the corpuscular or atomic level of reality). The isolation of the elements from each other was repeated at the level of the social. In conformity to the philosophy of possessive individualism, persons were reduced to so many interchangeable rights-bearing subjects (rather like billiard balls knocking about on the smooth surface of some pool table) who go about contracting, confident that the State will back them if a deal goes wrong. This was a great boon for the legal profession. It was also a great boon for capitalism.

To appreciate this last point, we need to go back and correct a misimpression in the preceding discussion where the Lockean state of nature was analogized to the Hobbesian state of nature. Actually, Locke's state of nature was a lot less dismal than Hobbes's: natural law prevailed, which is to say "God's Law," in Locke's view. Consequently, it is a wonder that anyone should have wanted to leave the state of nature, since God's law would presumably have brought out the best in them (according to Locke's convictions). So we must dig deeper to uncover the real motivation. Perhaps it was the lure of capital accumulation under the cover of "freedom of contract"—the banner cry of the liberal economist—that did it.[8] Indeed, in his promotion of capitalism, Locke can be seen as contributing to the nascent psychology of the marketplace.

The Fallout of the Cognitive Revolution

Danièle Dubois is a prominent French scholar in the field of cognitive psychology, with the added distinction of being one of that field's most ardent critics. She directs the Paris-based Languages, Cognitions, Practices, and Ergonomics research team of the Centre National de Recherche Scientifique (CNRS) and is the lead author of the book *Sensory Experiences: Exploring Meaning and the Senses* (2021).

In her introduction, Dubois notes how, in the history of psychology, the behaviorist revolution upset psychophysics; then, the cognitive revolution toppled behaviorism. Now, she states, within cognitive psychology, there is another revolution afoot: the sensory revolution. The resulting paradigm could be called "sensory cognitive psychology," or "sensuous cognition." By leading with the senses instead of, for example, "the categories of the understanding" (as defined by Kant), Dubois and her conspirators invite us to put our skin (and other senses) in the game. Thus, Dubois and company do not defer to "the brain" (as "revealed" through an MRI scan), or Kant's *a priori* categories, or Descartes's *esprit* (spirit). Indeed, Descartes famously "called away" his senses to arrive at the truth of his existence and cogitations (Synnott 1991), whereas Dubois and company *embrace* the senses.

Dubois beseeches her fellow psychologists to recognize that there is more, much more, to "sensory processing" than signal recognition or "information-processing." This word "information" abstracts and also flattens the senses: "information as abstract conceptualization of a stimulation" (with the idea of stimulation being left to the natural sciences to define) is fundamentally amodal and therefore at odds with the multimodality of sense *experience* as we humans know it.

According to Dubois, sensory processing involves "sensing" first and foremost. The term "sense" is rich in meaning. It includes in its spectrum of referents both sensation or stimulation *and* signification, both feeling *and* meaning (as in the "sense" of a word). The implication is that human beings sense and make sense of the world, and this process goes on at the level of the senses themselves, whatever their localization in the brain might be. The French term *sens* covers the same semantic field as the

English word "sense" and also encompasses "direction" (as in *sens unique*). The senses may thus be understood as giving our thinking (read: meaning-making) direction. Rudolf Arnheim understood this point well. In his book *Visual Thinking* (1969), he demonstrated how thinking (or cognition) can be construed as a continuation of seeing; vision is not the servant of cognition.

Dubois and company are highly critical of cognitivism and advocate a kind of *sensitivism* in its place. This brings the senses back in to our understanding of cognitive processes (by treating them as agents, rather than passive receptors) and thereby challenges Cartesianism, challenges the "neuromania" of cognitive neuroscience (Tallis 2011; Howes 2022), and also challenges the computationalism that has come over cognitive psychology in the wake of the *révolution numérique* ("digital revolution" in English)—the idea of the mind as programmed like a computer.

I admire the way Dubois and company ardently refuse to assimilate the deliverances of the senses to the idea of "information," or conceive of cognitive processes on the model of "computation," or assimilate our understanding of how the senses function to sensor technology (the mechanization of the senses, which hearkens back to Descartes). I particularly admire the way their approach abjures quantifying qualia (as in the psychophysical paradigm) and concentrates instead on the *qualification of qualia*—that is, on investigating how qualia are categorized, evaluated, lived, and communicated through "discourses." This focus on the categorization of sensations shifts the onus from the private and subjective to the public, for categories are *collective* representations. This move has the effect of bringing not only the senses but also the social back into our understanding of cognition. There is a strong synergy between Dubois's sensory cognitive psychology and sensory anthropology, as the following chapter will show. But first we need to fill in some of the background regarding how the operation of the senses came to be (re)conceptualized over the course of the twentieth century.

From Sensation to Computation

The philosopher Matt Nudds presents a brilliant overview of developments in his chapter on "The Senses in Philosophy and Science: From Sensation to Computation" in *A Cultural History of the Senses in the Modern Age, 1920–2000* (Howes 2014a). At the outset, Nudds (2014) observes, the conception of the senses and sense experience was broadly empiricist (i.e., unchanged since Locke). It was supposed that there was an isomorphic relationship between the stimulation of a sensory receptor or "transducer" (the retina, the cochlea, the tongue, etc.) and the resultant pattern of sensations produced in the mind of the perceiver. The search was on to uncover law-like connections between stimulation and sensation, and this was carried out by means of introspection. The verbal reports of sensation by the subjects of these experiments were often very rich and detailed (see, e.g., Titchener 1912), but the whole procedure was marred by the fact that there was no independent way to verify the accuracy of the subjects' reports, and in any event, any inferences as to law-like connections between the physical properties of the stimuli (e.g., brightness or wavelength in the case of light) and the corresponding qualities of the sensations (e.g., luminous intensity or color) were dependent on the very laws that the experimenter was seeking to discover, so the "explanations" were circular.

The Gestalt movement in psychology, centered in Germany, offered one way out of this methodological impasse. Gestalt psychologists proposed that the basic units of experience were not simple or "atomic" sensations but organized "wholes," or *gestalten*, and redirected attention to the laws that determined this organization, which were presumed to be rooted in the physiological organization of the brain. One such law was the law of closure, which holds that elements will be perceived as a "complete figure" even when some may be missing. For example, an array of dots may be perceived as forming a circle even though there is no continuous line connecting them. This very promising line of inquiry into the intrinsic organization of perception was, however, foreclosed by the rise of Nazism and the dismantling of the institutes in which such research was carried out (Nudds 2014, 132–33).

Another response to the methodological problems facing introspectionism was behaviorism, which rose to dominance in the United States. Within this paradigm, as propounded by B. F. Skinner (1938), the search for laws linking stimulation to sensation was suspended on the ground that it was impossible to measure "inner" states, and the focus shifted to the search for laws linking stimulation to overt behavioral response, or "S-R." This circumvention of subjective consciousness, with all its presumed vagaries, was highly influential on account of its directness and simplicity, but black-boxing the mind in this way did nothing to advance understanding of the content or organization of sense experience.

Beginning in the 1940s, advances in neurophysiology made it possible to measure the inner workings of the brain-mind by using electrodes to gauge neural activity. The focus shifted from the interface between sense organ and world to the activity of individual neurons within sensory pathways from sense organ to brain. Significantly, with regard to vision, it was found that receptor cells in the retina and in the terminal area in the brain (i.e., the visual cortex) respond not individually but as assemblages, and what they pick up on are actually particular "features"—such as movement, or the presence of an edge or slope—and not the simple sensations of the empiricist and introspectionist account.

In the postwar years, the drive was on to produce machines that could think (the idea of Artificial Intelligence was born), beginning with the problem of enabling machines to "see." This task proved far more difficult than was anticipated by the pioneers of computer vision, such as Marvin Minsky. In 1966, Minsky directed an undergraduate student by the name of Gerald Sussman to "spend the summer linking a camera to a computer and getting the computer to describe what it sees" (quoted in Nudds 2014, 137). The challenge consisted in figuring out how to write a program that could transform the two-dimensional image produced by the camera into a representation of the three-dimensional objects in the robot's environment. This task was simplified by restricting the input to "synthetic worlds," such as, for example, an array of variously shaped wooden blocks. For the robot to identify the blocks, however, required first identifying their edges (as distinct from their shadows, which could appear like edges) and which edges belonged to which objects, as well as taking into account how the shape of an object in an image varied with perspective.

This problem was eventually solved by David Marr (1982), who theorized that what the neurons were doing could be conceptualized on the model of a computational system. This redirected attention from sensation to the computational algorithms responsible for transforming one "representational state" (labeled input) into another (labeled output) in a series of steps from "features" to the "2 ½ D sketch" to the three-dimensional representation of objects. Marr's application of ideas from computation theory to the problem of understanding how the senses function helped substantiate the idea that the mind should be thought of as analogous to a computer program.

There were problems with the emphasis on serial information processing and the idea of perception as representation in Marr's model. The subsequent rise of connectionism sought to resolve these issues by introducing the notion of parallel distributed processing and the theory that the brain was made up of interconnected networks of neurons coupled with the suggestion that it is the strength of the connections between the information-processing units of the brain, rather than representations, that determine perception (see further Sacks 2017).

In his chapter, Nudds also traces the developments in the philosophy of perception over the course of the twentieth century. At the outset, he notes, the sense datum theory of consciousness prevailed: "the view that perceptual experience consists in the awareness of non-material objects (sense data) that instantiate the sensory qualities that are apparent in experience" (Nudds 2014, 134). The emphasis on appearances raised difficult questions as to whether sense data should be construed as "mind-independent" or "mind-dependent." The latter prospect raised the specter of solipsism and suggested that perception is basically a matter of belief in a mind-independent reality. This was not a satisfactory solution, and it was eventually dissolved thanks to the development of "naturalistic explanations of the semantic properties of thought and language . . . [that] aimed to show how thought and language could be accommodated within a scientific world view" (144).

According to Nudds, the upshot of all this was that "psychological evidence became relevant to philosophy in a way that it had not previously been" (146). That is a nice way to put it, but let me suggest an alternate take. The way I see it is that the *naturalization* of perception spelled the *end* of philosophy's autonomy, with the result that psychological theories came to *dominate* philosophical speculation. How philosophy has fallen!

Being a philosopher in the (English-speaking) analytic tradition, Nudds does not have much to say about developments in other branches of philosophy. But he nevertheless (if rather cursorily) acknowledges the contributions that Continental (French and German) philosophy—most notably, phenomenology—and feminist philosophy have made to our understanding of science and the senses. "Both these approaches," he writes,

> differ from the analytic approach in the attitude they take to the natural sciences.... Both are interested in analyzing sensory consciousness and in understanding the intentionality of the mind. But whereas philosophers working in the analytic tradition embrace the methods and results of the natural sciences and view sensory consciousness and perception as part of the natural order, phenomenologists bracket the methods and results of the natural sciences, and see their approach as neutral with respect to scientific results.... Feminist philosophers of science have elaborated a critical approach to the methods of the natural sciences. In particular, that the distinction between "the facts" as determined by science and non-epistemic (i.e., social, moral, and political) "values" is not clear-cut ... and that we should not uncritically rely on the results of empirical science. (126)

This is an admirably succinct statement, entirely to be expected of an analytic philosopher, but it is a little too dry.

Sensuous Critiques of the Scientific Attitude

Phenomenology and feminist philosophy each offer *profound* critiques of the scientific attitude, which are poles apart from the neutrality of analytic philosophy. Feminist scholars in particular have exposed how the scientific quest for truth was undergirded by a particular set of gender relations. Nature was framed as a female entity whose "secrets" could be revealed through the deployment of the experimental method. In the work of Francis Bacon, for example, we find similar inquisitorial techniques to those that were used to interrogate witches being deployed to probe and subdue Nature (Classen 2005b; see further Jordanova 1993). This resulted in the disenchantment and rationalization of the natural world and the triumph of a mechanistic conception of Nature's inner workings, in contrast to the more organic understanding that prevailed in premodernity (Merchant 1990).

In addition to exposing the masculine bias of scientific thinking, despite its much-touted value-neutrality and presumed objectivity, feminist scholars have laid bare its visual bias, stretching back to Plato (Keller and Grontkowski 1983). We caught a glimpse of this in our earlier discussion of the invention of linear perspective vision, and in particular how this technique "objectifies" the body—particularly women's bodies—as in Dürer's illustration (see fig. 2). The male draftsman in Dürer's drawing could stand for any "man of science" and the female model for any "object" of scientific investigation.

The predominance of the gaze has seriously restricted the scope of scientific knowledge. Consider Constance Classen's study in chapter 3 of *The Color of Angels* (1998) of the life and works of the seventeenth-century writer Margaret Cavendish, duchess of Newcastle (1623–1673). Cavendish was an auotodidact and a polymath who took up the pen instead of, as was the rule for women of her time, the needle. The eclectic oeuvre of this "learned lady" included plays and stories as well as diverse forays into natural philosophy.

Cavendish was a contemporary of Descartes but disagreed with his opinion that "all knowledge is in the Mind and none in the Senses" (Cavendish [1668] 1992, 185). Rather, "Cavendish argued that each part of the body and each sense has its own knowledge: 'the Eye is as knowing as the Ear, and the Ear as knowing as the Nose, and the Nose as knowing as the Tongue.' She similarly stated in favor of a bodily intelligence that "the Heads Braines cannot ingross all knowledge to themselves'" (Classen 1998, 101). This is an intriguing example of the democratization of the senses in contrast to the customary hierarchization. Significantly, Cavendish used the nonmonarchical image of a parliament or a commonwealth to describe the sensory order: "In the Commonwealth of the body the senses were given . . . [the] role of judges, accepting or rejecting the various sensations which came before them" (Classen 1998, 101–2).

In a story she published in 1668 titled *The Description of a New World Called The Blazing World*, Cavendish confronted the masculine scientific establishment, with its cult of "Optick Glasses." The story begins with a lady being kidnapped and transported aboard a boat bound for the North Pole. After various mishaps (which left her male captors dead), she steps into a new world peopled by anthropomorphic animals (bear-men, fox-men, bird-men, etc.). In short order, she is proclaimed the empress of this new world, and she proceeds to divide the populace into learned societies: the bird-men become astronomers, the bear-men experimental philosophers, and so forth. Significantly, the empress upbraids the latter for their reliance on the aforementioned glasses:

> In *Blazing World* the bear-men scientists try to understand nature by examining it through telescopes and microscopes. It soon becomes evident, however, that such magnifying lenses have a series of deficiencies which lead them to present a grossly distorted image

> of the world. For example, lenses can produce a magnified image of a louse, but not of a whale, they can operate in light but not in darkness, they can enhance one sense but are no use to any of the others. "Your glasses are false informers, and instead of discovering the truth, delude your senses," the Empress proclaims. "Wherefore I command you to break them." (Classen 1998, 104)

In the end, the empress gives in to the vociferous protests of the bear-men (who would be powerless without their glasses) and relents. However, Cavendish was not done. In the "Observations on experimental philosophy" that accompany *Blazing World*, she paints experimental science as a pursuit more suitable for housewives than for philosophers on account of the housewife being practiced "in Brewing, Baking, Churning, Spinning, Sowing" (Cavendish 1668, 102)—all processes that inhere in the natural world rather than being imposed on Nature, like the investigative procedures of the *Novum Organum*, or "Baconian method." Her husband, William, championed her daring to write on matters scientific by noting, as regards medicine, that even though she was not trained in the field, any "good Farmer's wife in the Country" would have access to medical knowledge as a result of caring for infants and invalids (in Cavendish 1655, An Epistle).

As Classen (1998, 104) observes, Cavendish's "homey portrayals of science served to diminish the masculine majesty of the field and bring it within the domestic realm of women." Margaret Cavendish offered an alternative understanding of the senses based on her knowledge of traditional women's work and her own insights. She was also arguably the first feminist philosopher of science. It would take several centuries for other feminist critiques of the scientific investigation-representation of the physical universe and masculinist constructions of the sensorium to achieve much traction. But the tide is definitely turning now, as evidenced by the works of Evelyn Fox Keller and Christine Grontkowski (1983), Ludmilla Jordanova (1989), Donna Haraway (1988), and, most recently, Karen Barad (2007).

For its part, phenomenology (after Merleau-Ponty) problematized the overwhelming adherence to the analytic, disembodied, third-person perspective that is inherent to the scientific attitude. In its place, Merleau-Ponty (1962) expounded on the synesthetic, embodied, and first-person perspective that is intrinsic to phenomenology. His insistence on the primacy of perception and embodied knowing offered an important corrective to the scientific attitude. There is no question of this. However, in what we regard as a profoundly reactionary, retrograde move, Merleau-Ponty's phenomenology has otherwise been mobilized by the anthropologist Tim Ingold (2000) to attack the anthropology of the senses. In addition to wielding the *Phenomenology of Perception* like a cudgel, Ingold draws on the "ecological psychology" of J. J. Gibson to undercut the anthropology of the senses and shore up his brand of "perception anthropology," or "activity theory." Here there are questions, serious questions, as will be discussed in the next chapter.

CHAPTER 5

Anthropology Contra Phenomenology, Ecological Psychology, and Sensory Science

This chapter begins with a rebuttal to the critique of the anthropology of the senses advanced by Tim Ingold in *The Perception of the Environment* (2000). In that work, Ingold champions the ecological psychology of J. J. Gibson and phenomenological philosophy of Maurice Merleau-Ponty as part of his "efforts to restore anthropology to life" (Ingold 2011, 4), as he grandiosely puts it.[1] In this opening section, our goal is to expose the many epistemological and political problems with Ingold's brand of "ecophenomenology" (Ingold 2022) and to show how sensory anthropology is better positioned to resolve them.

The latter part of the chapter examines the rise of the Sensory Evaluation Research Laboratory. Sensory evaluation, also known as "sensory science," is one of the "sciences of subjectivity" that forms part of what Steven Shapin (2012) has called the "aesthetic-industrial complex." The researchers who staff these laboratories were known as "organolepticians" at first but subsequently changed their title to "sensory professional." Their research methods are loosely derived from psychophysics (Ulloa, forthcoming). In the ensuing discussion, the methods of sensory science will be critiqued from the standpoint of sensory anthropology, and an alternative, ethnographically grounded approach to design advanced. It is offered as an antidote to the misperception (and misconstruction) of the senses and designer goods under the glare of sensory science, and, it is hoped, may provide a balm for the consumer's senses and conscience alike.

On the Mental Traps of Ecological Psychology and the Problems with Phenomenology

Tim Ingold's account of perception in *The Perception of the Environment: Essays on Livelihood, Dwelling and Skill* purports to further the perspectives of Maurice Merleau-Ponty and J. J. Gibson while questioning the work of a number of social and cultural anthropologists whose contributions had been highlighted in *The Varieties of Sensory Experience* (Howes 1991)—most notably, Edmund Carpenter (1973), Anthony Seeger (1975, 1987), Paul Stoller (1989), Alfred Gell (1977, 1995), and Constance Classen (1993a, 1997) as well as the present writer (see Ingold 2000, 249–53, 281–85). What united us in our efforts to elaborate an anthropology of the senses was a commitment to developing a cultural approach to the study of sense experience, with a corresponding emphasis on the cultural *mediation* of perception. Ingold, however, dismisses any thought of mediation and proposes "the idea of direct perception" in its place.

In a nutshell, Ingold alleges that at the heart of the anthropology of the senses is "a representationalist theory of knowledge, according to which people draw on the raw material of bodily sensation to build up an internal picture of what the world 'out there' is like" (Ingold 2000, 282).[2] He claims that it "upholds a notion of cultures as consisting in systems of collective representations, over and above the conditions and contexts of *practical life* within which people develop and embody their own skills of action and perception" (284, emphasis added). He further holds that the various senses are not separate faculties, not "separate keyboards for the registration of sensation," but "organs of the body as a whole, in whose *movement*, within an environment, the activity of perception consists" (268, emphasis added). In elaborating his own brand of "perception anthropology" (as it may be called, to distinguish it from the anthropology of the senses), Ingold champions Gibson's "nonrepresentational" theory of the senses as "perceptual systems," a focus on the contexts of "practical life" and individual skills of action and perception, and an idea of the body and perception as a "synergic whole" (following Merleau-Ponty) along with a focus on "movement" within some environment (following Gibson).

According to Ingold's rendition of Gibson (1966, 1979), the senses are to be considered as "means of active inquiry and of orienting oneself in the world," and from this perspective they are "interchangeable" (Ingold 2000, 245, 276–81). What the perceiver looks for when moving from place to place are constancies underlying the continuous modulations of the optical array. These constancies or invariants constitute "affordances," or so many "possibilities for action," which are not mental constructs but rather inherent in the environment itself. For example, a doorway is an affordance (something through which you can pass); a chair is an affordance (something on which you can sit).

Assuming the givenness of affordances, Ingold goes on to posit "the idea of direct perception." This idea holds that "living beings can find meaning in an environment unmediated by signs.... It asserts that we perceive things directly, as they come forward into presence and impinge on our [practical] activity, not indirectly through the signs they leave in their wake" (2018, 41). On this account, perception is "a mode of action" (2000, 166), not representation, and not interpretation: "Interpretation comes later" (2018, 41). As for culture, there is no room nor any need for it in Gibson's "ecological equation." "Like life, perception *carries on*," Ingold says, at what he presumes to be a pre- or infra-cultural level.

Gibson's theory of perception as "information pick-up" in an environment can appear attractive, if one is not too concerned by his instrumentalization of the senses or bothered by the extrapolation of his findings concerning visual perception to the rest of the senses, as if they were "interchangeable." There are those who have sought to show that what goes for vision also goes for audition, and so on (e.g., Clarke 2005). However, more discerning scholars (Hetherington 2003; Valiquet 2019) balk at this assimilation, with good reason. The fact that their objections typically fail to register has much to do with the vaunted status of vision in the Western sensory hierarchy: being the paragon sense, it is assumed to stand for all the senses, with the result that the "other" senses are either overlooked or else assimilated to a visual model without further ado.

By cleaving to the work of a psychologist, Ingold distances his perspective from the more socially minded and cross-culturally sensitive work of anthropologists (Carpenter, Gell, Stoller, etc.), whom he pillories for adopting a social constructionist approach to the study of perception. Ingold's rejection of this approach is a product of his "ontogenetical" fixation (Howes in Ingold and Howes 2011), which privileges "ontogeny"—the development of the individual—and trivializes or dismisses the role of "phylogeny"—the development of the species, including the state of society. Indeed, Ingold is so dismissive of the social that, as he would have it, "relations among humans, that we are accustomed to calling 'social,' are but a subset of ecological relations" (Ingold 2000, 5). Or, again, he appeals to the evidence of the senses (ironically) to rubbish the idea of society: "You can see and touch a fellow human being, but have you ever seen or touched a society? We may think we live in societies, but can anyone ever tell where their society ends and another begins?" (Ingold 2011, 238). On the contrary, people who live in small-scale societies can certainly distinguish the bounds of their society, and sense this as well, when, for example, they engage in communal song (see Guss 1989; Seeger 1987).[3] Nor does the fact that it may sometimes be difficult to distinguish where one society ends and another begins invalidate the whole notion of societies, any more than the fact that it may sometimes be difficult to tell where one color ends and another begins could be said to invalidate the use of different color terms or even the concept of color. Yet, Ingold (2011, 238) writes, "Granted that we are not sure what societies are, or even whether they exist at all . . ." Not so fast! The social anthropologist takes nothing for granted.

Ingold's agnosticism with respect to society, and the way he skips over the social when he prefers the term "field of relations" (without further specification) to that of social structure, is what makes him a post-social anthropologist. His methodical individualism is consistent with that of other British anthropologists, such as Nigel Rapport, author of *I Am Dynamite* (2003), and can be seen as rooted in the venerable tradition of "English individualism" (Macfarlane 1991). Of course, individualism is no less a *social* ideology for being individualist in orientation (Dumont 1980), but Ingold pays no heed to this fundamental "social fact" (Durkheim [1895] 1982).

As noted above, Ingold attaches a premium to "practical activity," to people "going about their business" or practicing their vocation. Being so disposed, he approved of the example that I gave in *The Varieties of Sensory Experience* (Howes 1991, 168) of the sensory specialization of the Western musician, who may develop a refined sense of hearing, or the chef with an equally subtle sense of taste, even though both belong to "a society that is inclined to describe the knowledge and judgement of each through metaphors of sight" (Ingold 2000, 283). "To his credit," Ingold wrote, "Howes does recognize that human beings are not simply endowed by nature with ready-made powers of perception, but that these powers are rather cultivated, *like any skill*, through practice and training in an environment" (283, emphasis added).

Ingold's theory of enskillment has inspired some fine ethnographic studies (e.g., Downey 2005; Marchand 2008, 2009; Schroer 2018), but I have serious reservations about the appositeness of using the term "skill." I prefer the term "technique" (following Mauss ([1936] 1979) as in "les techniques des sens" (Howes 1990b), or the even more encompassing concept of "way" as in "ways of sensing" (Howes and Classen 1991, 257; Howes 2003a, 32–34; Howes and Classen 2013). The main reason for my reservations is that Ingold's theory of skilled practice is devoid of the notion of style and any concept of moral value. By contrast, these concepts are crucial to the practice of sensory anthropology.[4] For example, in her highly perspicacious analysis of the Anlo-Ewe sensorium in *Culture and the Senses: Bodily Ways of Knowing in an African Community* (2003), Kathryn Linn Geurts notes how, because of the premium attached to balance, the Anlo-Ewe have an extensive vocabulary for different ways of walking, or *kinesthetic styles*, each of which carries a different *moral valence* (Geurts 2002a, chap. 4). How does Ingold view walking? In "Culture on the Ground," he reduces walking to "locomotion" (see Ingold 2011, chap. 3): the focus is on bodily mechanics and the cognitive concomitants thereof, not moral action. Yet the exercise of the senses is always and everywhere hedged in by moral norms. For example, the practice of looking is strictly curtailed and regulated in societies that subscribe to the notion of the "evil eye"; the act of eating is commonly circumscribed by the notion of gluttony (i.e., overeating) being a sin. The amorality of Ingold's approach to perception is a direct result of the instrumentalism and information-centric bias of ecological psychology.

Being mindful of the strictures entrained by Ingold's exclusive focus on "practical activity in an environment," I called him out in a debate we had in 2011 (Ingold and Howes 2011). I observed that his portrayal of the environment in "Stop, Look and Listen!" (Ingold 2000, chap. 14) is "one in which you can look, listen, and are always on the move, but not taste or smell" (Howes in Ingold and Howes 2011, 313). His response was telling. He protested that, despite the ostensible marginalization (or downright elision) of olfaction and gustation in *The Perception of the Environment*, "there is nothing in my argument [that] . . . rule[s] out taste and smell. I do not subscribe to the Aristotelian hierarchization of the senses"; he then goes on to reiterate the "interchangeability" hypothesis—namely, understood as a "mode of active, exploratory engagement with the environment . . . vision has much more in common with audition than is often supposed, and for that matter also with gustation and olfaction" (in Ingold and Howes 2011, 313–14). No evidence is presented for the latter part of this claim. Elsewhere, Ingold falls back on the doctrine that "my body is a ready-made system of equivalents and transpositions from one sense to another" (Merleau-Ponty 1962, 235) to scuttle any suggestion that it is necessary to attend to the full panoply of senses, their differences, or their interplay. In other words, the twin doctrines of the "prereflective unity" and "interchangeability" of the senses excuse him from having to pay detailed attention to the ways in which the senses are discriminated and combined in different ways in different cultures. This, in turn, serves to perpetuate the modern Western bias in favor of sight and hearing as they can supposedly stand in for all the senses.

As noted previously, Ingold is hostile to the idea of "signs," or semiosis, and this extends to "culture," too (as a corollary of his doctrine of direct perception.) For example, he is dismissive of any field of study that contains culture in its definition, such as "visual culture" (with its roots in art history), "auditory culture" (also known as soundscape studies), and "material culture" (or materiality). Thus, he is critical of art historians and anthropologists of art for "reducing" sight to the perusal of images. Images are but "reflex[es] of vision" in his estimation—that is, paintings and such are objectifications of visual processes, which convert the eyes into "instruments of playback" (Ingold 2011, 137). As far as Ingold is concerned, perusing images "has nothing to do with observation, with looking around in the environment . . . [or] with the experience of illumination" that makes vision possible in the first place (in Ingold and Howes 2011, 316).

Ever the iconoclast, Ingold (2011, chap. 11) also trained his sights on the concept of soundscape, building on his prior critique of visual culture. Here, he would appear to have the work of "The World Soundscapes Project," directed by R. Murray Schafer, which assembled a vast library of sounds from far-flung places, in his crosshairs (though it could equally be the sound recordings of Steve Feld, such as the latter's *Voices of the*

Rainforest). Ingold's objections in this case have to do with the way landscapes are reformatted as soundscapes—that is, as objects of analysis by means of some audio-recording technology. Thanks to the recordings, he states, the ears become "instruments of playback." As such they are diverted from their proper function as "organs of observation" in the same way that the eyes are "allegorized" (Ingold's term) when sight is confined to the contemplation of images in visual culture (Ingold in Ingold and Howes 2011, 316). Another of his objections to the concept of soundscape is expressed in terms of a variation on the interchangeability hypothesis: sound is "not the object but the medium of our perception. It is what we hear *in*" in the same way that "we do not see light but see *in* it" (Ingold 2011, 138; 2000, 265).

A moment's reflection will reveal the fallacy of these objections. First, Ingold presents a romanticized (ante-technological) philosophy of the innocent eye, untainted by the perusal of images, and the naked ear, unmediated by any audio-technology. This is a hopelessly naïve position, utterly divorced from the actual complexities of sensory experience. Second, images such as paintings *do* mediate our perception of the environment, even when we are not looking at them directly, the very idea of landscape being a case in point. As Ron Broglio shows in *Technologies of the Picturesque: British Art, Poetry, and Instruments, 1750–1830* (2008), the idea of landscape was born of a particular painterly style, mediated by the use of the handheld Claude glass or mirror. Third, R. Murray Schaffer (1977) offered an important correction to the visualism of landscape studies by inventing the concept of the soundscape and helping attune us to the other-than-visual dimensions of the environment. His insight, or better, insound, was picked up on by the geographer J. Douglas Porteous, author of *Landscapes of the Mind: Worlds of Sense and Metaphor* (1990), who introduced such concepts as the "smellscape," "bodyscape," and "tastescape" to add yet more other-than-visual dimensions to our perception (and analysis) of the environment.

Practitioners from a range of disciplines have since heightened our attention to the diverse sensory dimensions of the environment through developing such practices as the "soundwalk" (Polli 2017), "smellwalk" (Henshaw et al. 2017), and "touch tour" (Howes et al. 2013). Ingold is not impressed. He says he "deplore[s] the fashion for multiplying *scapes* of every possible kind" (2011, 136) and insists on the "power of the prototypical concept of landscape," which "lies precisely in the fact that it is not tied to any specific register" (Ingold 2011, 136).[5] However, the point of utilizing such techniques of attunement, or single-sense approaches, is precisely to allow for the diverse sensory "voices" that are otherwise drowned by the blare of the visual to be "heard" and appreciated. Sensory anthropology, in contrast to Ingold's perception anthropology, strives to create room for the experience and expression of "nonelite" sensations (Santos 2018).

Furthermore, Ingold is mistaken in his claim that we only see *in* light, for this overlooks the ways in which visual experiences are modulated by social values and personal states. According to Dutson (2010), we do see light, and it comes in many gradations: from melancholy or somber through dull or gloomy to radiant or brilliant. These gradations are what Nancy Munn (1986) would call "quali-signs of value" (see further Chumley 2017). Note how the first terms in this series (melancholy, somber) have a negative connotation or value while the last terms (radiant, brilliant) are positively valued and have cheerful or energetic connotations (Dutson, Myerson, and Gheerawo 2010; Bille 2017). Hence, there is a process of valuation at work in the way we see light, not just "information pick-up." So too with sound and other sensations. For example, we discriminate between sound and noise. Noise is unwanted sound, which again implies a process of valuation (Mopas 2019; Thompson 2017). Sound is, in fact, rarely neutral.[6]

Ingold makes explicit his debt to Merleau-Ponty when he writes, "I *am*, at once, my tasting, my listening, and the rest" (in Ingold and Howes 2011, 330). This is another way of saying, "I am my body." This is fine insofar as it bridges the Cartesian split between mind and body. However, the self-centeredness of this affirmation must give us pause, for while it may help resolve the mind-body split, it also occludes the many other divisions that must be considered in any properly social account of the constitution of the subject—such as the division of society along racial, class, and gender lines (Sekimoto and Brown 2020; Hsu 2020; Bourdieu 1987; Jaffe, Dürr, and Jones 2019; Classen 1998).

From a sociological perspective, the individual subject is not simply "an undivided centre of movement and awareness," as Ingold (2011, 136) avers, but a product of the intersection of social forces that shape how the senses are used and understood. Thus, in the premodern West, women were taught to guard their ears and keep their eyes downcast. In modernity, individuals were generally instructed to keep their hands to themselves and to dismiss or trivialize odors—unless such emanations signaled disease or social status. Social factors, therefore, along with individual abilities and environmental allowances, deeply influence our modes of seeing, hearing, smelling, and so on. To assert otherwise is not merely an act of gross naïveté; it is a sign of contempt for the ways in which individuals and social groups have had their senses constrained and their experiences disdained by the politics of perception put forward by the dominant class.

Ingold may well be giving an accurate account of his subjective experience when he writes, "I *am*, at once, my tasting, my listening," and so forth, or defines the self as "an undivided centre of movement and awareness." However, when he extrapolates his individual experience to all humanity, as those of a phenomenological persuasion are wont to do, he errs.[7] There is far too much evidence in the historical and ethnographic record of the *decentering of the self along sensory and social lines* for us to attach much credence to Ingold's position.[8]

The problem here is that Ingold's "perception anthropology" is largely oblivious to the ways in which selves are positioned socially and how mobility may be circumscribed for the less privileged. Tellingly, one of Ingold's most vaunted figures is that of the wayfarer (see Ingold 2011, 148–52). The wayfarer is a rootless being, of course. What is more, in Ingold's writing, the wayfarer is a generic/masculine character, as when in *The Life of Lines* he writes, "Let us imagine the walker . . . making his way over hills and through valleys"; or, again: "In walking the labyrinth, . . . the walker is under an imperative to go where it takes him" (Ingold 2015, 42, 132–33). Now, presumably, Ingold does not mean to exclude women, since women walk, too. He is merely (uncritically, unreflexively) subscribing to the convention that "he" includes "she," and "his" encompasses "her."

Ingold's generic use of the masculine pronoun makes for a certain economy of writing, but its obfuscatory and exclusionary aspects should not go unremarked. There are alternatives, such as using "they/their" in place of "he/his," or, to be resolutely inclusive and specific at once, using "auteur.e" or "théoricien.ne.s contemporain.e.s," *à la française*. More fundamentally, as recent advances in the context of medical research have shown, gender blindness of the sort displayed by Ingold can lead to the infliction of many hidden injuries, such as misdiagnosis, or drugs that treat male ailments but exacerbate female disorders (Holdcroft 2007). Men and women are not interchangeable.

Furthermore, most people, and especially most women, know only too well that wayfaring, and even walking in public, can hold particular dangers because of ingrained gender inequalities and stereotypes of women's place being in the home. Similarly, wayfaring while Black, or any other disadvantaged ethnicity, would be unlikely to be the same unfettered, carefree experience that Ingold appears to depict. Witness the murder of Ahmaud Arbery, a Black man who went jogging—or "wayfaring"—in a white American neighborhood. But there is no place for these kinds of "othered" embodied experiences, marked by oppressive social structures, in Ingold's asocial approach. By stripping anthropological research of its social dimensions, Ingold turns it into a branch of psychology—or natural science, even, unable to respond to, or even acknowledge, the complexities of social life.

In effect, what Ingold's perception anthropology does is roll back the discipline of anthropology to a stage that is, for all practical purposes, precultural and pre-Boasian (recalling our discussion of Boas's break with psychophysics in chapter 1). It is also post-social in its abstraction of social contexts, its privileging of the generic individual (as when the pronoun "he" is assumed to include "she"), and its treatment of the self as an undivided perceptual center. This abstracted (generic) self is of a piece with Ingold's abstraction of the senses under the guise of the "interchangeability" hypothesis. To understand the conceptual basis of such notions, we need to take a closer look at the philosophical underpinnings of his approach—that is, his debt to Merleau-Ponty, and, in particular, at how the experience of synesthesia, or "union" of the senses, is (mis)represented in the work of Merleau-Ponty.

Merleau-Ponty on Synesthesia

Ingold's twin notions of the "interchangeability" and "prereflective unity" of the senses would appear to be derived from the following passage in Merleau-Ponty's *Phenomenology of Perception*: "My body is a ready-made system of equivalents and transpositions from one sense to another. The senses translate each other without any need of an interpreter, and are mutually comprehensible without the intervention of any idea. ... Synaesthetic perception is the rule, and we are unaware of it only because scientific knowledge shifts the centre of gravity of experience, so that we have unlearned how to see, hear, and generally speaking, feel, in order to deduce, from our bodily organization and the world as the physicist conceives it, what we are to see, hear and feel" (Merleau-Ponty 1962, 235, 229). Merleau-Ponty's account of the primordial union of the senses can appear attractive, if one is not too concerned by the way he treats very different forms of sensory processing as interchangeable and lumps them under the same term—namely, synesthesia. On the one hand, there is synesthesia proper, a relatively rare condition in which a perception in one modality triggers a vivid experience in another modality, without any corresponding stimulus. Synesthetes report seeing sounds (C sharp is bright blue), tasting shapes, and so forth (Marks [1975] 2014; Cytowic 1998). It bears noting that the "union of the senses" here is total and that these "equivalents" are generally supposed to be completely arbitrary and utterly idiosyncratic (for example, it is typically said that every synesthete with color-grapheme synesthesia will differ regarding the equation of a given color with a given letter of the alphabet).[9] While synesthetic perception can to some extent be explained by reference to brain physiology (see, e.g., Ramachandran, Hubbard, and Butcher 2004), this fact does not interest Merleau-Ponty, since he is only concerned with describing "the phenomenal body."

On the other hand, Merleau-Ponty extrapolates the term "synesthesia" to refer to a range of situations where the perceptual process is actually one of *matching* a sensory feature in one modality with a corresponding feature in another modality. For example, he writes, "I hear the hardness and unevenness of cobbles in the rattle of a carriage, and we speak appropriately of a 'soft,' 'dull' or 'sharp' sound. . . . One sees the springiness of steel, the ductility of red-hot steel, the hardness of a plane blade, the softness of shavings" (Merleau-Ponty 1962, 229–30). Other examples of these sorts of sensory conjunctures include our tendency to match higher pitches with lighter colors and to associate fuller sounds with round shapes (Marks 1975; Abath 2017).[10] These instances are referred to as "cross-modal correspondences" in the terminology of the philosopher Ophelia Deroy (2017) and her frequent collaborator, the experimental psychologist Charles Spence, head of the Cross-Modal Research Laboratory at Oxford University (see Spence 2018a). What is at issue here is that one can "almost feel" the hardness and unevenness of the cobbles from the sound of the carriage passing over them, or "almost feel" the springiness of the steel without actually touching it. By contrast, for the synesthete, the perception of a C sharp *is* bright blue, not like bright blue: that is, the equivalence is *total*. For the synesthete, such joint sensations are not joint; they are *intrinsic* in that they have a "perceptual reality," or "subjective indistinguishability," that is lacking from the experiential reality of the more commonplace cross-modal correspondence (Abath 2017).

Merleau-Ponty's account of the body as "a ready-made system of equivalents and transpositions" is susceptible to criticism for the way it obscures the multiple other sorts of relations that can obtain among the senses. John Urry provides a helpful typology of some of these forms of sensory interconnection in the following passage: "*cooperation* between the senses; a *hierarchy* between different senses, as with the visual sense during much of the recent history of the West; a *sequencing* of one sense which has to follow on from another sense; a *threshold* of effect of a particular sense which has to be met before another sense is operative; and *reciprocal* relations of a certain sense with the object which appears to 'afford' it an appropriate response" (Urry 2011, 238, summarizing Rodaway 1994). These examples show how the senses may be united in relations of domination and subordination, or reciprocity, anticipation, and so forth (see further Howes 2022, 26; O'Callaghan 2019; Santos 2018, ch. 8). It is important to attend to the full panoply of such relations (especially the sequencing of sensations in different modalities) and not suppose that the sensorium is a ready-made totality. The senses are made, not merely given, and their deliverances may conflict, rather than coalesce. Consider the example of the stick half in water, which looks crooked to the eye but feels straight to the touch. The suggestion that "synaesthetic perception is the rule" (i.e., some sort of default setting) needs to be tempered by the recognition that everyday perception (as distinct from synesthetic perception proper) involves "labor" (Lahne and Spackman 2018; Lupton and Maslen 2018), the work of *forging* connections, the work of *making* sense.

In "Colour and Sound: Transcending the Limits of the Senses" (2018), the cultural historian Fay Zika documents how the *idea* of synesthesia has spurred numerous scientists to try to codify the correspondences between color and sound. By way of example, she points to Newton's theory of an accord between the seven primary colors and the seven musical tones of the (Western) seven-tone scale. The idea of synesthesia has also inspired many artists and inventors to attempt to induce synesthetic perceptions in their audiences, whence the "ocular harpsichord" developed by the French Jesuit Louis-Bertrand Castel in the 1720s, the "color organ" invented by the British painter Alexander Rimington in 1895, or the abstract paintings of Wassily Kandinsky in the early twentieth century.

Interestingly, Zika suggests that the ideal of fusing the senses was actually (in her estimation) realized in the latter part of the twentieth century in the context of experimentation with prosthetic devices. These devices included the tactile-visual substitution system (TVSS) invented by Paul Bach-y-Rita, a complex apparatus involving a head-mounted television camera linked to electrically driven vibrators attached to a square of skin on a blind person's back. The TVSS "throws" an image of the objects in the blind person's surroundings onto the patch of skin, and this tactile stimulation is transposed into visual information in the brain, which in turn enables the blind person to move in space without bumping into things. Another such device is the "eyeborg," which harnesses different colors (as light reflected from surfaces at different frequencies) to different sound frequencies, enabling the blind person—in a very basic way—to "see with their ears" (Zika 2018, 312). These examples may be taken to suggest that "information" is fundamentally amodal, since the brain is able to extract relevant "information" about the environment no matter which modality or sensory pathway is activated. However, as noted previously, the word "information" is suspect (see pp. 133–34). Furthermore, these supposed transpositions function at such a crude and restricted level that they cannot be used to support any notion of the interchangeability or unity of the senses. Rather, they point to the fact that—even in the most carefully tailored and technologically assisted contexts—one sense cannot completely or adequately replace another.

If everyday perception involves "sensory labor" (Lahne and Spackman 2018; Lupton and Maslen 2018), as we have seen in the preceding discussion of the work involved in forging sensory interconnections, then it must be equally conceivable and possible for these connections to be *undone*. In *Fluid Signs: Being a Person the Tamil Way* (1984), Valentine Daniel presents an intriguing example of a Tamil ritual, the purpose of which is to "overcome" or "vanquish" the senses one by one and thus open the way for a transcendental experience. This ritual speaks directly to this issue of undoing connections.

By way of background, in traditional Indian cosmology and sensory psychology, "the five elements are associated with the five senses, and act as the gross medium for the experience of sensations. The basest element, earth, created using all the other elements, can be perceived by all five senses—(i) hearing, (ii) touch, (iii) sight, (iv) taste, and (v) smell. The next higher element, water, has no odor but can be heard, felt, seen and tasted. Next comes fire, which can be heard, felt and seen. Air can be heard and felt. "Akasha" (aether) is beyond the senses of smell, taste, sight, and touch; it being accessible to the sense of hearing alone."[11] It is against this background that we are to read the account Daniel gives of the arduous six-mile pilgrimage in honor of Lord Ayyappan that he undertook with some Tamil friends. There is a definite sequence to the order in which the senses are "merged" or "collapsed" in the course of this ritual: this is supposed to enable the devotees to achieve union with the deity. This sequence corresponds, with certain variations, to the division of the elements and the senses in the cosmology described above. As Daniel recounts, first hearing goes, then smell, then sight, then "the sense organ *the mouth*" (taste and possibly speech), until finally, all these faculties having "merged" into the sense of touch (which itself feels nothing besides pain by this late stage), that sense too "disappears," along with any sense of self (Daniel 1987, 270–76).

Midway through the third stage of the trek, one of the pilgrims told Daniel: "I stopped smelling things after Aruda Nati." To which Daniel responded: "Did you not even smell the camphor and incense sticks offered at the various shrines on the way after Aruda?" His friend replied: "You might say I felt it. I didn't smell it" (Daniel 1987, 272). Parenthetically, when the last of the senses, that of pain, "goes" or "dissolves" close to the end of the pilgrimage, "love" is said to take its place.

How would Ingold, the perception anthropologist, have fared were he to have participated in this pilgrimage? Would he have been capable of doing the work of "vanquishing" each of his senses in the prescribed order, or would he have kept on affirming, "I *am*, at once, my smelling, my listening, and the rest" to the end of the trek? To carry on in this way would have been true to Merleau-Ponty's phenomenology, but it would also be to defeat the purpose of the pilgrimage (i.e., achieving union with Lord Ayyappan). More broadly, to persevere in practicing phenomenology prevents the perception anthropologist from achieving the "liberation from the senses" that is a precondition of spiritual enlightenment—and salvation in the Tamil and other religious traditions of the region.[12] To put this another way, which will also help clarify the principal difference between perception anthropology and the anthropology of the senses: by cleaving to the supposition of the "synergic system" of the body, and believing in the universality of the self as "undivided centre of movement and awareness," Ingold disables himself from ever experiencing *other* ways of sensing and making sense of the world or from ever attaining the state of "being of two sensoria" (Métraux) about things that is integral to the practice of "sensuous scholarship" (Stoller 1997). In effect, Ingold's theory drains the practice of ethnography of any sense and drastically diminishes our understanding of the diverse intersensorial dynamics of the sensorium.

The Birth of the Sensory Evaluation Research Laboratory and the Rise of the Sensory Professional

There is a class of experts who specialize in the analysis of the sensory qualities of commodities—the color, sound, smell, taste, and feel of things. The original name for this area of research was "organoleptics." Its origins can be traced to the 1930s, when the Arthur D. Little industrial consulting firm devised a "Flavor Profile Method" and "Hedonic Index" for use by commercial food and beverage companies. The field was given a major boost during World War II, when the US Army found that industrially produced troop rations, which had been designed for their nutritional value, were "not performing their role because the men didn't like how [the rations] tasted and looked" (Shapin 2012, 179). Various studies were commissioned to find out how to make the food more palatable (Pangborn 1964; Lahne 2016; Hisano 2019 and "Use Not Perfumery," forthcoming).

The title of "organoleptician" was later dropped and replaced by "sensory professional." The sensory evaluation of food products remains central to the practice of these professionals, but the scope of the products that now fall within their purview has expanded significantly to include everything from personal care to household cleaning products, and from home decor to automobiles (Postrel 2003; Howes 2005b; Bijsterveld 2010; Eklund 2019; Howes and Classen 2013, chap. 6). Sensory professionals have also lobbied hard to expand their role within the companies they work for, seeking to convince management that the application of sensory evaluation techniques is crucial to every stage of product development, from conception to consumption. They like to use the language of driving, as in "sensory properties drive consumer acceptance and emotional benefits" (Kemp, Hollowood, and Hort 2011), and it has had the desired effect. The science of sensory evaluation now forms an integral part of what Steven Shapin (2012) calls "the aesthetic-industrial complex." It is one of the "sciences of subjectivity" that, as he suggests, "are world-making" (Shapin 2012). But what sort of world are these professionals synthesizing out of our senses?

The science of sensory evaluation rests on a fundamental paradox. On the one hand, "most sensory characteristics of food can only be measured well, completely, and meaningfully by human subjects," as opposed to scientific instruments. On the other hand, it is considered important that human subjects behave as much like scientific instruments as possible: "When people are used as a measuring instrument, it is necessary to control all testing methods and conditions rigidly to overcome errors caused by psychological factors" (Poste et al. 1991, 1). In a similar vein, Morten Meilgaard affirms that the key to sensory analysis is "to treat the panelists as measuring instruments. As such, they are highly variable and very prone to bias but they are the only instruments that will measure what we want to measure so we must minimize the variability and control the bias by making full use of the best existing techniques in psychology and psychophysics" (Meilgaard, Carr, and Civille 2010, 1).

The controls in question include creating a sampling environment that is as sensorially neutral as possible with regard to such factors as temperature, color, sound, odor, and so on and ensuring that "irrelevant" sensory factors, such as the size of the samples, do not impinge on the panelists' judgments. Furthermore, panelists are trained to evaluate products "monadically"—that is, to assess one sensory characteristic at a time: the use of blindfolds, nose clips, and "ear defenders" is advised to ensure that panelists maintain the desired focus (Kemp, Hollowood, and Hort 2011, 2.2.1.5 and 3.2). Focus is also enhanced through isolating one panelist from another by having them perform their tasks in individual booths or cubicles (for illustrations of the design of such cubicles, see Meilgaard, Carr, and Civille 2010, 24–30). In addition, assessors are commonly instructed not to discuss samples before evaluation, since this might create expectations, which are considered one of the most serious potential sources of error. So too are they instructed to work in silence, since "comments or noises made out loud, e.g., urgh! or Mmmm! can influence [the] sensory judgments" of other assessors who may be within earshot (Kemp, Hollowood, and Hort 2011, 2.2.1.2). Panelists are otherwise advised to disregard their "subjective associations," since the objective is to "provide precise, consistent, and standardized sensory measurements that can be reproduced" (Poste et al. 1991, 15). And, above all, they are commanded to "be spontaneous!" (Teil 2019).

There are basically three kinds of tests used in sensory evaluation experiments. "Discriminative tests" determine whether or not a difference exists among samples. "Descriptive tests" identify sensory characteristics that are important in a product and give information on the degree or intensity of those characteristics. "Affective" or "hedonic tests" measure how much a panelist likes a product sample based on its sensory characteristics. There is at least one kind of test missing from this repertoire, as we shall see presently.

Finally, the variability of responses is controlled for through the use of standardized questionnaires and standard numerical scales (see, e.g., Stone, Bleibaum, and Thomas 2012; Meilgaard, Carr, and Civille 2010) as well as through statistical analysis of the results of the experiments, and the plotting of such results in the form of graphs and tables. Only those results that are "statistically significant" are considered "meaningful." In other words, while sensory evaluation experiments are concerned with assessing the qualities of products, it is the *quantification* of sensation that (really) counts. There are some cautionary voices:

"Statistical analysis is not a substitute for thinking"; hence, "just because one obtains a graphical display or a series of tables with associated statistical significance does not mean it has any meaning or external validity" (Stone et al. 2012, 2). Nevertheless, such cautions go largely unheeded, and, in the final analysis, the interpretation of results boils down to tabulating responses and pinpointing averages so that any trace of the "subjective associations" of individual panelists can be eradicated from the overall picture of a product's sensory qualities.

To an outside observer, it might appear difficult to distinguish the protocol of a sensory evaluation test from the protocol of the sensory deprivation experiments of the 1960s (see Zubek 1969). It is indeed remarkable the degree of sensory restriction to which the sensory professional is subjected in the interests of producing results that are precise, consistent—and *reproducible*.

A survey of the sorts of articles published in the *Journal of Sensory Studies*, one of the leading journals in the field of sensory science, reveals that many of the papers are concerned with the development of sensory lexicons. The construction of these vocabularies is important both to the standardization of communication among sensory professionals working in different countries and to the communication of sensory product attributes to the consuming public. The articles may otherwise be grouped according to whether they use trained panelists or so-called naïve panelists, whether they use forced-choice, projective mapping, or some other scaling method, and whether they are "unimodal" (e.g., El-Ghezal Jeguirim et al. 2010), "multimodal" (e.g., Jervis et al. 2014), or "cross-modal" (e.g., Piqueras-Fiszman and Spence 2012) in orientation.

From the standpoint advanced in this book, the ways in which sensory science abstracts sensations from social, environmental, and even sensory contexts is deeply problematic. Basically, it is difficult to imagine a more asocial or, practically speaking, more asensual environment and protocol than the environment and protocols of the sensory evaluation research laboratory. While the precision and control that such sensory evaluation specialists aim to achieve in the products they help engineer is impressive, there is a profound lack of any glimmer of social consciousness. Absolutely no account is taken of the environmental impacts of the food items so carefully and minutely assessed, of the working conditions of those involved in the production process, or of the welfare of the animals whose bodies become the stuff of the dainty savoring and chewing of sensory analysis. Moreover, the everyday, culturally situated life of the senses is completely annihilated in the laboratory—for who ever dines or drinks wine in a white cubicle?

Breaking Out of the Laboratory: Sensory Ethnography and the Design of Sensorially Appealing, Socially Meaningful, Aesth-Ethical Products

What if, instead of depending exclusively on methodologies derived from psychology and psychophysics, the methodologies of other disciplines, such as anthropology, were allowed into the practice of sensory science? There is, in fact, a rapidly growing body of research in sensory design anthropology (e.g., Pink 2004, 2009, 2014); the sensory anthropology of consumption (Howes 2017; Howes and Classen 2013, chap. 5; Lahne and Trubek 2014); and the sensory anthropology of marketing (Malefyt 2014, 2015). The methodology of choice for conducting this genre of research is sensory ethnography.

The principles that should, in principle, guide the sensory ethnographic approach to design contemplated here may be summarized as follows, based on the underlying understanding of perception as a cultural as well as biological and psychological act.

First, the sensory ethnographer gives primary consideration to analyzing the different impacts and contexts of the mode of production of a product, as well as to its reception and use by consumers. This enables the practice of sensory design to move from a simple examination of product aesthetics to what might be called *aesth-ethics*, or the joint aesthetic qualities and ethical implications of product creation and use.

Second, the sensory ethnographer wants to follow the product in development (or some prototype thereof) *beyond the laboratory* and into the home, the street, the bar, or whatever the "natural environment" of its use may be.

Third, rather than subjecting informants to some predetermined protocol and list of questions, the sensory ethnographer relies on participant sensation, or feeling along with informants, and seeks to elicit quotidian responses, so as to tap into local ways of sensing. This helps reveal the added value (undreamt of by the designer) that consumers bring to their experience of a product.

Fourth, the analysis of the distinctive sensory features of the product in development must be united to an investigation of associated ideas and attitudes.

Fifth, the sensory ethnographer wants to focus on how the senses interact with each other in culturally conditioned ways, rather than view them as independent channels, for the senses continuously modulate each other (i.e., enter into relations of domination, anticipation, sequencing, or, in some cases, translation).

Together, these principles enable the sensory and social aspects of commercial products to be considered within the broader cultural, environmental, and ethical context of their production, use, and significance. Attention to this broader context makes for the creation of products that are sensorially stimulating, socially meaningful, and, most importantly, "aesth-ethical."[13]

As observed previously, conventional laboratory sensory evaluation tests involve the construction of barriers among people, among the senses, and between the "subjective associations" of the assessors and their response to the sensory characteristics of the products tested. This is accomplished through training and through the architecture of the sensory research laboratory, with its individual booths and "neutral" atmosphere. Panelists are instructed to discriminate, describe, and express their preferences, but not associate. But do these firewalls work? They might seem to work in the context of the laboratory, even if they would scarcely work in everyday life. However, even in the laboratory it is dubious that the play of associations among the senses could be forestalled. For example, in one of the studies we reported on in *Aroma* (Classen, Howes, and Synnott 1994, 194) involving a test of facial tissues, it was discovered that respondents found pine-scented tissues to be "fresher" but also "rougher" than unscented facial tissues, even though there was no actual difference to the texture of the tissues used in the two samples. The most probable reason for this is that the respondents failed to dissociate the scent of pine from the feel of pine needles, which are, of course, prickly, hence "rough." This goes to the fourth and fifth principles mentioned above.

The polysemy of the word "sense" is lost on sensory professionals, since the signifying (or "symbolic") and social dimensions of perception are occluded by their research protocols. By limiting the sorts of tests they use to the discriminative, the descriptive, and the hedonic, they disable themselves from ever investigating the *semantics* of perception. (There are exceptions: see Alcántara-Alcover et al. 2014.) In effect, what their protocols lack is a fourth test, a semantic test, that could help "determine the meanings or mental associations stimulated by a given product's sensory characteristics" (Howes 2003b, 119). This goes to the fourth principle mentioned above. By way of example, in another study reported on in *Aroma*, respondents in a Chicago shopping mall were asked: What odors make you feel nostalgic? "People born in the 1920s, '30s and '40s said that such odours as rose, burning leaves, hot chocolate, cut grass and ocean air made them feel nostalgic. Persons born during the 1960s and '70s, in contrast, grow nostalgic at such scents as Downy fabric softener, hair spray, Play-Doh, suntan oil, Cocoa Puffs, and candy cigarettes" (Classen, Howes, and Synnott 1994, 202–3). The trending evidenced by this survey, when the responses are grouped by decade of birth, are significant: they suggest that there has been a shift away from "natural" odors toward artificial ones, and, what is more, many of the latter come already trademarked (see Howes and Classen 2013, 114–18). These considerations, which all have to do with associations entrained by the sensations, would all be classified as "extrinsic" factors by the sensory professional, though, for whom semantics do not count.

An article published in the food science journal *Appetite* can shed light on this question of "extrinsic" properties and "extrinsic associations." The article is the first of its kind, and it is in many respects surprising that it passed peer review. The article recounts a study of consumer perceptions of Vermont artisan cheese conducted by Jake Lahne and Amy Trubek (2014), the former a trained food scientist, the latter an anthropologist. In classic sensory ethnographic fashion, Lahne and Trubek theorize sensory perception as a learned and active practice (rather than passive reflex). They hold that sensations arise "neither from the food nor from the consumer, but from the encounter between them, that is, it is neither taste nor taster, but tasting"

(Lahne and Trubek 2014, 130, citing Hennion 2005). This shifts attention from the search for (putatively) universal, objective sensory qualities of food (as in conventional sensory evaluation research) to an exploration of the ways in which the sensory qualities of food "emerge" for a particular consumer in a particular context.[14]

The emphasis on context is carried further by Lahne and Trubek's insistence that "sensory experience is social experience." This is reflected in the way their preferred methodology involves holding focus-group discussions around a plate of cheeses instead of relegating participants to individual cubicles; their practice also involves inviting participants to recall past experiences instead of simply checking off boxes on a printed questionnaire. Furthermore, in Lahne and Trubek's study, "social experience" does not simply refer to the exchanges between the participants in the focus group but also extends to the geographic region or "terroir" of Vermont. They assert that part of what makes the artisan cheeses "taste better" is that they embody "the taste of place" (Trubek 2009). According to Lahne and Trubek (2014), this taste of place is conditioned both by the physical characteristics of a particular geography and what they call "cultural saturation"—that is, the ubiquity of artisan cheese in Vermont, such that it is impossible for a Vermonter not to be aware of this product (see also Paxson 2013).

While these innovations in product sense-making are to be lauded for taking sensory evaluation outside the walls of the laboratory, the enlargement of perspective that Lahne and Trubek achieve is nonetheless limited. This is because social, economic, and professional interests raise their own walls, which block out the wider effects of product creation. To briefly mention some of these effects in the case of Vermont dairy products, the Vermont dairy industry has hardly been immune to charges of exploitation of workers or of cruelty to animals. News articles abound on these topics, detailing "How Migrant Workers Took on Ben & Jerry's" (Orleck 2018), "Ben & Jerry's Remove Claim that Ice Cream Comes from 'Happy Cows' Amid Lawsuits" (Raum 2020), and so forth (see also "'Ag-Gag' Bill Stirs Debate" [Burgess 2013]). In point of fact, the Vermont dairy industry is responsible for extensive pollution of the environment, with its creation of enormous manure pits and algae-covered lakes (Dillon 2019; D'Ambrosio 2021). (Such environmental outcomes suggest a whole new range of sensations that could be associated with the "terroir" of cheesemaking.) Even if a product might taste good, therefore, these kinds of impacts do not leave one with a "good taste." When the investigative focus is simply on personal perceptions of a particular product, as in Lahne and Trubek's study, however, this crucial information remains hidden.

In order to address these important issues, sensory ethnography must not only employ a culturally grounded approach to understanding the sensory features of the commodities that pervade our lives but also bring a critical perspective to bear on (and within) the practice of sensory science by engaging with welfare and environmental concerns. This may seem a tall order, but it is nonetheless essential. As the anthropologist Sidney Mintz (1986) noted as regards the cultural history of sugar—one of the quintessential sensory products of modernity—the different uses and meanings that this enticing sweetener acquired within the context of eighteenth-century European society represent but one side of the sensory impacts of sugar. The other, nether side has to do with the sensory and social impacts of sugar production in colonial plantations that often relied on slave labor. It would clearly be remiss for an anthropologist (or historian) to focus solely on the sensory life of sugar among eighteenth-century European consumers without taking at least some account of its effects on the peoples and places that produced it. Anthropologists looking at the consumer reception of contemporary goods should likewise be prepared to delve into what is happening "behind the scenes." The resulting ethnographies will be all the richer and more meaningful for it. Hence, just as the anthropology of the senses has a vital role to play in countering the asocial generalizations of phenomenology (as discussed in the first section of this chapter), it also presents a corrective to the narrow assessments of sensory science by providing a more holistic understanding of the sensory and social lives of the products that we bring into our homes and place on our tables.

PART 3

BETWEEN HISTORY AND ANTHROPOLOGY

CHAPTER 6

Sensory Exchange
Crossing Disciplines

There is an ambiguity inherent in the word "history." At one level, it refers to the passage of time, the succession of events. At a second level, it refers to the record of events, usually by means of writing. At a third level, it refers to the interpretation of that record, which is where the discipline of history comes in. The discipline of history comprises many branches and approaches, one of which is the history of the senses. The French social historian Alain Corbin is commonly regarded as the chief instigator of this field. However, there were earlier intimations of the field now known as the history of the senses. This chapter opens with an examination of those overtures, the work of Corbin's precursors, before turning to consider Corbin's own oeuvre and the exchange he entered into with a certain practitioner of the anthropology of the senses, which in turn gave rise to the emergent field of the historical anthropology of the senses.

Overtures to the Senses

Lucien Febvre, who cofounded the journal *Annales d'Histoire Economique et Sociale* (1929) with Marc Bloch, was the author of one of the aforementioned overtures to the senses. It comes in a little section entitled "The Underdevelopment of Sight" toward the end of *The Problem of Unbelief* ([1942] 1982), Febvre's classic work on the mentality of sixteenth-century France. There, he observed that the sixteenth century was more attentive to smells and sounds than sights,[1] and he went on to suggest that "a fascinating series of studies could be done of the sensory underpinnings of thought in different periods" (quoted and discussed in Classen 2001).

The focus on the reconstruction of "mentalities" in the work of Febvre and the Annales School (e.g., Mandrou 1975) was supplanted by a focus on "discourse" in the work of the philosopher Michel Foucault, who dabbled in historical analysis (e.g., Foucault 1973, 1979), and the poststructuralists. Then, in the early 1980s, Alain Corbin intervened. He broke with both of the previous traditions by imagining a "history of the sensible" (Corbin and Heuré 2000), as exemplified first by *The Foul and the Fragrant* ([1982] 1986), which explored the social life of smell in nineteenth-century France, and continuing with *Village Bells: Sounds and Meanings in the Nineteenth-Century French Countryside* ([1994] 1998). Other works of relevance include Corbin's history of silence, his history of the lure of the sea, and a highly personal and illuminating memoir (or "sensory biography") of his boyhood during World War II.

I spent much of the summer of 1987 immersed in reading *The Foul and the Fragrant* in order to write a review of this book for the journal *Culture, Medicine, and Psychiatry*. The reason it took me so long was because Corbin has such a flair for writing (fittingly enough, since flair comes from *flairer*, "to smell"), and I wanted to do justice to the richness of his profoundly sensuous descriptions and analysis of the nineteenth-century smellscape and period nose. When my review appeared (Howes 1989), I sent a copy of it to Corbin, and we struck up a correspondence. All of his letters to me were handwritten in a beautiful cursive script, which mirrored the fluidity of his prose.

A few years later, I invited Corbin to write an article for a special issue of the journal *Anthropologie et Sociétés* on the theme of "Les cinq sens." He graciously agreed and offered an essay called "Histoire et anthropologie sensorielle" ([1990] 2005). This *essai* contains many keen observations regarding sensory history methodology. Although they were already cited in the introduction, these lines are worth quoting again here, so they remain front of mind. Thus, Corbin (2005, 135, 133) urges us to "take account of the habitus that determines the frontier between the perceived and the unperceived, and, even more, of the norms which decree what is spoken and what left unspoken"; he also highlights the dangers of "confusing the reality of the employment of the senses and the picture of this employment decreed by observers." In other words, the key to writing the history of the senses lies in sensing between the lines of written sources.

The interchange between anthropology and history that characterized my exchange with Corbin was not without precedent. There had been numerous exchanges between our respective disciplines in earlier decades. For example, the Oxford anthropologist E. E. Evans-Pritchard, in addition to being a great ethnographer, moonlighted as a historian when he wrote *The Sanusi of Cyrenaica* (1954). Meanwhile, a number of prominent historians took note of Evans-Pritchard's classic ethnography, *Witchcraft, Oracles and Magic Among the Azande* ([1937] 1982), and sought to draw out its lessons for analyzing the "mentality" of the historical periods they were interested in. As Alan

Macfarlane notes in "Anthropology and History" (1988), the period between 1960 and 1980 witnessed an important shift in historical writing as a result of the transplantation of anthropological techniques and interests into historical studies. The anthropological turn made everyday practices and popular beliefs fit topics for serious historical inquiry. These topics included "conflict, ceremony, work discipline, time, space, myths, folklore, style and fashion, oral and literate culture, birth, death, dreams, suicide, animals . . . [and, particularly, witchcraft and magical beliefs]. The formal historical documents usually conceal such topics, so that it was largely under the pressure of anthropology that a vigorous development of the study of past mentality and emotional structures took place, exemplified in the work of historians such as E. Hobsbawm, E. Le Roy Ladurie, E. P. Thompson, and Keith Thomas" (Macfarlane 1988, 13). As this roll call of luminaries attests, the corpus of historical work that emerged out of this "pressure" from anthropology was of extraordinarily high quality.

The US historian Mark M. Smith is a twenty-first-century historian who has been deeply influenced by anthropology. In 2007, Smith invited me to contribute an article to a roundtable on "The Senses in American History" for the *Journal of American History*. I was delighted to have the chance to return the favor that Corbin did for me, so I agreed. My contribution was called "Can These Dry Bones Live? An Anthropological Approach to the History of the Senses" (2008). In this and the chapters that follow, I would like to build on this ongoing exchange between history and anthropology by presenting two case studies in what could be called the historical anthropology of the senses.

Both of these studies center on "first contact" situations—that is, on moments when two civilizations meet for the first time. First contact situations are interesting to study because they throw the "sensory regimes" (Corbin) of the cultures concerned into relief and also testify to the techniques of negotiation deployed by agents on both sides of the cultural divide to carve out a common ground, or build a new *con-sensus*. There is always the risk that such a confrontation-conciliation will result in sensory and social homogenization/normalization, for globalization always comes at a price. However, by attending carefully to the written sources, and by sensing between the lines, one can develop a keen eye, and nose, and so forth for traces of the *ways of sensing* that prevailed at the initial conjuncture, and then follow their expression down to the current conjuncture. It is not always the case that cultures trade in their senses in the interests of trade —far from it, as we shall see.

For a Historical Anthropology of the Senses and Sensation

In this section, I present a brief historical anthropology of sense perception in China and the West, with a focus on the Spring and Autumn (771–476 BCE) and Warring States (475–221 BCE) periods in the case of China and on the classical and medieval periods in the case of the West. This exercise in excavating the sensory underpinnings of thinking about the cosmos, self, and society in the two cultures is intended both to serve as a primer for what is entailed in "doing sensory history" and to set the stage for the analysis of cultural exchange as sensory exchange in the early modern period in the chapter that follows. There, the focus will be on the sensory qualities of the commodities that were the object of commercial, intellectual, and artistic exchange between the two civilizations.

The history of the senses, like the anthropology of the senses, proceeds from the recognition that the senses are constructed and lived differently in different societies and historical periods. To put this another way, "the perceptual is *cultural and political*" (Bull et al. 2006). Thus, when we turn to examine the meanings and uses ascribed to the senses, historically or cross-culturally,

> we find a cornucopia of potent sensory symbolism. Sight may be linked to reason or to witchcraft, taste may be used as a metaphor for aesthetic discrimination or for sexual experience, an odour may signify sanctity or sin, political power or social exclusion. Together, these sensory meanings and values form the *sensory model* espoused by a society, according to which the members of that society "make sense" of the world.... There will likely be challenges to this model from within the society—persons and groups who differ on certain sensory values [or practices]—yet this model will provide the basic perceptual paradigm to be followed or resisted. (Classen 1997, 402)

The first step in eliciting a given society's sensory model is to determine how the senses are categorized and ranked. The idea of the senses being five in number, and of each sense as having its proper sphere, is a commonplace of Western thought, as we saw in chapter 4. However, early enumerations were far from uniform. For example, in one enumeration, Plato listed sight, hearing, and smell but left out taste and mentioned perceptions of hot and cold (though not touch); he also included sensations of pleasure, discomfort, desire, and fear (Classen 1993b, 3). It is to Aristotle that we owe the standard fivefold schema, but this was determined as much by cosmological considerations as anatomical facts. Aristotle posited an intrinsic relationship between the senses and the elements: for example, vision with water, smell with fire, and so on. While insisting that there were five senses and five senses only, Aristotle also posited the existence of a "common sense" (*koinē aisthēsis* or *sensus communis*), which was responsible for coordinating the deliverances of the other five (Howes 2009, 17).

According to Jane Geaney (2002), in the philosophical texts of the China of the Warring States period, we also find a fivefold classification. Much as in classical Greece, though, there was considerable diversity of opinion as to which bodily organs or emotional states were to count as senses. Most lists include eyes, ears, mouth, nose, and body (or form), but one continues with "trust, awe, and peace," while other lists may omit one or another of the abovementioned body parts and/or emotions (Geaney 2002, 16–17). Interestingly, in view of the highly bureaucratic character of the Chinese state, the standard model of the sensorium depicted the five senses as five "officials," with the "heartmind" (*xin*) as their ruler. "Ear, eye, nose, mouth, and form, each has its own contacts [lit. 'receptions' or 'meetings'] and does not do things for the others. Now, these are called the heavenly officials. The heartmind dwells in the central cavity and governs the five officials. Now this is called the heavenly ruler" (*Xunzi* quoted in Geaney 2002, 19; see further Blake 2019 on the evaluative role of the heartmind). There is an obvious parallel between the "heartmind" and "the common sense" of Aristotle, and Aristotle actually located the mind (or, sentience and reason) in the heart. However, the union of thinking and emoting that is given in the "heartmind" concept would eventually get split in the Western tradition, with the brain coming to be seen as the seat of the mind or intellect and the heart as the seat of the emotions (Santangelo 2005). This fusion/division can prove to be a major stumbling block to cross-cultural understanding.

The notion of a hierarchy of the senses, with sight at the apex, followed, in descending order, by hearing ("the second sense"), smell, taste, and touch, is another commonplace of Western thought (Classen 1998; Vinge 1975). Sight and hearing were commonly referred to as the "higher" or "intellectual" senses, in contrast to the "lower," "bodily," and even "bestial" senses of smell and taste and touch. The senses were hierarchized in classical Chinese thought as well, but not in the serial order one finds in the West. Rather, ear and eye, hearing and seeing, were treated as a pair and often functioned as a synecdoche for all the senses. According to Jane Geaney (2002, 43–49), the primary reason for their joint or shared supremacy had to do with their presumed complementarity: hearing gave access to words while sight registered actions. It was vital that words and actions be in accord. Interestingly, the word for action originally meant "walking." Hence it was important that people "walk the talk," as it were. When word and deed diverged, there could only be trouble. The "heartmind" was responsible for "validating" the concordance (or not) between what hearing and seeing reported.

There is some evidence of sight and hearing being considered superior and prevailing over the other senses in classical Chinese culture. For example, Cangjie, a mythological figure who is said to have created the pictographs that later developed as Chinese characters (a strongly visual system of communication), is represented with four eyes as a sign of his exceptional wisdom.[2] As another example, in the *Lunyu* there is a passage that states: "When the Master was in Qi, he heard the Shao music—for three months he did not know the taste of meat" (quoted in Geaney 2002, 28). This suggests that the Master's absorption in the spiritual delights of music enabled him to abstain from the more carnal pleasure of eating meat. Another manifestation of this complex of ideas is given in the association of the left side (which is considered superior to the right in China) with the breath and with music (Granet 1973).

Much as in classical Greece, ancient Chinese cosmology was a "sensory cosmology" (Classen 1993b, 1998). The universe was understood to be composed of five elements (metal, wood, water, fire, and earth); the human body of five major organs (heart, liver, spleen, lung, kidney); the year of five seasons; and space of five directions. To these divisions there corresponded five musical tones, five flavors, five colors, and so forth. Thus, the element of fire was associated with a smoky scent, a bitter taste, a red color, the musical tone *chih*, the season of summer and the direction of south. The element of water was associated with a rotten smell, a salt taste, the color black, the musical tone *yu*, the winter season, and the direction north (see Meade and Emch 2010, 436; Jütte 2005, 25–31).

This elaborate system of correspondences, or cross-modal associations, provided the underpinning for numerous domains of life, including medicine[3] and the ritual life of the emperor and his court. For example, one manual of court etiquette prescribed that in the first month of spring, "the Son of Heaven shall live in the apartment to the left of the Green Bright Hall. He shall ride in a belled chariot driven by dark green dragon [horses] and bearing green flags. He shall wear green clothes with green jade. He shall eat wheat and mutton" (cited by Henderson 2010). It bears underlining that because of the presumed interdependence of all these macrocosmic and microcosmic divisions (they were actually regarded as "phases," and perhaps "forces" would be the most apt term to describe them), action in one domain could affect the balance in all the others, setting off a concatenation of changes, but always tending (ideally) to the recovery of equilibrium.

The attention paid to ritually reproducing the proper relations *between* sensations in ancient Chinese culture was of a piece with the importance attached to maintaining the proper relations between persons. Just as traditional Chinese theories of perception and the cosmos suggest an "interrelational network" (Rošker 2019, 27), so did the understanding of the person. Indeed, the social philosophy of the Spring and Autumn period sage Confucius was distinguished by its "refusal to conceptualize individuals in any way other than relational—as children, parents, lovers, youngsters, oldsters, employees, employers and on and on" (Glenn 2010, 337). In the words of one Chinese official, "Heaven and Earth have their patterns, and people take these for their patterns. . . . [Among these patterns are] the five tastes, manifested in five colors and displayed in the five notes. When these are in excess, there ensue obscurity and confusion, and people lose their nature. That is why they were made to support that nature. . . . There were ruler and minister. . . . There were husband and wife, with the home and the world outside as their divided duties [the home being the female sphere]. There were father and son, elder and younger brother" (cited by Wang 2000, 184).

The sensory and social patterns deemed to be "laid up in Heaven" constrained both rulers and subjects, with every member of society expected to play their proper part. Each individual was a bundle of roles, a nexus of relationships, and these social relations mapped onto the relations between the senses. Thinking and living according to the established pattern of cross-modal connections provided a potent model for the maintenance of orderly and interdependent relationships within society. The relational understanding of the universe and of the person that prevailed in the China of the Spring and Autumn period would be reiterated in each succeeding dynasty down to the Ming

(1368–1644) and Qing (1644–1912) periods, which will concern us in the next chapter.

We find a similar emphasis on sensory integration in the cosmology and society of medieval Europe. As Constance Classen observes, "The medieval cosmos was an intricate tapestry of colors, sounds, and scents. In heaven saints and angels sing in an eternally flowering garden. In hell, damned souls cried out in a foul, fiery pit. This potent cosmic imagery was reinforced by the sensory dimensions of Christian ritual. Incense, music, vestments, and the savors of feasts and fasts helped to engage participants through all their senses. Medieval cosmology was not simply a feast for the senses, however. The medievals held that every sensory image embodied a spiritual truth and participated in a cosmic code of meaning" (Classen 1998, 13; see further Jørgensen, Laugerud, and Skinnebach 2015). This elaborate tapestry of sensations would come undone, however, with—among other things—the invention of the printing press, which privileged sight and a decidedly linear way of thinking (McLuhan 1962), the overthrow of the feudal social order because of the rise of capitalism, and the birth of the atomistic theory of the universe, such as we see in the "empirical," "corpuscular" philosophy of John Locke and Robert Boyle. Civil society came to be seen as rooted in contract rather than nature, its shape determined by "the invisible hand of the market" instead of any pattern laid up in Heaven. As observed in chapter 4, it is no accident that Locke was the architect of the political theory of "possessive individualism" (which reduced individuals to the status of so many billiard balls), a proponent of the atomistic theory of the universe (following Robert Boyle) and of what could be called the isolationist theory of the senses. As regards the latter, while Locke took over the fivefold classification of the senses from Aristotle, there was no room within his understanding for the Aristotelian notion of "the common sense." This is apparent not only from Locke's silence on this score (there is no mention of the *sensus communis* in his writings) but also from the little passage, discussed previously (see p. 129), in his *Essay Concerning Human Understanding* about the blind man who claimed to understand the meaning of "scarlet": it was like the sound of a trumpet, he professed. Locke dismissed this suggestion as utter nonsense, on account of his unwillingness to accept the possibility of a transposition of sensations.

Now, it is possible that a literatus from the Spring and Autumn or Warring States periods would have been just as officious as Locke regarding synesthesias. We have seen how bureaucratic the ancient Chinese conception of the sensorium could be. But it seems more likely that the literatus would have had little difficulty appreciating the correspondence between the color scarlet and the sound of a trumpet, because of their familiarity with making such cross-modal connections all the time in daily life. Associations of this ilk formed the basis of court etiquette, as we have seen. Aristotle would likely have had considerable sympathy for the blind man's suggestion as well, but his understanding of "the common sense" was lost on Locke, replaced by the idea of the mind as a *tabula rasa*. This is what is meant by referring to Locke's theory of the senses as isolationist, an understanding that continues to bedevil Western perceptual psychology.

This brief comparative analysis of the differences and similarities between the premodern Chinese and Western sensory and social orders points to how interesting and informative a full-fledged historical analysis would be.[4] There is, in fact, a rapidly growing professional historical literature on the history of the

Chinese sensory imaginary (Nelson 1998/1999; Goh 2010; Keuleman 2014; Gu 2020; Irvine 2020); the "sensuous surfaces" (e,g., the unctuousness of jade, the ring of bronze) of Chinese material culture (Hay 2010; Ko 2019); the sensory body of traditional Chinese medicine (Kuriyama 1999; Farquhar 2020); the sensuousness of the Chinese art of writing (Billeter 1990; Pearce, Best, and Hu 2018); and, last but not least, the Chinese pleasures of the senses (Brook 1999; Nylan 2018). A number of these sources, such as Goh's *Sound and Sight: Poetry and Courtier Culture in the Yongming Era* and Keuleman's *Sound Rising from the Paper*, challenge Western assumptions about the separation of the arts and the separation of the senses in interesting ways, while others, such as Irvine's *Listening to China: Sound and the Sino-Western Encounter, 1770–1839*, bring out how difficult it was for the two civilizations to "hear" each other. This burgeoning literature bodes well for the continuing expansion of the still-fledgling field of the comparative study of historical sensory orders going forward. Hopefully, there will soon come a day when scholars from around the world collaborate in the production of a global history of the senses. Two very promising intimations of such a new world reckoning include the recent special issue of *The Senses and Society* on the cultural history of the senses in the Islamic world, edited by Christian Lange (2022), and Peter Denney's "The Senses in World History" (forthcoming from Routledge).

In the next chapter, we turn from comparing the two traditions in broad strokes to exploring how they became entangled with each other in the wake of the uptick in East-West trade in the sixteenth and seventeenth centuries.

CHAPTER 7

Cross-Cultural Exchange as Sensory Exchange
The Encounter Between China and the West in the Early Modern Period

Cultural relations between China and the West intensified in the early modern period because of the opening of a sea route by the Portuguese, which stimulated the expansion of trade and the onset of missionary activity in China. Jesuit missionaries were particularly instrumental with respect to bridging the two cultures because they made a point of learning Mandarin and transporting knowledge as well as goods from Europe to China and vice versa. The exchange initiated by the missionaries was expanded by Dutch, French, and English traders.

The focus of the first section of this chapter is on the sensory dimensions of the commercial and intellectual exchange between the two civilizations during the sixteenth and seventeenth centuries. The commodities that changed hands are analyzed as bundles of sensory qualities and social values—that is, as embodying and giving expression to sensual relations conjointly with the social relations that went into their production, circulation, and consumption. Cultural exchange and sensory exchange are thus shown to have been intimately intertwined. The second section explores sensory and social aspects of the ongoing exchange of medical knowledge between China and the West.

Sing-Songs and Silk: The Balance of Trade and the Shifting Balance of the Senses

The list of items coming in and out of China through the medium of Europeans in the sixteenth and seventeenth centuries makes it clear that the goods that changed hands were largely valued because of their sensory qualities: "The Chinese imported dye, incense woods, jewels, and large quantities of pepper" (Mungello 1989, 39); they exported silk, sugar, gold, lacquerware, and porcelain. None of these goods are necessities of life. Their appeal lies in the pleasurable sensations they offer the senses of sight, touch, taste, and smell—and in their prestige value. Trade with China in the early modern period was thus very much a sensory exchange.

It is important to recognize, however, that multiple areas of the world, and not just Europe and China, were involved in this sensory exchange. As David Mungello observes:

> The Dutch operated out of their main Asian base at Batavia to oversee a widespread circuit of trade between Japan, China, Southeast Asia, India, Yemen and Holland. Taiwanese sugar was sold in Persia and Europe, while white silk from China was sold in Japan and Europe. The Dutch carried pepper and sandalwood to China

and bought gold, tutenag, raw silk and silk fabrics from the Chinese. The Dutch carried the Chinese raw silk and silk fabrics to Japan where they sold them for silver, taking the silver plus the Chinese gold and tutenag to India to buy cotton fabrics which were exchanged for spices in Indonesia. (Mungello 1989, 39)

Moreover, the same New World products, from potatoes to tobacco, that were transforming the life of the senses in Europe in early modernity would also play an important role in transforming the sensory life of China. As regards tobacco, for example, travelers to China in the eighteenth century were struck by how widespread the practice of smoking had already become among the populace, noting that "even children two feet high" smoked (Pomeranz 2000, 118).

These different commodities had complicated histories of production that included practices of colonization, environmental exploitation, and slavery, as well as traditions of craftwork and agricultural and technological innovations. By way of example, one sensuous commodity that was in high demand in China from the sixteenth century on was silver. China's primary use of silver was as currency; however, the metal was also employed in the creation of various kinds of silverwork. The huge global trade in silver in early modernity had important political as well as commercial ramifications in multiple countries and led to significant innovations in mining technology as well. However, the silver trade also had enormous ramifications for the lands where the commodity was produced. Some 80 percent of the silver that made its way around the world in early modernity came from the Andean region of South America, which had been conquered by the Spanish in the sixteenth century. Indigenous peoples toiled and died by the tens of thousands extracting this prized global commodity from the rich silver mines on the slopes of

Cerro Rico—which came to be known as "the mountain which eats men." The intense demand for mining labor in the region disrupted ancient social networks and cultural traditions. The local environment, and the people and animals who lived there, in turn, ended up poisoned by the mercury used in the processing of silver. The toxic effluents of silver mining in the Andes continue to be breathed in, drunk, and handled by the inhabitants today (Robins 2011). Thus, the enticing gleam that added to silver's attraction as a commodity had as its counterpart a whole range of deleterious corporeal, social, and environmental impacts.

In terms of what Europe itself brought to China, what was most valued by the Chinese was scientific and technological knowledge: mathematics, astronomy, cartography, and mechanics. The principal sensory effect of such knowledge lay in expanding the importance of the visual in China in the same way that the scope of vision had been expanded and intensified by modern science and technology in Europe. Maps, for example, transformed the sensory experience of space, with all its diverse odors, sounds, temperatures, and textures, into a static, unchanging, visual representation. An interesting example of such a sensory shift is provided by the introduction of the European mechanical clock.

Modern Europeans are used to looking at a clock or watch to find out the hour—and to the image of a clock face being used as a symbol for time itself. In premodern Europe, however, timekeeping was largely sonic: the day was ordered by church bells ringing out the hour. The importance of such sonic methods of timekeeping is evidenced by the fact that the English word "clock" originally meant "bell." In Europe, short periods of time were often related to the length of time it took to say Christian prayers; for example, the time it takes to recite an "Our Father." The last two words of the "Our Father" prayer in Latin, "Sancti

Amen," could be used to indicate a very short passage of time. Mechanical clocks were different. Although they too might sound out the hours, they privileged the visual "reading of time" over the older, sonic methods of timekeeping.

In China there were a variety of ways of telling time at the moment of first contact. Astronomical and water clocks were both used, while gongs and drums were employed to mark off periods of time within cities. One interesting folk custom involved looking into a cat's eyes to tell the time of day. The more light, the smaller the cat's highly sensitive pupils would become, and the less light, the larger.

The most widespread method of telling time, however, involved the use of incense (Bedini 1994). A popular expression in China was "in the time it takes to burn an incense stick." Burning incense was a common religious ritual, and its association with the passage of time may well have led to the development of the incense clock. These incense clocks, which could be simple or very elaborate, measured time in two basic ways. One way was that a passage of time would be indicated by an incense stick of a certain length burning out. Another way was that the fragrance emitted by the incense would change after a certain interval, so as to distinguish one period from another. Such incense clocks were widespread in China in early modernity and used in both homes and temples. This smell-based notion of time, as can be appreciated, provided a highly immersive experience: time was "in the air." One "breathed" time and did not simply "read" it on a clock face. As odors may carry memories and emotional associations, the "aromatic time" of the incense clocks could well also have been full of personal associations, in ways that were alien to the visual, impersonal time of the mechanical clock. Significantly, Bedini (1994) reports, the Chinese traditionally regarded the fragrance of incense as an aid to thoughtfulness, a stimulus to conversation, and a mental and physical purifier. Obviously, Western clocks, while very efficient at keeping time, could fulfill none of these other roles of the incense clock.

When clocks were brought to China by the Jesuits, they aroused great interest. This was largely due to their novelty as mechanical devices, however. As regards their sensory aspects, the Chinese at first seemed just as interested in the clocks' ability to ring out the hours as in their visual features. One sixteenth-century Chinese official, for example, eagerly asked the Jesuit missionaries to send him "a self-sounding bell" (*zimingzhong*), referring to a chiming clock. This Chinese interest in the mechanical production of sound through clockwork meant that an important item of European trade to China from the seventeenth to the early nineteenth centuries was what the British called "sing-songs": clocks and other devices—such as snuff boxes with mechanical birds that sang when the lid was opened—which appealed primarily through their novel auditory effects.

Mechanical clocks were largely regarded as novelties and luxury objects in China, therefore, and not as practical, everyday devices. Indeed, it took several centuries before Western-style clocks came to be widely used for timekeeping in China. By that time many clocks had become purely visual means for telling time. (A key factor in this transition was the adoption in 1912 of a national standard time in China, which was related to the international standard time.) Although the process was gradual, therefore, the adoption of mechanical clocks in China did eventually contribute to a new way of apprehending the world through visual, rather than sonic or olfactory, signs.

Early modern European travelers to China, for their part, often remarked on the importance of fragrance in Chinese culture. They did so in a disapproving way, however, for while the Chinese might think of fragrance as a way of clearing and elevating thoughts, from a European perspective, indulgence in fragrances was seen as a sign of irrational sensuality. One missionary wrote, for example, of "hot wafts of scent from flowers or incense working on minds open to bewitchment" (quoted in Bedini 1994, 48). Considering the high quality of the incense produced in China, it is a very interesting fact that it was not a major import good for Europe. This lack of European desire for incense indicates a decline in the importance of the sense of smell in modernizing Europe (Classen 1993b, chap. 1). Chinese incense was an interesting novelty, but it did not have the attraction of such luxury goods as Chinese silk, tea, or porcelain.

What was it about these Chinese goods that so appealed to the Western sensorium, that made them necessary luxuries, as it were? Silk comes from the cocoons of silkworms, which are killed by heat so that the threads of their wrappings may be extracted (Vainker 2004). This harsh process results in the soft, smooth fibers that are used to produce silk cloth. However, silk was made in Europe as well as in China, with the main difference being that China produced silk in far greater quantities and with attractively exotic designs. As silk was a luxury product, as well as being very soft and visually attractive, it served as a sign of the refinement of the European elite. Silk was used by the wealthy in articles of clothing and to cover the rough surfaces of walls with a shimmering softness. In the Middle Ages only the nobility were allowed to wear silk, and it remained a marker of social status in the following centuries. The European desire for silk, therefore, combined a desire for silky sensations with a desire for social prestige.

Tea became a popular beverage in Europe, and particularly in England, in the eighteenth century (Hohenegger 2006). Just as Europeans had altered the traditional spicy chocolate drink of the Aztecs in Mexico to produce their own variety of hot chocolate, so tea was altered to suit European tastes. In China tea was customarily served without anything added to it, whereas Europeans mixed sugar with their tea to reduce its bitterness. There was some resistance to tea drinking among those who felt that a "proper" man should call for wine in the evening, and not for tea, yet its nonalcoholic nature recommended the brew to social reformers who sought to reduce drunkenness. Along with the new drink came a desire for new cups in which to serve it. This fueled the demand for Chinese porcelain. The Chinese traditionally drank tea in bowls without handles: this let the warmth of the brew seep through to one's hands, and, at first, these tea bowls (rather than tea cups) were used in Europe as well. But because Europeans liked to drink their tea hot, they required cups with handles. Porcelain tea sets were therefore manufactured in China to European designs and shipped to Europe to meet the demand for elegant accessories to go with the exotic new drink.

Chinese porcelain had an allure for Europeans even before the rise of tea drinking, however. For example, consider the painting by the Venetian painter Andrea Mantegna entitled *Adoration of the Magi* (ca. 1495–1505). It shows one of the Three Kings presenting a porcelain cup to the Christ child. This indicates the extent to which porcelain was considered a rare luxury item and therefore a suitable gift for a god. In China, finely wrought pieces of porcelain were also regarded as luxury items. Antique pieces, for example, were extolled as being "brilliant as a mirror, thin as paper," and, interestingly, "sonorous as a king" (Degenhardt 2013, 198). This last auditory adjective suggests that the senses of sight and touch alone may be insufficient to appreciate all the qualities of porcelain pieces that were valued by peoples of earlier eras. (It probably refers to pinging a vase with one's finger.)

In Europe, porcelain was regarded as "the best earthen matter in all the world, for three qualities; namely, the cleannesse, the beauty, & the strength thereof" (150). There were myths circulating about porcelain taking a hundred years to mature in special mounds of earth. Other attributes included its capacity to stand up to "the heat of hot foods without cracking," its self-mending capacities, and its (alleged) ability to confer "a magical immunity to poison upon the food or liquor it contained" (151–52). All this suggests that porcelain was a substance that almost transcended materiality on account of its fineness. This would play into burgeoning class distinctions in Europe. As one snob put it, porcelain is prized by "those who appreciate elegance at their banquets rather than pompous display" (quoted in Degenhardt 2013, 151). Once porcelain began to be widely produced in Europe in the eighteenth century, however, it lost a good part of its social prestige.

It frustrated the European traders that—apart from "sing-songs"—the Chinese had no particular desire or use for the European products they could trade in return for the tea, silk, and porcelain they prized so highly. In the case of England, while the English were anxious to trade their wool to the Chinese, the Chinese had little use for it. This created a huge trade—and, one might say, sensory—imbalance. Furthermore, in the late eighteenth century Spain allied itself with the rebellious American colonies: this had the result of cutting off the supply of silver from Spanish America, which the British had used to pay for Chinese goods up to that point. This provoked a great crisis. The solution, from the guileful British perspective, was to sell opium produced in India to the Chinese. The popularity of opium as more and more Chinese became addicted to it gradually began to reverse the trade imbalance in the early nineteenth century. The Chinese desire for opium also served to reinforce Western stereotypes of the Chinese, and Asians in general, as a people given to "bewitchments of the senses." Hence, the situation arose that, in exchange for the gustatory and olfactory qualities of tea and the tactile and visual qualities of silk and porcelain, China was provided with dreamy sensations produced by opium, which was described as "the silken garment of the imagination" (Kane 1882, 61).

The sensory exchanges between Europeans and Chinese were not limited to those products that formed the bulk of Sino-European trade. In fact, the goods that Europeans most craved from China were *not* among those goods that the Chinese themselves most valued—namely, traditions of art, music, and literature. The latter were generally overlooked by Europeans. While in the modern era, Europeans would develop a taste for traditional Chinese art styles that would result in the "chinoiserie" decorative fashion, Europeans at first tended to disparage the artistic productions of the Chinese. The fact that Chinese pictures were often painted on silk or porcelain, or on fans or screens, reduced their value for Europeans by removing them from the purely visual aesthetic realm of fine art into the realm of the tactile and functional. Furthermore, Chinese art, from the European perspective, lacked the richness and visual interest of Western oil paintings, with their variegated lights and shadows and perspectival accuracy: "They [the Chinese] know nothing of the art of painting in oil or of the use of perspective in their pictures, with the result that their productions are likely to resemble the dead rather than the living," wrote the great Jesuit missionary and world traveler Matteo Ricci (quoted in Thompson 2015). Europeans viewed Chinese artists as mere copyists, adhering faithfully to traditional styles and designs without innovating.[1] The Chinese, however, found the visual realism of European paintings disturbing. The following was related of an Italian Jesuit who was employed as a painter by Emperor Kangxi: "One day [the Jesuit] had finished a large architectural picture in which were columns that appeared to recede in perspective, the Chinese were at first sight stupefied.... Even upon approaching the canvas they were scarcely convinced by the touch that it was a visual deception upon a flat surface. They then cried out, there is nothing more contrary to nature than to represent distances where there are actually none.... The picture was condemned. Whether from motives of policy, or contempt for strangers, the emperor refused permission to open a public school of painting" (Marryat 1857, 217). This response, perhaps somewhat exaggerated in the retelling by Europeans, was not simply evidence of a Chinese resistance to realism in art.[2] It indicated the extent to which Chinese art forms were related to social values and rules. Adopting foreign styles of painting would have created a rupture in the social training of the senses considered essential for the educated elite.

European and Chinese opinions on music were even more divergent than they were on painting. Matteo Ricci wrote of Chinese music that "it seems to consist in producing a monotonous rhythmic beat as they know nothing of variations of harmony that can be produced by combining different musical notes" (quoted in Thompson 2015, n.p.). The Chinese, for their part, found Western music overly complex. "European music cannot be heard with pleasure by a Chinese audience.... [Musical harmony] does not fit their taste and they feel an intolerable confusion," noted one commentator (cited in Gild 2012, 537).[3] Or, again: "Your concerts, especially if they are rather long, are violent exercises for those who perform them and small tortures for those who listen. After all, it is inevitable that European ears are built differently to ours. You like things that are complicated, we are fond of things that are simple. In your Music, you often run until you are out of breath, we always walk at a serious and measured pace" (Amiot quoted in Thompson 2015, n.p.). As with art, there was a close association between musical values and social values in China, with music serving as an auditory illustration of social and even cosmic order (Brindley 2006). As one Chinese author put it, "When the material principle of music (that is the instruments) is clearly and rightly illustrated, the corresponding spiritual principle (that is the essence, the sounds of music) becomes perfectly manifest, and the State's affairs are successfully conducted" (cited in Gild 2012, 535). This point of view made the perceived confusion of Western music deplorable from both an aesthetic and a social perspective. Given this mutual dislike of musical styles, it is not surprising that there was little in the way of a musical exchange between China and the West, but mainly just derogatory monologues (Irvine 2020).

The material covered in this chapter illustrates the complexity of the sensory interactions between China and the West. Particularly in the case of the Chinese, the senses, and their engagement through various art and craft forms, were linked to social values considered necessary for the proper ordering of the State. This made it difficult to adopt foreign styles and tastes without disrupting the integrity of the system. In the case of Europe, maintaining the integrity of a sensory cultural whole was less of an issue, and therefore imports from China could be more readily accommodated. However, the Chinese sensations imported by the West were highly selective: a taste here, a texture there—and virtually no music. Although Westerners became knowledgeable connoisseurs of Chinese porcelain, for example, as of tea, there was little understanding of the larger cultural context of these traditions or of the ways in which sensory practices were interrelated with social values.

An Interplay of Medical Systems

Among the goods put into circulation by European traders and missionaries were pharmaceuticals. An example of this is quinine, which was employed to treat fevers and malaria. This use of quinine originated among Indigenous peoples of South America, who employed the bitter bark of the cinchona tree as a febrifuge. The Spanish harvested and commercialized this valuable medicament (and in the process devastated Andean forests), marketing it around the world. In China, cinchona bark was notably employed by Jesuit missionaries to cure the emperor Kangxi, who had tried a range of traditional Chinese remedies for malaria in vain. The remarkable success of this bitter medicine enhanced the standing of Europeans in China. However, "the medical treatises introduced by Europeans were treated as curiosities by both Chinese and Indian medical scholars" (Jonsen 2008, 38).

The practice of traditional Chinese medicine included classifying medicaments by their sensory properties, an approach that one can find in premodern Western medicine as well but that was discarded with the rise of modern biomedicine (Howes and Classen 2013, chap. 2). Thus, the Scottish physician John Dudgeon wrote in his late nineteenth-century study of Chinese medicine: "We find the Chinese describing particular diseases according to particular planets, portioning out their relations to these heavenly bodies, to the five elements, colours, tastes, points of the compass, &tc., &tc.; and gravely assigning every disease to the predominance of one or other, and treating them accordingly. In this respect their pathology even to this day resembles Galen's, which depended on the four elements, the four humors, the four qualities, and these in combination" (Andrews 2014, 28).

It was in the late nineteenth century that Western medicine began to exercise more influence in China, as Western notions of physiology, microbiology, and surgical practices gained ground in the region (Jonsen 2008, 38). At this time, there was a backlash against traditional medicine by Chinese physicians schooled in modern Western medicine. One Chinese physician rejected the notion of any alliance between the two systems by saying,

"Why should modern medicine accept this marriage proposal from such a lazy, stupid wife with bound feet wrapped in yards of smelly bandage?" (39). Along with its explicit misogyny, this statement made it clear that traditional medicine was to be discarded together with other outdated cultural "relics," whose suspect nature was signaled by the reference to the unpleasant smell of old bandages.

Western physicians working in China often had to adapt their descriptions of diseases and treatments in order to better align them with the concepts of Chinese medicine. For example, one Chinese doctor advised his Western colleagues that "continued administration of the same drug for a length of time is sure to induce the patient to dispense with your services. . . . The doctor ought from time to time to alter the taste, odour or colour of the preparation" (cited in Andrews 2014, 60). The need for this sensory modulation had to do with the fact that illness and healing were considered to be interlinked in a dynamic process in China, making alterations to prescriptions over the course of a disease appear necessary.

Chinese physicians trained in Western medicine themselves often tried to make sense of the new learning by means of the old. For example, when describing the biomedical use of creosote to treat tuberculosis, the early twentieth-century Chinese physician Zhang Xichun noted that creosote was smelly and unpleasant, but that combining it with menthol gave it a cooling nature and pungent taste that "balanced" the prescription. Similarly, he described aspirin as cool in nature and sour in taste, which he thought enhanced its ability to dissipate fever (135). Other Chinese physicians, however, held that Chinese medicine needed to be "purified" of "absurd doctrines" that allied medicines with flavors and colors and emphasized feeling the pulse in diagnosis (176). After the Communist Revolution of the 1940s, however, Chinese medicine began to acquire an attractive savor of nationalism in elite society, and its practice was officially supported and systematized as traditional Chinese medicine (Taylor 2005).

In her book *Appetites* (2002) the anthropologist Judith Farquhar explores the gustatory life of Chinese medicine in contemporary China. Farquhar (2002, 32) holds that the task of ethnography is to "expose a body totally imprinted by history" à la Foucault. She fleshes out her theoretical position further in the following lines: "If bodies are capable of imagining, we should be able to carnally imagine other life worlds, or sensory realms, through an ethnographic description that attends to the concrete and the everyday.... Direct sensory experience, the material attributes of concrete things and mundane activities, can be invoked, and thereby imagined, but only by way of language and images and only in the context of times, places, and habitus that impose constraints on what can be experienced or imagined" (57). This notion of sensation as always already constrained and mediated by representation (language and images) is in keeping with the emphasis in other works in sensory anthropology (e.g., Laplantine 2015) on the dynamic, relational (intersensory, multimedia), and often conflicted nature of our everyday experience of the sensory world.

Farquhar devotes the second chapter of *Appetites* to a discussion of the theory of flavor causation in Chinese medicine. In China, the power of medicines is held to reside in their flavor and their thermal traits of "hot" or "cold." The five basic flavors of traditional Chinese medicine are pungent, sweet, sour, bitter, and salty, each of which is understood to have a different function. Sour, for example, has the function of "contracting and constricting," pungent that of "spreading and disseminating," sweet has the function of "replenishing and supplementing," and so forth (Farquhar 2002, 64–65). But how can the (subjective) experience of a flavor produce (objective) bodily changes of this nature? While medieval and early modern Europeans might have understood the concept, the modern Westerner balks at this suggestion. As Farquhar points out:

> English does not offer a language for whole-body responses to tastes or a theory of flavor causation of this kind. Perhaps the closest we come is the notion of "heavy" or "light" meals affecting our alertness, or learning that certain foods "disagree" with our stomachs. The idea that flavor could have powerful physiological efficacies is odd enough to have been politely ignored by most of the English-language literature on Chinese herbal medicine. In North American nutritional lore, we tend to relegate tastes to that domain in which the (relatively isolated) human subject receives sensory input, registering pleasure or revulsion in response to food. We think of those forces and entities that actually alter our bodies as properties of the food that are quantifiable (e.g., fat, vitamin, or protein content) and inhere in the food whether we eat it or not. (66)

Thus, while flavors may be "secondary qualities" or subjective sensations in Western psychology, they are *primary* qualities and objective forces in Chinese ontology and medicine: "sweet herbals build up ... overworked spleens and pungent drugs mobilize energies that steady ... fluttering hearts," and so on (75). In this way the body becomes a "flavourful temporal formation," very different from the body image in (Western) biomedicine.[4] Above all, the body is interpellated as the *subject* of experience, rather than the patient. Farquhar avers that coming to appreciate how the apparently ephemeral (e.g., flavor) is actually essential proved crucial to her subsequent understanding of the "experiential" dimensions of Chinese medicine: "This experiential side to Chinese medicine encourages a personal micropolitics, as patients [in concert with their physicians] seek to govern themselves and their immediate environment using techniques that fuse thinking and feeling, forming habits that make sense to their own senses" (66).

The sensations that are linked to curative regimes in traditional Chinese medicine are stimulated by the different substances that make up the materia medica. These medicaments are made both from plants and animal body parts. Bear bile, for example, is said to be bitter in taste and cold in nature and to have the power to detoxify and clear the body of heat (Zeng and Zhao 2017, 160). The demand for animal materia medica in China and elsewhere in Asia has unfortunately resulted in the intensive hunting and smuggling of animals with valued body parts and the exploitation of captive animals in "factory farms." Thus, thousands of bears are kept in cramped cages on bear farms where their bile is extracted to satisfy the public's appetite for this traditional medicament (Denyer 2018). Western medicine is hardly free of such practices—consider the exploitation of pregnant mares for estrogen, which is extracted from their urine and marketed as a therapy for menopause. The unspeakable cruelty of such practices should not go unremarked. It is precisely by delving into such backstories that sensory ethnography can go the extra mile and deliver full-bodied—and multibodied, multispecies—accounts of the life of the senses.

Because of modern trends of migration and globalization, traditional Chinese medicine now figures as an "alternative' or "supplementary" medicine in many Western countries. As a result, it has become part of the complex range of sensory interchanges that has taken place over the centuries between East and West. Perhaps partly in response to the positioning of Chinese medicine as an alternative medicine in the West, attempts have been made to similarly marginalize biomedicine in China in a cross-cultural quid pro quo. Consider the following statement issued by a meeting of traditional Chinese medicine (TCM) practitioners in Beijing in 2001: "There is sufficient evidence of Western medicine's effectiveness to expand its use into TCM and to encourage further studies of its physiology and clinical value. Western medicine shows promise as adjunctive treatment to TCM. As a stand-alone medicine, however, its efficacy is mainly in the areas of acute and catastrophic care that comprise a relatively minor percentage of total patient complaints" (cited in Barcan 2011, 8). A Western physician might well be surprised to see biomedicine represented in this way; however, it illustrates how medical systems are cultural products that are subject to different interpretations and uses across cultures. Indeed, just as one can now find Chinese versions of Western biomedicine in China, so can one find Western versions of Chinese medical practices in the West. An example of the latter is Western medical acupuncture, which combines Chinese acupuncture techniques with Western notions of physiology and disease. Such medical amalgams, while distinct in their uses, can be likened to the Chinese refashioning of European clockwork techniques to convey Chinese decorative and temporal values (Pagani 1995), or the European refashioning of the Chinese craft of porcelain to create European dishware with local motifs. In their different ways, these novel products illustrate how cross-cultural exchange not only functions as sensory exchange but can also stimulate new ways of mixing media and meanings. However, as we have seen, these products are very much the stuff of politics as well, for they all involve appropriating and manipulating power in various ways at the same time as they appropriate and manipulate the different sensations generated through their complex histories and social and material contexts.

CHAPTER 8

Smoke and Mirrors
A Sensory Analysis of Indigenous-Settler Commerce and Covenants in North America

The first section of this chapter will explore how Indigenous/settler interchanges in the colonial period in the land now known as North America involved negotiating sensory values. The second section moves this discussion into the present by examining how the differing sensory values and customary law of Indigenous societies and the formal legal culture of the nation-state have interacted and clashed in recent court cases dealing with Indigenous territorial and sovereignty claims in Canada.

The colonial record of settler contacts with Indigenous peoples in North America makes frequent reference to the interest shown by Indigenous inhabitants in what, from the European perspective, were "trinkets." Near the start of the colonial era in the early sixteenth century, Hernando Cortés repaid offerings of gold and other substantial gifts from the Indigenous inhabitants of what is now Mexico with "glass beads, looking glasses, scissors, knives, pins, &c., which pleased them much" (Cortes 1843, 26). In the early seventeenth century, the explorer John Smith declared that the Indigenous inhabitants of present-day Virginia were "generally covetous of copper, beads, & such like trash" (cited by Miller and Hamell 1986, 311). As a result, it was possible to trade a few pounds of copper and assorted low-cost goods for hundreds of bushels of wheat, peas, and beans. These representations play up the cunning rationality of the European traders. This perception has persisted. According to Christopher Miller and George Hamel, "It is difficult to think of colonial era ... contact without envisioning Peter Minuit's buying Manhattan Island for twenty-four dollars' worth of costume jewelry" (312). But were the trade items really all that worthless, and the relationship between Indigenous peoples and newcomers truly that asymmetrical? Following Peter Charles Hoffer's lead in *Sensory Worlds in Early America* (2006),[1] this chapter seeks to "sense between the lines" of the written record to explore how the parties to the conjuncture made sense of each other's presence, engaged in trade, and negotiated treaties. As we shall see, the treaty-making process involved bridging sensoria but was often fraught with misunderstanding and/or willful misreading.

The written word played a central role in mediating the encounter between Indigenous peoples and newcomers throughout the Americas.[2] Consider what Columbus meant when he recorded in the diary of his 1492–93 voyage to the West Indies that he "spoke to the Indians." Speaking did not mean conversing (Columbus had no interpreter, nor did his interlocutors have anyone who could speak any of the European languages he understood). It meant pronouncing—that is: "He spoke in their presence. It was not important, at first, whether they understood or could reply, for part of the Spanish process for taking control of territory—that is, claiming it for the Spanish crown—was to read aloud a legal document announcing that the Spanish were the rightful owners of the land on which the Spanish conqueror stood" (Hoffer 2006, 50).

Double Vision: The View from Both Sides of the Ledger

A different understanding of intercultural relations emerges when exchanges of goods between Indigenous inhabitants and European colonizers are viewed from the other side of the ledger. Indeed, what the Europeans sometimes saw as commercial transactions, the Indigenous peoples often understood to be ritual ceremonial exchanges. Ethnohistorical research has revealed that many goods of European provenance were valued for their luster and reflective quality (Turgeon 1997; Saunders 1999). These qualities might be seen as giving them a kind of spiritual aura. Moreover, it was not simply the novelty of the glass beads, mirrors, and the like that made them desirable to many Indigenous peoples, but the ways in which they lent themselves to traditional uses and meanings. This is suggested by the way these foreign items were used alongside Indigenous copper, siliceous stone, and shell beads to fashion gorgets, or neck bands, and pendants in northeastern North America. Further research (Miller and Hamell 1986) has revealed that the latter items (and by analogy the European goods that were associated with them) were believed by certain peoples of the region to be of otherworldly origin and supposed to be guarantors of long life, physical and spiritual well-being, and good fortune for those who possessed them. They were the sorts of gifts that "Other World Grandfathers" and other supernatural beings typically bestowed on their supplicants. This gave the wares that the Europeans traded for Indigenous products a whole other meaning and value. Though the focus here is on Indigenous perspectives, it is also important to recognize that at least some of the local goods desired by Europeans also had more than monetary value for them. This is notably the case with gold, which was attributed alchemical powers and moral and medicinal virtues in early modernity.

Gift economies are predicated on a very different principle than market economies—namely, the principle of reciprocity (Mauss 1967). The former are keyed to the creation and maintenance of longstanding, symmetrical relations of equilibrium, whereas the latter are more short-term, or one-off, and asymmetrical, geared to the accumulation of capital. As the Indigenous peoples were drawn into increasingly unequal mercantile relations and their dependence on European trade goods increased, they balked at the asymmetricality of their relations with the settlers.

In *Natives and Newcomers: Canada's 'Heroic Age' Reconsidered* (1986), archaeologist Bruce G. Trigger debunks the myth of there ever having been a "Heroic Age" of exploration and colonization by stalwart and self-sufficient pioneers in North America. The European discoverers, traders, and settlers in fact depended heavily on the Hurons and other Woodland peoples not only for sustenance (corn, etc.) but also for alliances in the wars among the Spanish, the English, and the French that were transposed from the Old World to the New World. Treaties had to be forged both for military purposes and for colonization to proceed.

We can catch a glimpse of the treaty-making process in this sketch of the peace treaty that was concluded between Massasoit, leader of the Wampanoag Confederacy, and John Carver, governor of Plymouth Colony, in March 1621 (see fig. 12). Both the Wampanoag and the pilgrims, who had arrived aboard the *Mayflower* only three months earlier, were in a weakened state because of the predations of disease and worried about being overrun by the Narragansett.

Fig. 12 Massasoit, sachem of the Wampanoag Confederacy, handing a ceremonial pipe to John Carver, governor of Plymouth Colony, Massachusetts, March 1621. From J. C. Ridpath, *A Popular History of the United States of America, from the Aboriginal Times to the Present Day* (Cincinnati: Jones Brothers, 1881).

The sketch depicts an indoor scene, in which all the walls are at right angles. A grandfather clock looms in the background, signaling the instauration of a lineal temporal regime unhinged from the seasonal cycle. Some of the pilgrims are seated on chairs, while the Indigenous dignitaries remain standing. The terms of the treaty are being dictated by a man in a dark frock coat reading from a paper. At the center of the scene, Massasoit and Carver are portrayed as seated on a mat on the floor. This arrangement would perhaps have had resonance for the Wampanoag sachem on account of his being in contact with the ground, the earth, and Governor Carver being brought to the same level, as if on a par. Massasoit holds a tankard, which would have contained "fire water," and it is well known that the Europeans plied their Indigenous counterparts with alcohol to gain an advantage. Equally if not more significant, however, is the gesture Massasoit makes with the long-stemmed pipe. He invites Carver to smoke with him.

Within the Wampanoag Confederacy, tobacco was considered to be both pleasurable and spiritual at once. The pleasure stemmed in part from the tobacco's being mixed with other aromatic ingredients, such as juniper and red willow bark, sumac leaves, and like, to create what is called *kinnikinnick*. Meanwhile, the ethereality of tobacco smoke makes it a suitable vehicle for offerings to the spirits (though tobacco is often used in solid form as well). Smoke may, indeed, be seen as a medium of communication analogous to writing in its presumed capacity to carry messages and its binding power. This understanding can be pieced together from the following historical accounts quoted by James Warren Springer in his classic analysis of "the smoking complex" in eastern North America:

> Tobacco was regarded as a gift from the *manido*, and for this reason it was supposed to have "magic power," in that it increased the efficacy of a request and made an obligation or agreement more binding. Thus a gift of tobacco accompanied a request and its acceptance signified a promise to grant the request. The smoking of tobacco by both parties was an essential part of the making of a treaty [quoting Densmore (1928), "Uses of Plants by the Chippewa Indians"].
>
> They believe there is nothing so suitable as Tobacco to appease the passions; that is why they never attend a council without a pipe or calumet in their mouths. The smoke, they say, gives them intelligence, and enables them to see clearly through the most intricate matters [quoting the Jesuit missionary Jean de Brébeuf (1629) in the *Jesuit Relations*].

> The Iroquois believed that tobacco was given to them as a means of communication with the spiritual world. By burning tobacco they could send up their petitions with its ascending incense, to the Great Spirit, and render their acknowledgments acceptably for his blessings. Without this instrumentality, the ear of Ha-wen-ne-yu could not be gained. In like manner they returned their thanks at each recurring festival to their Invisible Aids, for their friendly offices, and protecting care [quoting Morgan (1851), *League of the Ho-de-no-sau-nee*]. (Springer 1981, 232)

These quotations bring out well how the smoking of tobacco was an "essential part" of treaty making (whereas for the Europeans, it was the "X" or signature on paper that sealed a deal). They also reveal how the consumption of tobacco enabled the Indigenous participants "to see clearly through the most intricate matters" (unlike alcohol, which clouds judgment), and how tobacco was instrumental to opening a channel of communication with supernatural beings in ritual contexts, as with other human beings in the context of diplomacy.

In his article on "the smoking complex," Springer goes on to discuss two other core elements (apart from *kinnikinnick* and the smoke that is offered the spirits and inhaled by all the ceremonial participants, thereby uniting them). These elements are the pipestem, often adorned with feathers, and the pipe bowl, together referred to as "the calumet" (an old French word). As Springer states, "A village would entertain and honor the visiting leader of a foreign tribe (or a group of Europeans) with a series of dances and songs, by sharing the smoke of the calumet, and by giving the calumet to the guest" (222) as a token of the alliance. It is important to note that the calumet was not just smoked. It was also sung and danced. In other words, it was at the center of a multisensory ritual.

Another common means of communicating and recording alliances used in the Eastern Woodlands and Great Lakes region was the ceremonial wampum belt, decorated with symbolic designs in beads. This belt had to be touched, as well as seen, by the parties involved for the alliance to be formally ratified. Ritual speech and singing also formed an essential part of the process: "In Iroquois tradition the 'word,' the essence of oral tradition and of wampum, had a life to it that paper (written documents) just did not have, regardless of its assumed durability" (Druke 1985, 92; see also Rath 2014). What made the wampum ceremonial more "durable" than writing was its multisensoriality—the way it impressed itself on each of the senses and forged memorable associations.

Some colonial officials were alert to this and accordingly incorporated elements of Indigenous legal practice into the treaty-making process in an attempt to ensure greater compliance (Howes 2017, 61–63). For the most part, however, the colonizers considered it sufficient to obtain a signature, an "X." Nonplussed by this, many Indigenous leaders came to regard the settlers' fixation on writing, and its suspicious effects, such as the alienation of territory, as so much "pen-and-ink witchcraft"—in the words of the Odawa chief Egushawa, commenting on the textual treaty-making process in 1791 (Howes 2017, 62; Mann 2004, 136–37).

In the Pacific Northwest Coast region, we find a different complex, popularly known as the potlatch. The potlatch ceremony was an important means for forging alliances and affirming social standing as well as for distributing wealth and resolving conflicts. It provided an occasion for members of a clan and their neighbors to join in marking an important event through communal feasting. During the potlatch, speeches would be made concerning territorial rights and clan histories, and gifts would be given to the guests. Dances and songs figured prominently and were central means of expressing and experiencing social authority and unity. A chief of the Wet'suwet'en summed up "the way the feast works" with these words: "My power is carried in my House's histories, songs, dances and crests. It is recreated at the Feast when the histories are told, the songs and dances are performed, and the crests are displayed. With the wealth that comes from respectful use of the territory, the House feeds the name of the Chief in the Feast Hall. In this way, the law, the Chief, the territory, and the Feast become one" (Wa and Uukw 1992, 7). Participating in the feast—eating, drinking, dancing, hearing the speeches and songs, witnessing the hereditary symbols, and accepting the gifts—was deemed to obligate the guests to respect the traditions and uphold the territorial rights of their hosts. The potlatch was a legal, as well as social and aesthetic, ceremony in which people experienced the ordering of society through all of their senses. It was a total sensory phenomenon as well as a "total social phenomenon" (Mauss 1967).

From the point of view of the Canadian government, however, potlatches encouraged wasteful spending. They were therefore outlawed from the late nineteenth to the mid-twentieth centuries. The protest of one First Nations chief at this stifling of traditional practices was recorded by an anthropologist: "We want to know whether you have come to stop our dances and feasts.... Is this the white man's land? We are told it is the Queen's land; but no! It is mine! ... We will dance when our laws command us to dance, and we will feast when our hearts desire to feast.... It is a strict law that bids us dance. It is a strict law that bids us distribute our property among our friends and neighbors. It is a good law. Let the white man observe his law, we shall observe ours" (quoted in Trosper 2009, 2). In order to understand a legal system that can be eaten or danced, such as we encounter in the potlatch or the calumet dance, we need to expand our understanding of law as "code" or as "discourse" and even as "hearing" to law as *sensed*. Adopting a sensori-legal approach to law (Howes 2019; Hamilton 2020) is particularly crucial to understanding the dynamics of the judicial process in situations of legal pluralism, such as persist in the current conjuncture.

From the Initial Conjuncture to the Current Conjuncture

In Canada, the resilience of the potlatch was crucial to the late twentieth-century Aboriginal title case known as *Delgamuukw v. British Columbia* (hereafter *Delgamuukw* 1997). In 1984, the hereditary chiefs of the Gitksan and Wet'suwet'en brought a suit for "ownership and jurisdiction," which is to say unextinguished Aboriginal title and entitlement to govern by Aboriginal laws, over an assortment of territories in northwest British Columbia that totaled fifty-eight thousand square kilometers. Unlike in other parts of Canada, the colonial administration had never bothered to treat with the Indigenous inhabitants of the region to secure the extinguishment of their title. The case was heard by Allan McEachern, chief justice of the BC Supreme Court, in both the town of Smithers and the provincial capital, Victoria, over 369 days between 1987 and 1991, and generated reams of transcripts, in addition to a 760-page decision, *Delgamuukw v. A. G.* (hereafter *Delgamuukw* 1991).

In accordance with precedents, most notably *Calder v. British Columbia* (1973), the plaintiffs had to establish that they and their ancestors constituted an "organized society" that had occupied the disputed territory continuously and exclusively since before the declaration of British sovereignty (ca. 1870).

The Wet'suwet'en chiefs (like their Gitksan counterparts) supported their claim with direct testimony of their connection to the land as evidenced by their sacred oral tradition—the *kungax*, or spiritual songs and stories that formed the basis of their authority over specific territories and people. They also engaged expert witnesses, including the anthropologists Antonia Mills and Richard Daly, to document their tradition and explain to the court the workings of the Feast Hall.

In her expert opinion report, later published as *Eagle Down Is Our Law* (1994), Mills, who spent three years gathering material, described the feasts she had been permitted to attend: "One by one, [the head chiefs] stood up, donned the ceremonial robes that they had been given when they took their respective [titles], and talked about their territory, its location and boundaries, and how it is associated with the title and the robes, songs and crests" (Mills 1994, 47). At the end of each feast, after any boundary disputes had been resolved through consensus and gifts had been distributed to the guests, the assembled company would be sprinkled with eagle down, symbolizing peace and the end of discussion.

So intimate is the Wet'suwet'en connection with the land that, in the words of Johnny David, the first Wet'suwet'en chief to give testimony on behalf of the plaintiffs, "If you know the territory well, it is like your own skin. Sometimes you can feel the animals moving on your body as they are on the land, the fish swimming in your bloodstream.... If you know the territory well enough, you can feel the animals" (Mills 2005, 3). Significantly, in the lead-up to the deposition, the chief had gone out and walked his clan territory, naming each of its distinctive features and recounting the stories associated with each one, and his words were recorded on an audiocassette. When Johnny David was subsequently shown archival photographs of key village sites, he complained that the light and his poor eyesight prevented him from "see[ing] the pictures clearly," and he frequently could not identify them. Mills surmises that this was due to the disjuncture between the medium of photography and the physical presence of the landmarks (Mills 2005, 30), since Johnny David's eyesight was otherwise fine. Also significant is the fact that, when Johnny David occasionally performed a song, the transcript simply reads: "THE WITNESS SINGS THE SONG AND PLAYS DRUM" (*Delgamuukw* 1991, 24, 269).

The elision of the songs was symptomatic of the clash of media and knowledge systems that underlay the court proceedings. According to Brian Thom, "Oral histories must be seen as 'cultural forms that organize perceptions about the world,' not merely containers of brute facts which may be laid on the table for judges to interpret in a 'common-sense' way" (Thom 2001, 10). There is a world of difference between traditions that are handed down by word of mouth (and literally ingested in the context of the feast) and those that rely on writing as their means of transmission. The former are adjudged to constitute hearsay from the viewpoint of the latter (see Mills 2005, 30–35). This view fails to recognize that, in the case of the Wet'suwet'en, the narratives would have been "authenticated" each time they were performed in the Feast Hall.

Chief Justice McEachern relaxed the hearsay rule to some extent by allowing the narratives to be introduced into court instead of excluding them outright, but in the end, he discounted the direct testimony of the Gitksan-Wet'suwet'en chiefs on account of the allegedly indeterminate and putatively self-serving nature of this testimony. The chief justice went on to point out that "much of the plaintiffs' historical evidence is not literally true" because the narratives included elements of myth (*Delgamuukw* 1991, 49). Then, in a blatant example of the scriptocentrism of the Western legal profession (and the conventional Western understanding of history as written record), he concluded that the Gitksan-Wet'suwet'en had "some minimal levels of social organization, but the primitive condition of the natives described by early observers is not impressive" (24). The observers in question included traders and colonial administrators who had kept journals. The journals were introduced into court by the historians hired by the defense. Of the latter, McEachern wrote, "Generally speaking, I accept just about everything they put before me because they were largely collectors of archival, historical documents . . . [which] largely spoke for themselves" (52).

McEachern's blind spot becomes glaringly apparent in the following quote from his reasons for judgment: "The plaintiffs' ancestors had no written language, no horses or wheeled vehicles, slavery and starvation was not uncommon, and there is no doubt, to quote Hobbs [sic] that aboriginal life in the territory was, at best 'nasty, brutish and short'" (13). This statement interpellates a Western myth concerning the so-called state of nature as envisioned by Thomas Hobbes (how ironic that McEachern got the spelling of Hobbes's name wrong!), and conveniently overlooks the fact that slavery and starvation were common in European history. It also assumes that what are taken to be key elements of Western civilization—writing, horses, and wheeled vehicles—are necessary to civilization everywhere, regardless of the fact that, for example, there were no horses in the Americas (before the arrival of the Europeans). The lack of writing, one suspects, was particularly damning to a man who was ready to accept the biases of colonial documents without question (as "speak[ing] for themselves," even!) but found the oral testimony of the Aboriginal witnesses to be self-serving and unreliable.

By admitting cultural evidence but then privileging the written record over Gitksan-Wet'suwet'en oral tradition, the court (effectively) heard only one side of the case. Not surprisingly,

McEachern went on to dismiss the claim. He found that the Gitksan-Wet'suwet'en did not use the territories (except in the vicinity of their villages, which were already identified as reserved lands) sufficiently intensively or uninterruptedly to establish any more than use rights to the broader territory, and certainly not the proprietary rights that were claimed.

The BC Supreme Court decision was appealed to the BC Court of Appeal and then appealed again to the Supreme Court of Canada. In the Supreme Court of Canada, Chief Justice Antonio Lamer set aside the trial judge's findings of fact on the ground that "a court must take into account the perspective of the aboriginal people claiming the right . . . while at the same time taking into account the perspective of the common law," and he went on to affirm that "the laws of evidence must be adapted in order that this type of evidence [i.e., Aboriginal oral history] can be accommodated and placed on an equal footing with the types of historical evidence that courts are familiar with, which largely consists of written documents" (*Delgamuukw* 1997, 1065 and 1069). Only by "bridging" perspectives could the ultimate goal of reconciliation between Indigenous peoples and the State be achieved, according to the chief justice.

Chief Justice Lamer's decision is to be lauded for opening the ears of the court to nonliterate, sensorial modes of legal transmission, though it fell short of extending full faith and credit to the Indigenous definition of the legal process in terms of "the way the feast works" (Mills 1994). That would have involved turning the courtroom into a feast hall.

The Supreme Court of Canada decision in the *Delgamuukw* affair ushered in a highly creative and volatile period in Canadian jurisprudence regarding the legal definition of Aboriginal rights and title—a period in which orality became the new medium and occasionally buried the parol evidence rule: "The parol evidence rule dictates that if parties make an agreement in writing, that writing, if unambiguous, becomes legally definitive. All prior or contemporaneous utterances of the parties become immaterial. Instead of being considered as parts of a single expressive event, 'relevant' writing is separated from 'irrelevant' speech" (Hibbitts quoted in Howes 2017, 59). In *Regina v. Marshall* (1999), for example, which concerned the proper construction to be placed on the terms of a 1760–61 treaty between the Mi'kmaq and the English, the Supreme Court held that treaty arrangements "must be interpreted in a manner which gives meaning and substance to the oral promises made by the Crown during the treaty negotiations," and that what the Mi'kmaq heard in 1760–61 and passed on could trump what the British negotiators wrote down. Here, the spoken word prevailed over the written word.

At the start of this chapter, we saw how the sensory traits of goods take on new meanings when they cross cultural borders, and how this extends more broadly to sensory practices in general. Likewise, in the context of Indigenous-settler legal interactions, a written treaty establishing settler powers over Indigenous peoples may be viewed as "pen-and-ink witchcraft" from an Indigenous perspective, while an Indigenous song that offers a powerful account of the relationship of a people with their land becomes "nonsense" in a formal court context—incapable of being transcribed into the court record. In the decisions of the Supreme Court of Canada discussed above, we can see how Indigenous "ways of sensing" have now achieved some modest acceptance at the Court because of a new recognition of the importance of engaging in what I have elsewhere called "cross-cultural jurisprudence" (Howes 2005c).[3] This is a form of legal reasoning that looks at "the law" from various perspectives—within and without, formal and informal, the so-called common law and Indigenous practice—and strives for the "enlargement of mind" of which the political philosopher Hannah Arendt speaks (as discussed in the prologue) before passing judgment.

It must be noted that Western courts are not neutral bodies, capable of appreciating different legal and cultural perspectives objectively. They are, after all, creatures of the formal State system and thus upholders of that system. Given this situation, it is doubtful that a wholesome (which is to say a multi- and intermodal, legal and extralegal) comprehension of Indigenous practice could ever be fully realized within the confines of the courtroom. Nonetheless, the possibility exists that the divide between settler and Indigenous worldviews, and settler and Indigenous sensory values, can at least be bridged to some degree within transactional contexts through cultivating an awareness of how relationships with other communities and with the physical world, whether in terms of goods or of land, can be fashioned and experienced through multiple modalities by different cultures at different times. That is the touchstone of multicultural justice, which hinges on the interpellation of multiple sensoria.

Epilogue
The Senses of Justice

Sensorial Investigations highlights the need for a multi- and intersensory approach to analyzing societies and cultures (both past and present) and underlines the importance of contextualization for understanding sensory experience in history. Context alters perception. The senses are made, not given.

History and anthropology are foundational to this new understanding because of their attunement to sensory diversity over time and across cultures and their insistence on "the politics of the sensible" (Laplantine 2015). As such, these twin disciplines challenge the hegemony of modern Western perceptual psychology, from Lockean empiricism to cognitive neuroscience, by foregrounding the sociality of sensation and the cultural mediation of perception over and against the privatization and individuation of the senses, and of the reduction of "sensory processing" to "patterns of brain activity." The focus in the brain sciences on the neural pathways from receptor organ to brain needs to be offset by an equally attentive focus on the intercourse between the senses and the world, which is where the action is. The action—or "enaction"—of perception is modulated by all sorts of extrasomatic factors, from environmental to technological to social. Following Mauss ([1924] 1979), we need to put psychology in its place and stop it from occupying the whole field of perception.[1]

The recent rise in popularity of the "extended mind hypothesis" (Clarke 2008) is a case in point. What is needed is a theory of the extended sensorium. Such a theory would be able to accommodate the perceptual philosophies and practices of those cultures that do not ascribe the same centrality to the neural cortex. For example, the Cashinahua of Peru, when asked "Does the brain have knowledge?" say: "It doesn't . . . the whole body knows" (see p. 59). Similar views have been voiced by diverse renegade Western thinkers, such as Margaret Cavendish in her critique of Cartesianism (see pp. 140–41), and non-Western thinkers, such as Léopold Sédar Senghor (1964) (see further Santos 2016: ch. 8). With them we aver *sentio ergo sum*.

By contrast, Descartes ([1641] 1973) "called away" his senses to arrive at the truth of his own existence, *cogito ergo sum*. The mind (or *l'esprit*), according to Descartes, has no extension in space. It is confined to a separate (metaphysical) plane, inside the head. The extended mind hypothesis flips this positionality, by turning the inside out. It is no less mental for all that—that is, for all the hypothesis's insistence on the "distribution of cognition." It has no room for other persons, or, to put a finer point on it, for relations *between* persons. By contrast, in her highly perspicacious account of the Anlo-Ewe sensorium in *Culture and the Senses: Bodily Ways of Knowing in an African Community*, Kathryn Linn Geurts describes a "culturally elaborated form" of consciousness within which "Anlo people attend to and interpret their own bodies while simultaneously orienting themselves to the bodies of those around them" (Geurts 2002a, 167; see also Geurts 2002b).

Interpersonal relations can be conflictual as well as consensual, just as relations among the senses can admit of *dis-sensus* as well as *con-sensus*, a point beautifully illustrated by the seventeenth-century play *Lingua: Or the Combat of the Tongue and the Five Senses for Superiority* (see p. 122). The sensorium is multifaceted, which makes any attempt to theorize it as an undivided whole (e.g., Merleau-Ponty's synesthetic theory) a conversation-stopper that only serves to shut down inquiry into the varieties of sensory experience. The centrifugal tendencies of the sensorium deserve no less attention than the centripetal.[2] Only in this way can we arrive at an understanding of the intersensorial dynamics of the perceptual apparatus and a holistic, multifarious understanding of human sensuousness. The senses are "relationally produced" (Dawkins and Loftus 2013).

The chapters in part 1 of this book trace the history of research on—and later, with—the senses in anthropology. Chapter 1 shows how this field of inquiry was initially subordinate to the racialized science of psychophysics, before certain anthropologists of the first half of the twentieth century (Leenhardt, Mauss, and Mead) and turn of the twenty-first century (Stoller, Howes, Geurts, and others) redefined sensation as a social affair, which meant focusing on the cultural meanings and uses of the senses. In this way, the original emphasis on physiology was supplanted by a focus on practice—that is, on techniques of the senses, or *ways of sensing*. Chapter 1 concludes with a discussion of how the discredited but never extinguished tradition of psychophysical measurement made a comeback in the twenty-first century thanks to the proliferation of mobile digital self-tracking devices, whereby bodily "performance" came to be registered as abstract information on a screen. The invention of the "quantified self" was interpreted by some scholars as having obliterated the qualified self. Yet while quantification has certainly taken command of our consciousness and contributed substantially to supplanting bodily ways of knowing through datafication, the challenge of "*making sense* of data" persists (see pp. 43–46).

Chapter 2 charts the emergence of a full-bodied cultural anthropology of the senses in the 1990s. This revolution in anthropological scholarship is grounded in the critique of visualism and an equally incisive critique of textualism. Sensory anthropology has come to stand for "summoning all the senses," and for sensing cultures in place of "writing culture." Paradoxically, a major part of the impetus for displacing the definition of anthropology as a "discipline of words," as exemplified by the ethnographic monograph, came from the meteoric rise of visual anthropology (e.g., Lucien Castaing-Taylor's [1996] critique of the "linguification of meaning" and characterization of life as "pro-filmic"), only for visual anthropology to be dissolved into "multimodal anthropologies" in the last decade. As discussed in chapter 3, the multimodal turn dovetailed with the groundswell in the practice of sensory ethnography (Pink 2009) or sensorial fieldwork (Robben and Sluka 2007, part 8), which positioned the senses as the means of inquiry. This development opened the way for widespread experimentation with embodied practices, from walking (the soundwalk, smellwalk, taste tour, etc.) to live performance, and with diverse technologies of sensory augmentation, from virtual reality and augmented reality to video gaming. Some of these ethnographic techniques had been afoot for some time but have now become *de rigueur*. Sensualization has taken pride of place in the anthropological tool kit, as shown by all the experiments in sense-making currently being pursued by next-generation sensory anthropologists discussed in the concluding section of chapter 3 (e.g., implanting magnets, crafting sensory tables, writing poetry, designing immersive sensory environments). The space "between art and anthropology" (Schneider and Wright 2010) that their experiments in research-creation opened up have disclosed all manner of other ways of knowing and being.

The chapters in part 2 offer a series of reflections on psychological, philosophical, and juridical topics from a combined anthropological-historical perspective. The marriage of history and anthropology is shown to have tremendous power with respect to upsetting common-sense assumptions. It makes for *un*common sense—that is, for putting (Western) psychology in its place and laying the foundations for a *cross-cultural* psychology and *cross-cultural* jurisprudence, both of which are grounded in the polysensoriality of human existence.

Chapter 4 delves into the sensuous underpinnings of the Aristotelian worldview and then traces how the senses came unhinged from the elements—that is, how psychology came to be dissociated from cosmology. It also tracks how the category of the person was subjected to a process of involution. Whereas the term "individual" formerly referred to the individual as the "indivisible unit" of society, it gradually morphed into the notion of individuals as agents or "wills" who contract with each other to *make up* a society or civil compact. As a corollary to this, the concept of justice devolved from the idea of "what we are fitted for" to "what we bargain for, or make," and doing justice ceased to denote "to render each human being their due"; now it means "to treat everyone the same" in the name of equality—justice "as fairness."

This would have been for the better were it not for the fact that individuals are not all the same, not all interchangeable, rights-bearing entities (as per liberal democratic theory), because of the differential social factors that advantage some individuals or groups and disadvantage others. The liberal democratic ideal of "equality of opportunity" does not adequately address these differends. There is an alternative—namely, the social democratic ideal of *equality of result*. Such a regime would give meaningful expression to the archaic understanding of justice as calling us "to render each human being their due" through the creation of affirmative action programs, or through paying reparation to disadvantaged and historically disempowered classes of people.[3]

What is needed is a theory of "complex equality" keyed to the sorts of questions Michael Walzer asks in *Spheres of Justice* (1983), such as: "What choices have we already made in the course of our common life? What understandings do we (really) share?" (Walzer 1983, 5).[4] Walzer's approach articulates a vision of distributive justice that consigns social goods such as wealth, political office, quality education, and medical care to separate "spheres," each with its own distributive principle. The upshot of his analysis is that "it is wrong that the *wealthy* have so much *political power*," "access to quality *education* should not be based on economic or social *status*," the provision of medical services should be tied to need, not ability to pay, and so forth. Walzer's vision of "pluralism *and* equality" remains vulnerable to the criticism that it is not sufficiently critical of our "shared understandings,"[5] and not cross-cultural enough, but it nevertheless represents an eyes-wide-open stance, unlike the vision of justice "as fairness" that John Rawls conjured from behind his "veil of ignorance."

Part 3 of *Sensorial Investigations* opens with a chapter that celebrates the marriage between history and anthropology proposed by Alain Corbin in "Histoire et anthropologie sensorielle" (1990). It postulates a historical anthropology (or anthropological history) predicated on the method of "sensing between the lines" of written sources. In the ensuing chapter, this method is applied to the study of trade relations between China and the West in the early modern period. This investigation exposes the clash of sensibilities between the Chinese and Europeans that resulted in a substantial trade imbalance, since the kinds of goods the Europeans had to offer did not, for the most part, possess the same sense appeal as the goods emanating from China (wool versus silk, iron versus porcelain).

In the final chapter, the focus shifts to the treaty-making process between the sovereign Indigenous societies of North America and European settler society during the colonial period. This investigation highlights the clash of sensibilities—oral versus literate, or law as "the way the feast works" versus law as written document. It questions whether there could ever have been a true "meeting of minds" (the *sine qua non* of any binding contractual agreement) when the mentalities—or better, sensoria—of the contracting parties were at such loggerheads. "Pen-and-ink witchcraft" is the way one Indigenous leader characterized the settler insistence on "getting it in writing"—the "it" being consent (see above, pp. 215, 222).

The alienation of aboriginal rights in land and suppression of the right to self-determination instigated by the treaty process progressed apace until the Indigenous sovereignty movements of the latter half of the twentieth century. In Canada, this resurgence of Indigeneity was sparked by the "White Paper" (1969), which announced the federal government's intention to "achieve equality among all Canadians by eliminating *Indian* as a distinct legal status [through abolition of the Indian Act] and by regarding Aboriginal peoples simply as citizens with the same rights, opportunities, and responsibilities as other Canadians."[6]

Indigenous peoples promptly started taking to the courts to defend their Aboriginal and treaty rights, and they also mounted a pressure campaign that resulted in the adoption of a signal provision when the Canadian Constitution was patriated from the Parliament of Westminster in 1982—namely, section 35 of The Canadian Charter of Rights and Freedoms (1982), which states, "(1) The existing aboriginal and treaty rights of the aboriginal peoples of Canada are hereby recognized and affirmed. (2) In this Act, 'aboriginal peoples of Canada' includes the Indian, Inuit and Métis peoples of Canada" (section 35). The scope of these rights was left undefined at the time but has since been fleshed out through a series of Supreme Court decisions, which had already begun with *Calder v. British Columbia* (1973), continued with *Regina v. Van der Peet* (1996), and culminated in *Delgamuukw v. British Columbia* (1997). The latter case broke the silence of the official (written) record and turned the tables by holding that "the laws of evidence must be adapted in order that this type of evidence [i.e., Aboriginal oral history] can be accommodated and placed on an equal footing with the types of historical evidence that courts are familiar with, which largely consists of written documents" (see p. 221). In other words, it recognized the continuing existence of a "sensory archive," in Jennifer Biddle's apt phrase (Biddle 2016), alongside the state archive, and instituted a framework for cross-cultural jurisprudence, which is at the same time a multimodal jurisprudence. Doing justice to and by the senses of other people(s) is the better part of justice. The "time of the senses" (Bendix 2005) is now.

Notes

Prologue

1. The standard introduction to the anthropology of the senses is Classen 1997. The subsequent development of this field has been surveyed by Hsu (2008), Pink (2009), Porcello et al. (2010), Cox (2018), Gould et al. (2019), and Howes (2003a, 2015, and 2018, vol. 1), among others. The anthropology and history of the senses played a leading role in the creation of sensory studies (Bull et al. 2006). The definitive account of the origin and development of the latter field of inquiry is given in *The Sensory Studies Manifesto* (Howes 2022).

2. The standard history of Western perceptual psychology is Boring 1942. For a general introduction to sensory history, see Classen's "The Senses" (2001). The most comprehensive overview of the field is given in *A Cultural History of the Senses* (Classen 2014a). This set is divided chronologically: antiquity (Toner 2014); the Middle Ages (Newhauser 2014); the Renaissance (Roodenburg 2014); the Enlightenment (Vila 2014); the nineteenth century, or Age of Empire (Classen 2014b); and the twentieth century, or Modern Age (Howes 2014a)—and by domain, with individual chapters in each volume devoted to the analysis of the senses in the city, the marketplace, medicine, philosophy and science, literature, the arts, media, and religion. The history of the senses has also been surveyed by the medical historian Robert Jütte (2004) and the social historian Mark Smith (2008).

3. Stoller references Ong's media theory in the chapter on "Sound in Songhay Sorcery" in *The Taste of Ethnographic Things* (1989, chap. 7).

4. Madeline Schwartzman's *See Yourself Sensing: Redefining Human Perception* (2011) presents numerous further examples of technological and sensory experimentation in contemporary art. See also Arning 2006.

5. This phrase "archaeology of perception" was first introduced by Michel Foucault (1973), but whereas Foucauldians view knowledges (*épistemes*) as "discursive formations," the approach advocated here treats them as sensory formations (Howes 2003a). See further Hamilakis (2014) and Skeates and Day (2020) for a veritably archaeological approach to the study of perception.

6. This book does not present a sensory history of law and legal institutions in anything like the same detail as the sensory history of anthropology and psychology it offers. This is because we have already presented a sketch of what such a legal sensory history would involve elsewhere—namely, the chapter on "The Feel of Justice" in *Ways of Sensing* (Howes and Classen

2013, chapter 4). Other pertinent secondary sources include *A Cultural History of Law in the Modern Age* (Sherwin and Celemajer 2021); *Sensing the Nation's Law: Historical Inquiries into the Aesthetics of Democratic Legitimacy* (Huygebaert et al. 2018); *Synaesthetic Legalities: Sensory Dimensions of Law and Jurisprudence* (International Roundtable for the Semiotics of Law 2015); the publications of the Westminster Law and Theory Lab (https://www.westminster.ac.uk/research/groups-and-centres/westminster-law-and-theory-lab/publications/westminster-law-and-senses-series); and the "Probes" page of the Law and the Senses website (http://lawandthesenses.org/probes).

7. Simmel's insight regarding the sociality of sensation in "Sociology of the Senses" ([1921] 1997) lay fallow for much of the twentieth century. We owe it to Anthony Synnott for recuperating it and repositioning the body at the center of sociology in *The Body Social: Symbolism, Self and Society* (1993), the book that (re)launched the sociology of the senses (see Howes 2022, chap. 2).

8. The title, *Sensorial Investigations*, also resonates with the subtitle of Lionel Bently and Leo Flyn's groundbreaking edited collection *Law and the Senses: Sensational Jurisprudence* (1996). The present book is equally concerned with enucleating the connection between sensory studies and sociolegal studies. *Sensorial Investigations* is otherwise aligned with Paul Stoller's *Sensuous Scholarship*, which advocated using the idiom of the senses to enliven anthropological writing, or render the "process of textualization" more vivid. At the same time, the present book insists on the necessity of drilling down to analyze how sensation itself is culturally mediated.

Chapter 1

1. Myopia was something of an occupational hazard for the intellectual class, given their study habits, though by characterizing it as a "disease of civilization" it became a badge of honor (Dias 2006). It was even more of a hazard for seamstresses, but their work was regarded as manual, not intellectual, by the men of the SAP, and so it did not count.

2. In point of fact, Benedict, Mead, and Sapir were all poets, in addition to being anthropologists, though they tended to keep the two identities separate (Reichel 2021).

3. In *Sensory Experiments: Psychophysics, Race, and the Aesthetics of Feeling* (2020), Erica Fretwell discusses the uptake of psychophysics in the culture at large.

4. Marcel Mauss was a student (and also the nephew) of Émile Durkheim, the founder of French sociology.

5. This account owes much to my conversation with Florencia Marchetti (Marchetti and Howes 2020), and I am particularly indebted to her for bringing Debaene's book to my attention.

6. Of course, the social is never completely weeded out in the laboratory, as research in the sociology of laboratories has shown (e.g., Lahne and Spackman 2018; Latour 1987). Research protocols introduce their own social rules, and these have important

implications for knowledge production, as will be discussed further in chapter 5.

7. This notion of "sensory work" or "sensory labor" has been arrived at independently by a number of leading theorists in the anthropology and sociology of the senses, such as Lahne and Spackman (2018), Lupton and Maslen (2018), and Vannini, Waskul, and Gottschalk (2012), who call it "somatic work."

8. Lupton and Maslen thus draw attention to the infratechnological techniques of the senses and making sense that subtend and persist despite the all-embracing technologization of perception in "the sensor society" (see further Pink and Fors 2017; Salter 2022).

Chapter 2

1. This analysis builds on the critique of the textual revolution presented in chapter 2 of *Sensual Relations* (2003a; for an earlier statement, see Howes 1990a). I sent a copy of that chapter to Clifford Geertz. His response to it is on record in the form of a letter he wrote to me, reprinted (with the permission of his widow and literary executor Karen Blu) in "Boasian Soundings" (Howes 2018). In the letter, Geertz graciously but firmly and ever so loquaciously rebukes me for failing to pick up on the sensuous nuances of his hermeneutics. I stand corrected! In this chapter, I am also critical of the work of the late Steven Tyler. I hasten to add that while I stand by my critique, I remain in awe of Tyler for the way he stared down visualism in "The Vision Quest in the West, or What the Mind's Eye Sees" (Tyler 1984) and went on to plumb the depths of postmodernism (a school of thought that is more known for its shallowness, and fascination with surfaces) in "Postmodern Ethnography" (Tyler 1986).

2. "Sensory cosmology" is another key concept for the anthropology of the senses, first introduced by Classen (1993b, 1998): it is used in preference to "worldview."

3. Roseman's book is subtitled "Temiar Music and Medicine." Research in medical anthropology has been another major contributor to the development of the anthropology of the senses. Everywhere, the practice of medicine is grounded in sensuous techniques of diagnosis and healing, although in the West, insofar as diagnosing illness is concerned, the technologization of the medical gaze has tended to push aside the other senses, and as for treatment, the accent is more on anesthesia than synesthesia (compare Laderman and Roseman 1996; Howes and Classen 2013, chap. 2). Some exemplary case studies in the "anthropology of medical sensations" (Hinton et al. 2008) include Rice (2013), and Harris (2016, 2020).

4. For a profoundly sensuous critique of Kantian formalism, see Gernot Böhme's *Aisthétique* ([2001] 2020).

5. Other subfields of anthropology that have contributed significantly to the genesis and ongoing development of the anthropology of the senses include political anthropology (Feldman 1994; Hannerz 2006; Lamrani 2021); the anthropology of art (Biddle 2016; Voegelin 2018); the anthropology of religion and ritual (Meyer 2009; Bell 2002); and the

anthropology of food (Sutton 2001, 2010; Adapon 2008; Rhys-Taylor 2017).

Chapter 3

1. The reader is referred to *Honouring the Truth, Reconciling for the Future* (2015), which summarizes the findings and "calls for action" of the TRC Commission (see also p. 231).

2. For an account of the new *con-sensus*, see *Sensory Studies Manifesto* (Howes 2022).

3. This definition comes from a grant application written by Chris Salter. See further Howes 2022, chap. 8.

4. Lambert has published two books of poetry and won the coveted Félix-Antoine Savard Prize in 2017. Her poetry work is funded by the Canada Council for the Arts and Conseil des arts et des lettres du Québec, while her anthropological research is sponsored by the Fonds de recherche du Québec—Société et culture.

5. ExperiSens is a sensory evaluation research laboratory attached to the Institut de tourisme et d'hôtellerie du Québec, which provided partial funding for the project. Collins hired a sound artist and a smell artist to assist her with the sonic and olfactory compositions; the drinks and visuals she mixed herself.

Chapter 4

1. This definition highlights the relationality of every sensation. It may be compared to de Saussure's relational definition of the linguistic sign (Howes 2022, 209n6).

2. Aristotle held that there were three types of souls: the vegetative or nutritive (shared by all living beings); the sensitive or sensuous (shared by most animals and humans); and the rational or intellective soul (unique to humans).

3. For example, humoral theory underlay the practice of medicine (both diagnosis and healing) from antiquity (Wootton 2007) down to the invention of the anatamo-clinical method (Howes and Classen 2013, 38–45, 46–50; Foucault 1973, 146).

4. It is apparent that Locke saw microscopic vision as transgressive, whence its thrill. He goes on to observe that we should be thankful that we do not have eyes "acute enough" to discern corpuscles, since it would be terribly distracting to the formation of ideas if we did, and in any event our senses function the way God intended them to. The microscope was not diabolical, exactly; nor was it quite yet normal. See further Hacking 1981.

5. George Parkin Grant (1918–1988) was a Canadian political philosopher. He came from an establishment family. His archconservatism bordered on radicalism: he was a "red Tory." In some scholars' estimation, Grant's grasp of the whole of Western philosophy was unparalleled (see Donovan 1984 and Davis 1996). Incidentally, Grant dedicated his magnum opus, *English-Speaking Justice* (1985), to the painter Alex Colville and the poet Dennis Lee, "two artists who have taught me about justice."

6. Actually, Rawls (1971) introduced the trope of the "veil of ignorance" into his depiction of the

"original position" in order that it would appear to be in all of the contractors' self-interest to design a "fair" society, since they could not know their position or condition in the society to come. This is called "rational choice" theory, ironically.

7. Grant writes, "In the western tradition it was believed that the acting out of justice in human relationships was the essential way in which human beings are opened to eternity. Inward and outward justice were considered to be mutually interdependent, in the sense that the inward openness to eternity depended on just practice, and just practice depended on that inward openness to eternity. When public justice is conceived as conventional and contractual [as per Rawls], the division between inward and outward is so widened as to prevent any such mutual interdependence" (Grant 1985, 85).

8. As Grant (1985, 76) would have been quick to point out, capital accumulation conflicts with Christianity's "insistence on the primacy of charity," hence the desire, and indeed necessity, to escape the dominion of the Lord.

Chapter 5

1. Ingold advances his own conception of "life" in such works as *Being Alive* (2011) and *The Life of Lines* (2015). Traditionally, anthropologists were more concerned with enucleating local "vernacular" understandings of life (Coupaye 2018) than with spouting their own views on the subject. In the post-social world of Ingold's perception anthropology, however, such social (and cultural) anthropological efforts to access and evoke local ways of sensing have been suspended, and those who do pursue them are scorned for laboring under "the deadweight of Durkheim's sociologism" (Ingold 2011, 235).

2. Reading this quotation, a discerning reader will pause and wonder: Would a sensory anthropologist really conceptualize perception as reducible to "build[ing] up an internal picture of what the world 'out there' is like," or is this a case of Ingold putting words in someone else's mouth? It is the latter, of course. Ingold's writings are full of such willful misconstructions. (I shall have to leave it to the reader to see through Ingold's ruses, since it would take too much space to pick all his straw men apart.) For the record, sensory anthropology is no more wedded to one theory of mind than it is to one theory of life. It is open to all.

3. For an example of how the collective representations of large-scale societies such as Canada and the United States can be subjected to comparative analysis, using their constitutions as a key, and shown to reflect society back to the individual, see the studies of American versus Canadian painting, poetry, classical and popular music, and literature on the Canadian Icon website (http://canadianicon.org).

4. Ingold's elision of style is manifest in his account of basketry as a product of the "unfolding of the morphogenetic field" (Ingold 2000, chap. 18) where everything is a matter of "force." Compare the discussion of Desana basketry in "Sensory Basket Weaving 101" (Howes 2007), which is a lot less forceful and a lot more

style-conscious, as well as sensuous in orientation. Consider further Ingold's analysis of a painting by Bruegel, where he flatly asserts, "My purpose is not to analyse the painting in terms of style, composition, or aesthetic effect. Nor am I concerned with the historical context of its production" (Ingold 2000, 201). A visual studies scholar would be aghast at this.

5. Ingold (2011, 136) goes on to state: "In ordinary perceptual practice these [sensory] registers cooperate so closely, and with such overlap of function, that their respective contributions are impossible to tease apart." This is a weaker version of the interchangeability hypothesis, but not by much.

6. The harsh social reality of this fact (i.e., the nonneutrality of sound) is brought out by Jennifer Stoever in *The Sonic Color Line* (2016), where she discusses how the sounds and rhythms of Black English Vernacular have long been disparaged by speakers of Standard American English.

7. This criticism of phenomenology is not new: "Because of its focus on a body presumed to be universal and individual, depicted from the point of view of the subject, embodiment [in the tradition of phenomenology as evinced by Ingold] can lack both historical depth and sociological content" (Farquhar and Lock 2007, 6–7; see further Santos 2018: 171).

8. As an example of the division (or decentering) of the self along gender lines and the implications this has for freedom of movement, see Omri Elisha's discussion of how, in the charismatic Christian churches of inner New York City, women are permitted and even exhorted to "dance the Word" but are forbidden to "preach the Word," since that is deemed the preserve of men (Elisha 2018).

9. In fact, this point is overstated. Breaking research suggests that there are consistencies across synesthetes (Association for Psychological Science 2008). This overdetermined construction, with its stress on individual uniqueness, points to the need for a more cultural approach to the phenomenon (see Howes and Classen 2013, chap. 6).

10. Regarding fuller sounds being round, the Bouba/Kiki test comes to mind, the classic test purporting to demonstrate a connection between sound and shape. But this understanding is partial. If one says these words to oneself, one will find that they involve certain contortions of the mouth that may be described as round (bouba) or jagged (kiki). Hence, the shapes are not just formal, they are also corporeal—an example of iconicity (Feld 1996), rather than synesthesia, in the abstract (see further Howes and Classen 2013).

11. This account of Hindu sensology and cosmology, which comes from Wikipedia (https://en.wikipedia.org/wiki/Classical_element), finds support in Sarukkai (2014) but requires further substantiation.

12. This is according to the classical *Sāmkhya* system of Indian thought, where "we find the idea that the senses are within the world of un-liberated souls, whereas the liberated one is devoid of senses and feelings (as well as without words and consciousness)" (Michaels and Wulf 2014, 10). It bears noting that the *Sāmkhya* system is one model of structuring the senses, but there are others that are not so negative

regarding the usefulness of the senses for purposes of liberation (see Horstmann 2014; Sarukkai 2014).

13. This term, "aesth-ethic," was proposed by my doctoral student Jayanthan Sriram. He cobbled it together out of a reading of Laplantine (2015, 121–23), Böhme ([2001] 2020, 17), and Diaconu (2005, 43). It is also possible to hear echoes of Proposition 6.421 of the *Tractatus*—"Ethics and aesthetics are one" (Wittgenstein 1922)—in this term. I look forward to exploring the polysemy of this neologism further together with Jayanthan in future publications. I should note that we are still working on how best to spell this hybrid concept.

14. Summing up the assumptions that inform their approach to sensory analysis, Lahne and Trubek (2014, 130) state: "Through an active, iterative, and social practice of sensory perception, consumers integrate their past personal experiences, socially transmitted and valued information about producer practices, and the material properties of the cheese into a single instance of sensory experience" (see further Lahne, Trubek, and Pelchat 2014).

Chapter 6

1. Febvre may have overstated his case, according to the anthropologists John Leavitt and Lynn Hart (1990), who claim that his reading of the historical record was highly biased and selective. This is not to suggest that Febvre should be stripped of his title as the great precursor to Corbin. However, a strong case could be made for Johan Huizinga, author of "The Task of Cultural History" ([1929] 2014) and *The Autumn of the Middle Ages* ([1919] 1996), being the prescient one. Huizinga was influenced by the Dutch literary genre known as Sensitivism. This helps explain why he wrote so feelingly, colorfully, and sonorously about the Burgundian Moyen Âge. I am indebted to Jogada Verrips for drawing my attention to Huizinga's sensuous approach to writing history. See further Ankersmit (2005) on how Huizinga sought to capture and convey the "historical sensation" of the late medieval period.

2. See the Wikipedia entry for Cangjie: https://en.wikipedia.org/wiki/Cangjie.

3. Traditional Chinese medicine, or TCM, as it has come to be known in modern times, is very much a sensuous practice in terms of both diagnosis and treatment. In *A Way of Life: Things, Thought and Action in Chinese Medicine* (2020), Judith Farquhar contrasts the "*zheng* pattern" of TCM with the "ontological disease" of Western biomedicine. The "*zheng* pattern" is defined in a standard TCM dictionary as "what is composed from a set of interconnected symptoms and bodily signs (including tongue image, pulse image, etc.) and reflects certain patterns of illness change" (quoted in Farquhar 2020, 32–33). Farquhar provides the following exegesis:

> First of all, [the *zheng* pattern] is *composed*—though the definition does not say by whom. But the ingredients of which it is composed suggest a particular agency, that of the observant doctor: these interconnected symptoms and bodily signs are *images* legible to the physician, with his trained

perception. "Tongue image, pulse image, etc." are signs that are read from the surface of the body; and it is an essential part of this reading process (which relies on the doctor's own senses of vision, touch, hearing, etc.) to discover that these images form "an interconnected set." But the set is not out there in wild nature, as an ontological disease [as with the nosology of, say, syphilis in Western biomedicine], somehow (implausibly) freestanding and unchanging. Patterns come to the clinic one by one, expressed in the individual and idiosyncratic bodies and histories of patients.... [B]oth doctor and patient probably see the *zheng* pattern as already being gathered together into a sort of thing-hood that predates its presentation in the clinic. But medicine takes over the composing process, finding a way to express the materiality of the disorder as a pattern that can be treated. (33)

In TCM, diseases are composed, rather than ontologized, and patients present patterns, unlike in biomedicine where they become "a case of syphilis," or "the liver in room 202." (Elizabeth Hsu's [2010] account of pulse taking in early Chinese medicine also brings out well the techniques of sensory attunement that are so fundamental to TCM.) The sensorial dynamics of treatment within TCM will be addressed toward the end of the next chapter.

4. The comparative study of sensory orders in history and across cultures was integral to the fields of the history and anthropology of the senses at the outset, as exemplified by Constance Classen's *Inca Cosmology and the Human Body* (1993a) and *Worlds of Sense* (1993b), both published in the same year. But the comparative method was quickly abandoned (perhaps understandably, since it requires great rigor) and is only now making a comeback (e.g., Lange 2022, Denney forthcoming). Throughout this fallow period, Classen has persevered, coauthoring *Aroma: The Cultural History of Smell* (Classen, Howes, and Synnott 1994) and *Ways of Sensing* (Howes and Classen 2013) and editing *The Book of Touch* (Classen 2005a). She is the standard-bearer for this whole endeavour.

Chapter 7

1. The question of cultural copying is a complex one, and gauging cultural innovation is equally complex. For an intriguing study of innovation in the timeless art of Chinese calligraphy, see Pearce et al. (2018) and Billeter (1990). Pondering how change accretes in a practice that is supposed to be unchanging is a good place to start.

2. The cross-cultural perception of linear perspective drawing and painting, and "realism" in general, is a fascinating topic. Other pertinent sources include Kleutghen (2015a, 2015b) and Gu (2020.)

3. There is a venerable tradition of reflecting on "the pleasures of the senses" in China: Brook (1999); Goh (2010); Nylan (2018).

4. There is a radical incommensurability to Chinese and Western models of the body. This aporia has been brilliantly analyzed by Shigehisa

Kuriyama in *The Expressiveness of the Body and the Divergence of Greek and Chinese Medicine* (1999) and Judith Farquhar in *A Way of Life: Things, Thought and Action in Chinese Medicine* (2020).

Chapter 8

1. Commenting on the English way of "processing sensory novelties," Hoffer (2006, 41) writes, "anticipated use directed the eye and tutored the ear." As he goes on to relate, the explorers and settlers harbored a vision of the New World "transformed by permanent colonization. These perceptions differed from [Indigenous peoples'] dreams and prophecies [e.g., "vision-quests"]. The English imagination did not wander into the spirit world or hear the voices of the forest. Instead, the visitors pictured colonies of busy workers harvesting staple crops for export" (42, 72). The "busy workers" were to be drawn from England's homeless and unemployed, or "numbers of idle men" (Hakluyt quoted in Hoffer 2006, 42). On the rationality behind this scheme, see "Property, God and Nature in the Thought of Sir John Beverley Robinson" (Howes 1985).

Hoffer observes that the English employed a kind of "sensory imperialism" to try to subdue Indigenous populations: "Change the way the land looked, alter the terrain, levy an English scenery upon the wild settings of the New World. Begin with fortification" (55). The "geometrically precise" fort, with its straight sight lines, elevations, and declinations, looked out of place on purpose; it was meant to stand out. Referring specifically to the fort Ralph Lane had built on Roanoke Island, Hoffer surmises that it was "hurtful" to the Indigenous gaze, that it "disturbed whatever natural spirits lived on the island, and violated the natural shapes of dune, marsh, grassy park and woods" (61).

The "contest of the senses" of which Hoffer writes has never really ended, even if the English might seem to have established "a sensory dominion . . . upon the land and its living things" (73) in much of North America. See Audra Simpson's *Mohawk Interruptus: Political Life Across the Borders of Settler States* (2014).

2. Classen (1991) relates how, in the Andean region of South America, writing was regarded as a form of "anti-culture." Such a representation of literacy is unthinkable from within a literate mindset.

3. Cross-culturalizing justice (and legal education) has long been central to the work of the "McGill School" (of which I am a member), whether with regard to formal law and "everyday law," the civil law and common law traditions, the syncretic legal practices of "rebel courts," or, as here, the relations between the State and Indigenous societies. See Macdonald 2002; Glenn 2010; Howes 1987, 2002; Kasirer 2002, 2003; Janda 2005; Jukier 2006; Provost 2017, 2021. See further Justice Kasirer's decision in *C. M. Callow v. Zollinger* (2020).

This "polyjural" approach has important implications for the regulation and adjudication of differends not only between Indigenous societies and the State but across all of the divisions of the polity, including those between so-called minority cultures and the culture of the majority. A promising opening in the direction of cross-cultural jurisprudence is given in Alison Dundes Renteln's treatise *The Cultural Defense* (2005). As I have argued elsewhere, cross-cultural jurisprudence hinges on "culturally-reflexive legal reasoning" (after Geertz):

> Culturally-reflexive legal reasoning is increasingly necessary to the meaningful adjudication of disputes in today's increasingly multicultural society. It involves recognizing the interdependence of culture and law (i.e., law is not above culture but part of it). Judges ought to acknowledge and give effect to cultural difference, rather than override it. Deciding cases solely on the basis of some abstract conception of individuals as interchangeable rights-bearing units would have the effect of undermining our humanity. It is our cultural differences from each other that actually make us human. However, in extending judicial recognition to such difference, judges must be careful to take cognizance of their personal culture, and not just that of "the other." Reflexivity, not mere sensitivity, is the essence of cross-cultural jurisprudence. (Howes 2005c, 10).

Epilogue

1. Mauss's essay entitled "Real and Practical Relations Between Psychology and Sociology" ([1924] 1979) should be essential reading for every student of physiology, psychology, and sociology (including anthropology), for all three dimensions—body, mind, and society—are integral and irreducible components of "the total man," or rather, person: "It is at the frontiers of the [disciplines], at their outer limits, as often as in their principles, their nucleus and centre, that they make their advances . . . [through] acts of collaboration . . . from our different points of view" (Mauss [1924] 1979, 10–11).

2. Cracks are beginning to appear in the cognitive science literature, such as Jesper Aagaard's brilliant critique of the overwhelming emphasis on harmony in "4E cognition" (Aagaard 2021). It is about time. The four Es of 4E cognition "initialize its central claim: cognition does not occur exclusively inside the head, but is variously *embodied, embedded, enacted,* or *extended* by way of extra-cranial processes and structures" (Carney 2020, 77). 4E cognition might seem to overlap with the concept of the sensorium as a focus for cultural studies proposed in this book. However, there is at least one "E" lacking from 4E cognition: namely, enculturation. Other problems and lacunas include the fetishization of information, the privileging of intelligence over sentience, the overreliance on evolutionary psychology, and the fixation on harmony (which leaves no room for the study of conflict).

3. On how affirmative action programs can contribute to the achievement of equality of result, see the entry "Affirmative Action" in the *Stanford Encyclopedia of Philosophy* (https:/ plato.stanford.edu/entries/affirmative-action) and the entry on "Equality Through Affirmative

Action—Section 15(2)" on the website of the Centre for Constitutional Studies (https://www.constitutional studies.ca/2019/07equality-through -affirmative-action-section-152). On paying reparation to disadvantaged people, see the action taken by the Government of Canada pursuant to the recommendations of the Truth and Reconciliation Commission: "Delivering on Truth and Reconciliation Calls to Action" (https://www.rcaanc-cirnac .gc.ca/eng/1524494530110/15575114 12801). That is for the Government of Canada's perspective.

4. Michael Walzer is a prominent American political philosopher who participated in the same intellectual circle as Clifford Geertz at the Institute for Advanced Study at Princeton University. His approach to conceptualizing justice in *Spheres of Justice* may be described as anthropological for the way it builds on everyday understandings. It is diametrically opposed to George Grant's teleological conception of justice, on the one hand, and John Rawls's "rational choice" theory on the other.

5. For a radical critique of the notion of "shared understandings" (such as Walzer imports through his use of the term "we"), see Alasdair MacIntyre's *Whose Justice? Which Rationality?* (1988) as well as Boaventura de Sousa Santos's *The End of the Cognitive Empire: The Coming of Age of Epistemologies of the South* (2018).

6. Policy papers are called "white papers" in the Canadian legislature. The official title of this particular white paper was "Statement of the Government of Canada on Indian Policy." See https://indigenousfoundations.arts.ubc .ca/the_white_paper_1969.

References

Aagaard, J. 2021. "4E Cognition and the Dogma of Harmony." *Philosophical Psychology* 34 (2): 165–81.

Abath, A. J. 2017. "Merleau-Ponty and the Problem of Synaesthesia." In *Sensory Blending: On Synaesthesia and Related Phenomena*, edited by O. Deroy, 151–065. Oxford: Oxford University Press.

Adapon, J. 2008. *Culinary Art and Anthropology*. Oxford: Berg.

Alcántara-Alcover, E., M. Artacho-Ramírez, T. Zamora, and N. Martinez. 2014. "Exploratory Study of the Influence of the Sensory Channel in Perception of Environments." *Journal of Sensory Studies* 29 (4): 258–71.

Anderson, B. (1991) 2006. *Imagined Communities: Reflections on the Origin and Spread of Nationalism*. London: Verso.

Anderson, B. 2009. "Affective Atmospheres." *Emotion, Space, and Society* 2 (2): 77–81.

Andrews, B. 2014. *The Making of Modern Chinese Medicine, 1850–1960*. Vancouver: UBC Press.

Angéras, A. 2022. "La dimension sensorielle de l'espace de l'habiter dans l'habitat leger: (Re-)appropriations et representations." In Calapi et al., *Sensibles ethnographies*.

Ankersmit, F. 2005. *Sublime Historical Experience*. Stanford: Stanford University Press.

Appadurai, A., ed. 1986. *The Social Life of Things: Commodities in Cultural Perspective*. Cambridge: Cambridge University Press.

Arendt, H. 1961. *Between Past and Future: Six Exercises in Political Thought*. London: Faber & Faber.

———. 1982. *Lectures on Kant's Political Philosophy*. Chicago: University of Chicago Press.

Aristotle. (350 BCE) 1908. *De Sensu et Sensibili* (On Sense and the Sensible). Translated by J. I. Beare. The Internet Classics Archive. http://classics.mit.edu/Aristotle/sense.2.2.html.

———. (350 BCE) 1932. *De Anima* (On the Soul). Translated by J. A. Smith. The Internet Classics Archive. http://classics.mit.edu/Aristotle/soul.html.

———. (350 BCE) 1999. *Politics*. Kitchener: Batoche Books.

Arnheim, R. 1969. *Visual Thinking*. Berkeley: University of California Press.

Arning, B. 2006. "Sissel Tolaas." In *Sensorium: Embodied Experience, Technology, and Contemporary Art*, edited by C. A. Jones, 98–103. Cambridge: MIT Press.

Association for Psychological Science. 2008. "Consistencies Found in Synaesthesia: Letter 'A' Is Red for Many; 'V' Is Purple." *Science Daily*, April 30, 2008.

Barad, K. 2007. *Meeting the Universe Halfway: Quantum Physics and the Entanglement of Matter and Meaning*. Durham: Duke University Press.

Barcan, R. 2011. *Complementary and Alternative Medicine: Bodies, Senses, Therapies*. Abingdon: Routledge.

Barth, F. 1975. *Ritual Knowledge Among the Baktaman of New Guinea*. New Haven: Yale University Press.

Bedini, A. 1994. *The Trail of Time: Time Measurement with Incense in East Asia*. Cambridge: Cambridge University Press.

Bell, C. 2002. *Ritual: Perspectives and Dimensions*. Oxford: Oxford University Press.

Bendix, R. 2005. "Time of the Senses?" *Current Anthropology* 46 (4): 688–89.

Berlin, B., and P. Kay. 1969. *Basic Color Terms: Their Universality and Evolution*. Berkeley: University of California Press.

Bertuzzi, E. 2022. "Un dévouement sans fin: Qualités de présence dans les chants et dans la danse du *Debaa*. Analyse d'un 'mode majeur' d'agir." In Calapi et al., *Sensibles ethnographies*.

Biddle, J. 2016. *Remote Avant-Garde: Aboriginal Art Under Occupation*. Durham: Duke University Press.

Bijsterveld, K. 2010. "Acoustic Cocooning: How the Car Became a Place to Unwind." *Senses and Society* 5 (2): 189–211.

Bille, M. 2013. "Lighting Up Cosy Atmospheres in Denmark." *Emotion, Space and Society* 15:56–63.

———. 2017. "Ecstatic Things: The Power of Light in Shaping Bedouin Homes." *Home Cultures* 14 (1): 25–49.

Bille, M., and T. Sørenson, eds. 2016. *Elements of Architecture: Assembling Archaeology, Atmosphere, and the Performance of Building Spaces*. London: Routledge.

Billeter, J.-F. 1990. *The Chinese Art of Writing*. New York: Rizzoli.

Blake, S. 2019. "Perception and Its Disorders in Early China." In *The Senses and the History of Philosophy*, edited by B. Glenney and J. F. Silva, 33–48. Abingdon: Routledge.

Boas, F. (1889) 2018. "On Alternating Sounds." *American Anthropologist* A2 (1): 47–54.

———. 1916. "New Evidence in Regard to the Instability of Human Types." *Proceedings of the National Academy of Sciences of the United States of America* 2 (12): 713–18.

Böhme, G. (2001) 2020. *Aisthétique: Pour une esthétique de l'expérience sensible*. Translated from the German by M. Kaltenecker and F. Lemonde. Paris: Les presses du réel.

———. 2017. *The Aesthetics of Atmospheres*. Edited by J.-P. Thibaud. London: Routledge.

Boon, J. 1983. "Functionalists Write, Too." *Semiotica* 46 (1/2): 131–49.

Boring, E. 1942. *Sensation and Perception in the History of Experimental Psychology*. New York: Appleton-Century-Crofts.

Born, G., and A. Barry. 2010. "Art-Science: From Public Understanding to Public Experiment." *Journal of Cultural Economy* 3 (1): 103–19.

Bourdieu, P. 1987. *Distinction: A Social Critique of the Judgment of Taste*. Cambridge: Harvard University Press.

Boyle, R. (1666) 2017. "The Origin of Forms and Qualities." https://www.earlymoderntexts.com/assets/pdfs/boyle1666.pdf.

Boyle, S. 2020. "Fragrant Walls and the Table of Delight: Sensory (Re)construction as a Way of Knowing, the Case of Thornbury Castle, 1508–1521." PhD diss., Concordia University.

Brindley, E. 2006. "Music, Cosmos and the Development of Psychology in Early China." *T'oung Pao* 92:1–49.

Broglio, R. 2008. *Technologies of the Picturesque: British Art, Poetry, and Instruments, 1750–1830*. Lewisburg: Bucknell University Press.

Brook, T. 1999. *The Confusions of Pleasure: Commerce and Culture in Ming China*. Berkeley: University of California Press.

Bull, M., P. Gilroy, D. Howes, and D. Kahn. 2006. "Introducing Sensory Studies." *Senses and Society* 1 (1): 5–7.

Burgess, N. 2013. "'Ag-Gag' Bill Stirs Debate." *Stowe Reporter*, 2 May. https://www.vtcng.com/stowe_reporter/news/ag-gag-bill-stirs-debate-senator-supports-effort-to-punish-whistleblowers/article_6f9b8fba-b340-11e2-a6c9-0019bb2963f4.html.

Calapi, S. 2022. "Quand l'Inti Raymi est la: Euphories collectives lors des Visperas de Turucu." In Calapi et al., *Sensibles ethnographies*.

Calapi, S., H. Korzybska, M. Mazzella di Bosco, and P. Peraldi-Mittelette, eds. 2022. *Sensibles ethnographies: Décalages sensoriels et attentionnels dans la recherche anthropologique*. Marseille: Éditions Petra.

Calder v. British Columbia. 1973. Supreme Court Reports 313.

Candlin, F. 2010. "Sensory Separation and the Founding of Art History." In *Art, Museums and Touch*, 9–27. Manchester: Manchester University Press.

Carpenter, E. 1973. *Eskimo Realities*. Toronto: Holt, Rinehart and Winston.

Carney, J. 2020. "Thinking Avant la Lettre: A Review of 4E Cognition." *Evolutionary Studies in Imaginative Culture* 4 (1): 77–90.

Castaing-Taylor, L. 1996. "Iconophobia: How Anthropology Lost It at the Movies." *Transition* 69:64–88.

Castaing-Taylor, L., and V. Paravel, dirs. 2012. *Leviathan*. New York: Cinereach; New York: Creative Capital; n.p.: Arrête ton Cinéma.

Cavendish, M. 1655. *The Philosophical and Physical Opinions*. London: J. Martin and J. Allestyre.

———. (1668) 1992. *The Description of a New World Called The Blazing World. . . .* London: William Pickering.

Chapman, O. B., and K. Sawchuk. 2012. "Research-Creation: Intervention, Analysis and 'Family Resemblances.'" *Canadian Journal of Communication* 37 (1): 5–26.

Chumley, L. 2017. "Qualia and Ontology: Language, Semiotics and Materiality—An Introduction." *Signs and Society* 5 (S1): S1–S20.

Clarke, A. 2008. *Supersizing the Mind: Embodiment, Action and Cognitive Extension.* Oxford: Oxford University Press.

Clarke, E. 2005. *Ways of Listening: An Ecological Approach to the Perception of Musical Meaning.* Oxford: Oxford University Press.

Classen, C. 1991. "Literacy as Anticulture: The Andean Experience of the Written Word." *History of Religions* 30 (4): 404–21.

———. 1993a. *Inca Cosmology and the Human Body.* Salt Lake City: University of Utah Press.

———. 1993b. *Worlds of Sense: Exploring the Senses in History and Across Cultures.* London: Routledge.

———. 1997. "Foundations for an Anthropology of the Senses." *International Social Science Journal* 153:401–12.

———. 1998. *The Color of Angels: Cosmology, Gender and the Aesthetic Imagination.* London: Routledge.

———. 2001. "The Senses." In *Encyclopedia of European Social History*, edited by P. Stearns, 4: 355–64. New York: Charles Scribner's Sons.

———, ed. 2005a. *The Book of Touch.* Abingdon: Routledge.

———. 2005b. "The Witch's Senses: Sensory Ideologies and Transgressive Femininities from the Renaissance to Modernity." In Howes, *Empire of the Senses*, 70–84.

———, ed. 2014a. *A Cultural History of the Senses.* 6 vols. London: Bloomsbury.

———, ed. 2014b. *A Cultural History of the Senses in the Age of Empire, 1800–1920.* London: Bloomsbury.

———. 2017. *The Museum of the Senses: Experiencing Art and Collections.* London: Bloomsbury.

Classen, C., D. Howes, and A. Synnott. 1994. *Aroma: The Cultural History of Smell.* London: Routledge.

Clifford, J. 1983. "On Ethnographic Authority." *Representations* 2:118–46.

Clifford, J., and G. Marcus, eds. 1986. *Writing Culture: The Poetics and Politics of Ethnography; A School of American Research Advanced Seminar.* Berkeley: University of California Press.

C. M. Callow v. Zollinger. 2020. Supreme Court of Canada 45.

Collins, S. G., M. Durington, and H. Gill. 2017. "Multimodality: An Invitation." *American Anthropologist* 119 (1): 142–53.

Connor, S. 2015. "Literature, Technology and the Senses." In *The Cambridge Companion to the Body in Literature*, edited by D. Hillman and U. Maude,

177–96. Cambridge: Cambridge University Press.

Corbin, A. (1982) 1986. *The Foul and the Fragrant: Odor and the French Social Imagination.* Cambridge: Harvard University Press.

———. 1990. "Histoire et anthropologie sensorielle." *Anthropologie et Sociétés* 14 (2): 13–24.

———. (1994) 1998. *Village Bells: Sound and Meaning in the Nineteenth-Century French Countryside.* New York: Columbia University Press.

———. 2005. "Charting the Cultural History of the Senses." In Howes, *Empire of the Senses*, 128–39.

Corbin, A., and G. Heuré. 2000. *Alain Corbin: Historien du sensible; Entretiens avec Gilles Heuré.* Paris: Editions la Découverte.

Cortes, H. 1843. *The Despatches of Hernando Cortes.* Edited and translated by George Folsom. New York: Wiley and Putnam.

Coupaye, L. 2018. "'Yams have no ears!': Tekhne, Life and Images in Oceania." *Oceania* 88 (1): 13–30.

Cox, R. 2013. "The Political Affects of Military Aircraft Noise in Okinawa." In *Sound, Space and Sociality in Modern Japan: A Sensory Ethnographic Tour,* edited by J. Hankins and C. Stevens, 57–71. Abingdon: Routledge.

———. 2018. "Senses, Anthropology of." In *International Encyclopedia of Anthropology,* edited by H. Callan, vol. 10, 5411–22. New York: Wiley.

Cox, R., A. Irving, and C. Wright, eds. 2016. *Beyond Text? Critical Practices and Sensory Anthropology.* Manchester: Manchester University Press.

Crary, J. 1992. *Techniques of the Observer: On Vision and Modernity in the Nineteenth Century.* Cambridge: The MIT Press.

Csordas, T. 1990. "Embodiment as a Paradigm for Anthropology." *Ethos* 18 (1): 5–47.

———. 1993. "Somatic Modes of Attention." *Cultural Anthropology* 8 (2): 135–56.

Cundy, A. 2017. "War, Memory and the Senses in the Imperial War Museum, 1920–2014." In *Modern Conflict and the Senses,* edited by N. Sauders and P. Cornish, 361–74. London: Routledge.

Cytowic, R. E. 1998. *The Man Who Tasted Shapes.* Cambridge: MIT Press.

D'Ambrosio, D. 2021. "How Vermont Dairy Farms Have Changed." *Burlington Free Press,* 11 May. https://www.burlingtonfreepress.com/story/news/2021/05/11/herd-size-vermont-dairy-farms-getting-bigger-and-more-efficient/5034739001.

Daniel, V. 1987. *Fluid Signs: Being a Person the Tamil Way.* Berkeley: University of California Press.

Davis, A., ed. 1996. *George Grant and the Subversion of Modernity: Art, Philosophy, Religion, Politics and Education.* Toronto: University of Toronto Press.

Davis, C. 1976. *Body as Spirit: The Nature of Religious Feeling.* New York: Seabury.

Dawkins, A., and A. Loftus. 2013. "The Senses as Direct Theoreticians in Practice." *Transactions of the Institute of British Geographers* 38 (4): 665–77.

Debaene, V. 2014. *Far Afield: French Anthropology Between Science and Literature*. Chicago: University of Chicago Press.

Debord, G. 1994. *The Society of the Spectacle*. New York: Zone Books.

Degenhardt, J. H. 2013. "Cracking the Mysteries of 'China': China(ware) in the Early Modern Imagination." *Studies in Philology* 110 (1): 132–67.

Delgamuukw v. A. G.: Reasons for Judgement. 1991. No. 0843 Smithers Registry.

Delgamuukw v. British Columbia. 1997. 3 Supreme Court Reports 1010.

Denyer, S. 2018. "China's Bear Bile Industry Persists Despite Growing Awareness of the Cruelty Involved." *Washington Post*, June 3. https://www.washingtonpost.com/world/asia_pacific/from-hemorrhoids-to-hangovers--bears-bile-is-treasured-in-china-and-thats-bad-for-captive-bears/2018/06/02/fdb431da-5363-11e8-b00a-17f9fda3859b_story.html.

Deroy, O., ed. 2017. *Sensory Blending: On Synaesthesia and Related Phenomena*. Oxford: Oxford University Press.

Descartes, R. (1641) 1973. *The Philosophical Works of Descartes*. Translated by E. Haldane and G. R. T. Ross. Cambridge: Cambridge University Press.

Descola, P. 2013. *Beyond Nature and Culture*. Chicago: University of Chicago Press.

Despland, M. 1987. *Christianisme, dossier corps*. Paris: CERF.

Dewdney, A. K. 1984. *The Planiverse: Computer Contact with a Two-Dimensional World*. New York: Copernicus.

Diaconu, M. 2005. *Tasten—Riechen—Schmecken. Eine Ästhetik der anästhesierten Sinne*. Würzburg: Königshausen & Neumann

Dias, N. 2006. *La mesure des sens: Les anthropologues et le corps humain au XIXe siècle*. Paris: Flammarion.

Dillon, J. 2019. "'It's the Dairy Farm Sewer.'" NPR News, 9 December. https://www.vpr.org/vpr-news/2019-12-09/its-the-dairy-farm-sewer-neighbors-say-state-is-failing-to-regulate-agricultural-pollution.

Doerksen, M. 2017. "Electromagnetism and the Nth Sense: Augmenting Senses in the Grinder Subculture." *Senses and Society* 12 (3): 344–49.

———. 2018. "How to Make Sense: Sensory Modification in Grinder Subculture." PhD diss., Concordia University. http://centreforsensorystudies.org/how-to-make-sense-sensory-modification-in-grinder-subculture.

Donovan, J. 1984. *George Grant and the Twilight of Justice*. Toronto: University of Toronto Press.

Douglas, M. 1966. *Purity and Danger: An Analysis of Concepts of Pollution and Taboo*. London: Routledge.

———. 1973. *Natural Symbols: Explorations in Cosmology*. New York: Vintage.

Downey, G. 2005. *Learning Capoeira: Lessons in Cunning from an Afro-Brazilian Art*. Oxford: Oxford University Press.

Drazin, A., and S. Küchler, eds. 2015. *The Social Life of Materials: Studies in Materials and Society*. Abingdon: Routledge.

Druke, M. 1985. "Iroquois Treaties: Common Forms, Varying Interpretations." In *The History and Culture of Iroquois Diplomacy: An Interdisciplinary Guide to the Treaties of the Six Nations and Their League*, edited by F. Jennings, 85–98. Syracuse: Syracuse University Press.

Dubois, D., C. Cance, M. Coler, A. Paté, and C. Guastavino. 2021. *Sensory Experiences: Exploring Meaning and the Senses*. Amsterdam: John Benjamins.

Dudley, S., ed. 2010. *Museum Materialities: Objects, Engagements, Interpretations*. London: Routledge.

———, ed. 2012. *Museum Objects: Experiencing the Properties of Things*. London: Routledge.

Dumit, J. 2004. *Picturing Personhood: Brain Scans and Biomedical Identity*. Princeton: Princeton University Press.

Dummett, D. 1993. *The Origins of Analytical Philosophy*. London: Duckworth.

Dumont, L. 1980. *Homo hierarchicus: The Caste System and Its Implications*. 2nd ed. Chicago: University of Chicago Press.

———. 1992. *Essays on Individualism: Modern Ideology in Anthropological Perspective*. Chicago: University of Chicago Press.

Durkheim, E. (1895) 1982. *The Rules of Sociological Method*. New York: Free Press.

Dutson, C., J. Myerson, and R. Gheerawo. 2010. *Light Volumes, Dark Matters*. London: Royal College of Art.

Edensor, T., and S. Sumartojo. 2015. "Designing Atmospheres: Introduction." *Visual Communication* 14 (3): 251–65.

Edwards, E., C. Gosden, and R. Phillips, eds. 2006. *Sensible Objects: Colonialism, Museums and Material Culture*. Abingdon: Routledge.

Ei-ichi deForest, K. 2015. "Angus Carlyle and Rupert Cox: Air Pressure: Aircraft Noise and Perceptions of the Environment." *Senses and Society* 9 (1): 108–12.

Eklund, A. A. 2019. "Harmonising Value in a Car's Interior Using Sensory Marketing as a Lens." PhD diss., Linnaeus University.

El-Ghezal Jeguirim, S., A. B. Dhouib, M. Sahnoun, M. Cheikhrouhou, N. Njeugna, L. Schacher, and D. Adolphe. 2010. "The Tactile Sensory Evaluation of Knitted Fabrics: Effect of Some Finishing Treatments." *Journal of Sensory Studies* 25 (2): 201–15.

Elisha, O. 2018. "Dancing the Word: Techniques of Embodied Authority Among Christian Praise Dancers in New York City." *American Ethnologist* 45 (3): 380–91.

Elliott, D., and D. Culhane, eds. 2017. *A Different Kind of Ethnography:*

Imaginative Practices and Creative Methodologies. Toronto: University of Toronto Press.

Evans-Pritchard, E. E. (1937) 1982. *Witchcraft, Oracles and Magic Among the Azande*. Oxford: Oxford University Press.

———. 1954. *The Sanusi of Cyrenaica*. Oxford: Clarendon.

———. 1965. *Theories of Primitive Religion*. Oxford: Clarendon Press.

Farquhar, J. 2002. *Appetites: Food and Sex in Post-Socialist China*. Durham: Duke University Press.

———. 2020. *A Way of Life: Things, Thought and Action in Chinese Medicine*. New Haven: Yale University Press.

Farquhar, J., and M. Lock, eds. 2007. *Beyond the Body Proper*. Durham: Duke University Press.

Febvre, L. (1942) 1982. *The Problem of Unbelief in the Sixteenth Century: The Religion of Rabelais*. Cambridge: Harvard University Press.

Feld, S. 1982. *Sound and Sentiment: Birds, Weeping, Poetics and Song in Kaluli Expression*. Philadelphia: University of Pennsylvania Press.

———. 1988. "Aesthetics as Iconicity of Style, or, 'Lift-Up-over-Sounding,' Getting into the Kaluli Groove." *Yearbook for Traditional Music* 20:74–113.

———. 1991. "Sound as a Symbolic System: The Kaluli Drum." In Howes, *Varieties of Sensory Experience*, 79–99.

———. 1996. "Waterfalls of Song: An Acoustemology of Place Resounding in Bosavi, Papua New Guinea." In *Senses of Place*, edited by S. Feld and K. Basso, 91–135. Santa Fe: School of American Research Press.

———. 2005. "Places Sensed, Senses Placed: Toward a Sensuous Epistemology of Environments." In Howes, *Empire of the Senses*, 179–91.

Feld, S., and D. Brenneis. 2004. "Doing Anthropology in Sound." *American Ethnologist* 31 (4): 461–74.

Feldman, A. 1994. "From Desert Storm to Rodney King via ex-Yugoslavia: On Cultural Anaesthesia." In *The Senses Still: Perception and Memory as Material Culture in Modernity*, edited by C. N. Seremetakis, 87–108. Boulder: Westview Press.

Finnegan, R. 2002. *Communicating: The Multiple Modes of Human Interconnection*. London: Routledge.

Fortune, R. 1963. *Sorcerers of Dobu: The Social Anthropology of the Dobu Islanders of the Western Pacific*. New York: E. P. Dutton.

Foucault, M. (1963) 1973. *The Birth of the Clinic: An Archaeology of Medical Perception*. Translated by A. M. Sheridan Smith. New York: Random House.

———. (1975) 1979. *Discipline and Punish: The Birth of the Prison*. Translated by A. Sheridan. New York: Vintage Books.

Fretwell, E. 2020. *Sensory Experiments: Psychophysics, Race, and the Aesthetics of Feeling*. Durham: Duke University Press.

Friedner, M., and S. Helmreich. 2012. "Sound Studies Meets Deaf Studies." *Senses and Society* 7 (1): 72–86.

Fulford, R. 1983. "Painter Laureate." *Saturday Night*, July 1983, 5-6.

Gadoua, M.-P. 2014. "Making Sense Through Touch: Handling Collections with Inuit Elders at the McCord Museum." *Senses and Society* 9 (3): 323–41.

Galison, P., and C. A. Jones, eds. 2014. *Picturing Science, Producing Art*. London: Routledge.

Geaney, J. 2002. *On the Epistemology of the Senses in Early Chinese Thought*. Honolulu: University of Hawai'i Press.

Gearin, A. K., and O. C. Sáez. 2021. "Altered Vision: Ayahuasca Shamanism and Sensory Individualism." *Current Anthropology* 62 (2): 138–63.

Geertz, C. 1957. "Ethos, World-View and the Analysis of Sacred Symbols." *Antioch Review* 14 (4): 421–37.

———. 1973. *The Interpretation of Cultures*. Boston: Basic Books.

———. 1983. "Common Sense as a Cultural System." In *Local Knowledge: Further Essays in Interpretive Anthropology*. Boston: Basic Books.

———. 2001. "The Uses of Diversity." In *Available Light: Anthropological Reflections on Philosophical Topics*, 68–88. Princeton: Princeton University Press.

Gélard, M. L., ed. 2016. "Contemporary French Sensory Ethnography." Special issue, *Senses and Society* 11 (3).

Gell, A. 1977. "Magic, Perfume Dream . . ." In *Symbols and Sentiments: Cross-Cultural Studies in Symbolism*, edited by I. M. Lewis, 25–38. London: Academic.

———. 1995. "The Language of the Forest: Landscape and Phonological Iconism in Umeda." In *The Anthropology of Landscape: Perspectives on Place and Space*, edited by E. Hirsch and M. O'Hanlon, 232–54. Oxford: Clarendon.

Geurts, K. L. 2002a. *Culture and the Senses: Bodily Ways of Knowing in an African Community*. Berkeley: University of California Press.

———. 2002b. "On Rocks, Walks and Talks in West Africa: Cultural Categories and an Anthropology of the Senses." *Ethos* 30 (3): 178–98.

———. 2005. "Consciousness as 'Feeling in the Body': A West African Theory of Embodiment, Emotion and the Making of Mind." In Howes, *Empire of the Senses*, 164–78.

Gibson, J. J. 1966. *The Senses Considered as Perceptual Systems*. Boston: Houghton Mifflin.

———. 1979. *The Ecological Approach to Visual Perception*. Boston: Houghton Mifflin.

Gild, G. 2012. "Mission by Music: The Challenge of Translating European Music into Chinese in the Lulu Zuanyao." In *In the Light and Shadow of an Emperor: Tomas Pereira, the Kangxi Emperor and the Jesuit Mission to China*, edited by A. K. Wardewga and A. Vasconcelos de Saldanha,

532–45. Newcastle, UK: Cambridge Scholars Press.

Glenn, H. P. 2010. *Legal Traditions of the World: Sustainable Diversity in Law.* Oxford: Oxford University Press.

Goh, M. 2010. *Sound and Sight: Poetry and Courtier Culture in the Yongming Era (483–493).* Stanford: Stanford University Press.

Golding, V. 2010. "Dreams and Wishes: The Multi-Sensory Museum Space." In *Museum Materialities: Objects, Engagements, Interpretations*, edited by S. Dudley, 224–40. London: Routledge.

Goodman, S. 2010. *Sonic Warfare: Sound, Affect, and the Ecology of Fear.* Cambridge: MIT Press.

Gould, H., R. Chenhall, T. Kohn, and C. S. Stevens. 2019. "An Interrogation of Sensory Anthropology of and in Japan." *Anthropological Quarterly* 92 (1): 231–58.

Graif, P. 2018. *Being and Hearing: Making Intelligible Worlds in Deaf Kathmandu.* Chicago: HAU Books.

Granet, M. (1930) 1996. *Chinese Civilization.* London: Routledge.

———. 1973. "Right and Left in China." In *Right and Left: Essays on Dual Symbolic Classification*, edited by R. Needham, 43–58. Chicago: University of Chicago Press.

Grant, G. P. 1985. *English-Speaking Justice.* Toronto: House of Anansi.

Grimshaw, A. 2001. *The Ethnographer's Eye: Ways of Seeing in Modern Anthropology.* Cambridge: Cambridge University Press.

Gu, Y. 2020. *Chinese Ways of Seeing and Open-Air Painting.* Cambridge: Harvard University Asia Center.

Guss, D. 1989. *To Weave and Sing: Art, Symbol and Narrative in the South American Rainforest.* Berkeley: University of California Press.

Hacking, I. 1981 "Do We See Through a Microscope?" *Pacific Philosophical Quarterly* 62 (4): 305–22.

Halpern, O. 2015. *Beautiful Data: A History of Vision and Reason Since 1945.* Durham: Duke University Press.

Hamilakis, Y. 2014. *Archaeology and the Senses: Human Experience, Memory and Affect.* Cambridge: Cambridge University Press.

Hamilton, S. N. 2010. *Impersonations. Troubling the Person in Law and Culture.* Toronto: University of Toronto Press.

———, ed. 2020. "Sensuous Governance." Special issue, *Senses and Society* 15 (1).

Hammer, G. 2019. *Blindness Through the Looking Glass: The Performance of Blindness, Gender, and the Sensory Body.* Ann Arbor: University of Michigan Press.

Hannerz, U. 2006. "Afterthoughts: World Watching." In *Neo-Nationalism in Europe and Beyond: Perspectives from Social Anthropology*, edited by A. Gingrich and M. Banks, 271–82. New York: Berghahn Books.

Haraway, D. 1988. "Situated Knowledges: The Science Question in Feminism and the Privilege of Partial Perspective." *Feminist Studies* 14 (3): 575–99.

Harris, A. 2016. "Listening-Touch: Affect and the Crafting of Medical Bodies Through Percussion." *Body and Society* 22 (1): 31-61.

———. 2020. *A Sensory Education*. Abingdon: Routledge.

Hay, J. 2010. *Sensuous Surfaces: The Decorative Object in Early Modern China*. London: Reaktion Books.

Heller-Roazen, D. 2007. *The Inner Touch: Archaeology of a Sensation*. New York: Zone Books.

———. 2008. "Common Sense: Greek, Arabic, Latin." In *Rethinking the Medieval Senses: Heritage, Fascinations, Frames*, edited by G. Nichols, A. Kablitz, and A. Calhoun, 30–50. Baltimore: Johns Hopkins University Press.

Henderson, J. B. 2010. "Cosmology and Concepts of Nature in Traditional China." In *Concepts of Nature: A Chinese-European Cross-Cultural Perspective*, edited by H. U. Vogel and G. Dux, 181–97. Leiden: Brill.

Hennion, A. 2005. "Pragmatics of Taste." In *The Blackwell Companion to the Sociology of Culture*, edited by M. Jacobs and N. Hanrahan, 131–44. Malden: Blackwell.

Henshaw, V., K. McLean, D. Medway, C. Perkins, and G. Warnaby, eds. 2017. *Designing with Smell: Practices, Techniques and Challenges*. London: Routledge.

Herzfeld, M. 2001 *Anthropology: Theoretical Practice in Culture and Society*. Oxford: Blackwell.

Hetherington, K. 2003. "Spatial Textures: Place, Touch and Praesentia." *Environment and Planning A* 35 (11): 1933–44.

Heywood, P. 2019. "The Ontological Turn: An Anthropological Exposition." In *The Cambridge Encyclopedia of Anthropology*. Cambridge: Cambridge University Press. https://www.anthroencyclopedia.com/entry/ontological-turn.

Hinton, D., D. Howes, and L. Kirmayer. 2008. "Toward a Medical Anthropology of Sensations: Definitions and Research Agenda." *Transcultural Psychiatry* 45 (2): 142–62.

Hirsch, A. R. 1995. "Effects of Ambient Odors on Slot-Machine Usage in a Las Vegas Casino." *Psychology and Marketing* 12 (7): 585–94.

Hisano, A. 2019. *Visualizing Taste: How Capitalism Changed the Look of What We Eat*. Cambridge: Harvard University Press.

———. Forthcoming. "'Use Not Perfumery to Flavor Soup': The Science of the Senses in Aesthetic Capitalism." In *Capitalism and the Senses*, edited by R. L. Blaszczyk and D. Suisman. Philadelphia: University of Pennsylvania Press.

Hobbes, T. (1651) 1996. *Leviathan*. New York: Cambridge University Press.

Hoffer, P. C. 2006. *Sensory Worlds in Early America*. Baltimore: Johns Hopkins University Press.

Hohenegger, B. 2006. *Liquid Jade: The Story of Tea from East to West*. New York: St. Martin's Press.

Holdcroft, A. 2007. "Gender-Based Bias in Research: How Does It Affect Evidence Based Medicine?" *Journal of the Royal Society of Medicine* 100 (1): 2–3.

Horstmann, M. 2014. "Managing the Senses in Sant Devotion." In *Exploring the Senses: Asian and European Perspectives on Ritual and Performativity*, edited by A. Michaels and C. Wulf, 78–94. New Delhi: Routledge.

Howes, D. 1985. "Property, God and Nature in the Thought of Sir John Beverley Robinson." *McGill Law Journal* 30 (3): 365–414.

———. 1987. "From Polyjurality to Monojurality: The Transformation of Quebec Law, 1875–1929." *McGill Law Journal* 32 (3): 523–58.

———. 1989. "Scents and Sensibility: A Review of *The Foul and the Fragrant* by Alain Corbin." *Culture, Medicine and Psychiatry* 13:89–97.

———. 1990a. "Controlling Textuality: A Call for the Return to the Senses." *Anthropologica* 32 (1): 55–73.

———. 1990b. "Les techniques des sens." *Anthropologie et Sociétés* 14 (2): 99–115.

———, ed. 1991. *The Varieties of Sensory Experience: A Sourcebook in the Anthropology of the Senses*. Toronto: University of Toronto Press.

———, ed. 1996. *Cross-Cultural Consumption: Global Markets, Local Realities*. London: Routledge.

———. 2002. "Maladroit or Not? Learning to Be of Two Minds in the New Bijural Law Curricula." *Journal of Legal Education* 52:55–60.

———. 2003a. *Sensual Relations: Engaging the Senses in Culture and Social Theory*. Ann Arbor: University of Michigan Press.

———. 2003b. "Evaluation sensorielle et diversité culturelle." *Psychologie française* 48 (4): 117–25.

———, ed. 2005a. *Empire of the Senses: The Sensual Culture Reader*. Abingdon: Routledge.

———. 2005b. "HYPERAESTHESIA, or, The Sensual Logic of Late Capitalism." In Howes, *Empire of the Senses*, 281–303.

———. 2005c. "Introduction: Culture in the Domain of Law." *Canadian Journal of Law and Society* 20 (1): 9–42.

———. 2006. "Charting the Sensorial Revolution." *Senses and Society* 1 (1): 113–28.

———. 2007. "Sensory Basket Weaving 101." In *Neocraft: Modernity and the Crafts*, edited by S. Alfoldy, 216–24. Halifax: The Press of the Nova Scotia College of Art and Design.

———. 2008. "Can these Dry Bones Live? An Anthropological Approach to the History of the Senses." *Journal of American History* 95 (2): 442–51.

———. 2009. Introduction to *The Sixth Sense Reader*, edited by D. Howes, 1–49. Abingdon: Routledge.

———, ed. 2014a. *A Cultural History of the Senses in the Modern Age, 1920–2000*. London: Bloomsbury.

———, ed. 2014b. "Sensory Museology." Special issue, *Senses and Society* 9 (3).

———. 2015. "Senses, Anthropology of the." In *International Encyclopedia Social and Behavioral Sciences*, 2nd ed., edited by J. D. Wright, 615–20. Oxford: Elsevier.

———. 2016. "Sensing Cultures: Cinema, Ethnography and the Senses." In *Beyond Text? Sensory Anthropology and Critical Practice*, edited by R. Cox, A. Irving, and C. Wright, 173–88. Manchester: Manchester University Press.

———. 2017. "How Capitalism Came to Its Senses—and Yours." Paper presented at "Capitalism and the Senses," Harvard Business School, 29 June. http://centreforsensorystudies.org/how-capitalism-came-to-its-senses-and-yours-the-invention-of-sensory-marketing.

———, ed. 2018. *Senses and Sensation: Critical and Primary Sources*. 4 vols. Abingdon: Routledge.

———, ed. 2019. "Troubling Law's Sensorium: Explorations in Sensational Jurisprudence." Special issue, *Canadian Journal of Law and Society* 34 (2).

———. 2022. *The Sensory Studies Manifesto: Tracking the Sensorial Revolution in the Arts and Human Sciences*. Toronto: University of Toronto Press.

Howes, D., and C. Classen. 1991. "Conclusion: Sounding Sensory Profiles." In Howes, *Varieties of Sensory Experience*, 257–88.

———. 2013. *Ways of Sensing: Understanding the Senses in Society*. London: Routledge.

Howes, D., K. Morgan, M. Radice, and D. Szanto. 2013. "The Sensory City Workshop: Sensing the City Through Touch and Taste." http://centreforsensorystudies.org/the-sensory-city-workshop-sensing-the-city-through-touch-and-taste.

Hsu, E. 1999. *The Transmission of Chinese Medicine*. Cambridge: Cambridge University Press.

———, ed. 2008. "The Senses and the Social." Special issue, *Ethnos* 73 (4).

———. 2010. *Pulse Diagnosis in Early Chinese Medicine: The Telling Touch*. Cambridge: Cambridge University Press.

Hsu, H. 2020. "The Sensorial Bioaccumulation of Race." *Senses and Society* 15 (2): 247–50.

Hughes, H. C. 2001. *Sensory Exotica: A World Beyond Human Experience*. Cambridge: The MIT Press.

Huizinga, J. (1919) 1996. *The Autumn of the Middle Ages*. Chicago: University of Chicago Press.

———. (1929) 2014. "The Task of Cultural History." In *Men and Ideas: History, the Middle Ages, the Renaissance*, 17–76. Princeton: Princeton University Press.

Hume, D. 1975a. *Enquiries Concerning Human Understanding and*

Concerning the Principles of Morals. Oxford: Clarendon Press.

———. 1975b. *A Treatise of Human Nature*. Oxford: Clarendon Press.

Huygebaert, S., A. Condello, S. Marusek, and M. Antaki, eds. 2018. *Sensing the Nation's Law: Historical Inquiries into the Aesthetics of Democratic Legitimacy*. Cham, Switzerland: Springer International.

Ingold, T. 2000. *The Perception of the Environment: Essays on Livelihood, Dwelling and Skill*. London: Routledge.

———. 2011. *Being Alive: Essays on Movement, Knowledge and Description*. London: Routledge.

———. 2013. *Making: Anthropology, Archaeology, Art and Architecture*. London: Routledge.

———. 2015. *The Life of Lines*. London: Routledge.

———. 2018. "Back to the Future with the Theory of Affordances." *Hau* 8 (1/2): 39–44.

———. 2022. Response to David Howes. *Journal of Material Culture* 27(3): 336–40.

Ingold, T., and D. Howes. 2011. "Worlds of Sense and Sensing the World." *Social Anthropology* 19 (3): 314–31.

International Roundtable for the Semiotics of Law. 2015. *Synaesthetic Legalities: Sensory Dimensions of Law and Jurisprudence*. http://www.sensorystudies.org/wordpress/wp-content/uploads/2009/12/Synesthetic-Legalities-CFP.pdf. June 1, 2015.

Irvine, T. 2020. *Listening to China: Sound and the Sino-Western Encounter, 1770–1839*. Chicago: University of Chicago Press.

Jackson, M. 1983a. "Knowledge of the Body." *Man* (n.s.) 18:327–45.

———. 1983b. "Thinking Through the Body: An Essay on Understanding Metaphor." *Social Analysis* 14:127–48.

Jaffe, R., E. Dürr, and G. A. Jones. 2019. "What Does Poverty Feel Like? Urban Inequality and the Politics of Sensation." *Urban Studies* 57 (5): 1015–31.

Janda, R. 2005. "Toward Cosmopolitan Law." *McGill Law Journal* 50:967–84.

Jay, M. 1993. *Downcast Eyes: The Denigration of Vision in Contemporary French Thought*. Berkeley: University of California Press.

———. 1999. "Must Justice Be Blind? The Challenge of Images to the Law. In *Law and the Image: The Authority of Art and the Aesthetics of Law*, edited by C. Douzinas and L. Nead, 19–35. Chicago: University of Chicago Press.

Jervis, S. M., P. Gerard, S. Drake, K. Lopetcharat, and M. A. Drake. 2014. "The Perception of Creaminess in Sour Cream." *Journal of Sensory Studies* 29 (4): 248–57.

Jonaitis, A. 2006. "Smoked Fish and Fermented Oil: Taste and Smell Among the Kwakwaka'wakw." In *Sensible Objects: Colonialism, Museums and Material Culture*, edited by E. Edwards, C. Gosden, and R. Phillips, 141–68. Abingdon: Routledge.

Jonas, H. (1954) 1982. "The Nobility of Sight: A Study in the Phenomenology of the Senses."

Philosophy and Phenomenological Research 14 (4): 507–19.

Jones, C. A. 2006a. *Eyesight Alone: Clement Greenberg's Modernism and the Bureaucratization of the Senses*. Chicago: University of Chicago Press.

——. 2006b. "The Mediated Sensorium." In *Sensorium: Embodied Experience, Technology and Contemporary Art*, edited by C. A. Jones, 5–48. Cambridge: The MIT List Visual Arts Center and MIT Press.

Jonsen, A. R. 2008. *A Short History of Medical Ethics*. Oxford: Oxford University Press.

Jordanova, L. 1989. *Sexual Visions: Images of Gender in Science and Medicine Between the Eighteenth and Twentieth Centuries*. New York: Harvester Wheatsheaf.

Jørgensen, H. H. L., H. Laugerud, and K. L. Skinnebach. 2015. *The Saturated Sensorium: Principles of Perception and Mediation in the Middle Ages*. Aarhus: Aarhus University Press.

Joyce, K. A. 2008. *Magnetic Appeal: MRI and the Myth of Transparency*. Ithaca: Cornell University Press.

Jukier, R. 2006. "Transnationalizing the Legal Curriculum: How to Teach What we Live." *Journal of Legal Education* 56 (2): 172–89.

Jütte, R. 2004. *A History of the Senses: From Antiquity to Cyberspace*. Malden, MA: Polity Press.

Kane, B. 2018. "Sound Studies Without Auditory Culture: A Critique of the Ontological Turn." In Howes, *Senses and Sensation*, 4:277–96.

Kane, H. H. 1882. *Opium-Smoking in America and China*. New York: G. P. Putnam's.

Kapoor, S. 2021. "The Violence of Odors: Sensory Politics of Caste in a Leather Tannery." *Senses and Society* 16 (2): 164–76.

Kasirer, N. 2002. "Bijuralism in Law's Empire and in Law's Cosmos." *Journal of Legal Education* 52:29–41.

——. 2003. "Legal Education as Métissage." *Tulane Law Review* 78:481–501.

Kearney, R. 1988. *The Wake of Imagination: Toward a Postmodern Culture*. London: Routledge.

Keller, E. F., and C. R. Grontkowski. 1983. "The Mind's Eye." In *Discovering Reality: Feminist Perspectives on Epistemology, Metaphysics, Methodology and Philosophy of Science*, edited by S. Harding and M. B. Hintikka, 207–24. Dordrecht: Reidel.

Kemp, S., T. Hollowood, and J. Hort. 2011. *Sensory Evaluation: A Practical Handbook*. Oxford: Blackwell.

Keuleman, P. 2014. *Sound Rising from the Paper: Nineteenth-Century Martial Arts Fiction and the Chinese Acoustic Imagination*. Cambridge: Harvard University Press.

Kirmayer, L. 1992. "The Body's Insistence on Meaning: Metaphor as Presentation and Representation in Illness Experience." *Medical Anthropology Quarterly* 6 (4): 323–46.

Kleutghen, K. 2015a. "Bringing Art to Life: Giuseppe Castiglione and

Scenic Illusion Painting." In *Portrayals from a Brush Divine: A Special Exhibition on the Tricentennial of Giuseppe Castiglione's Arrival in China*, edited by C. He, 324–37. Taipei: National Palace Museum.

———. 2015b. "From Science to Art: The Evolution of Linear Perspective in Eighteenth-Century Chinese Art." In *Qing Encounters: Artistic Exchanges Between China and the West*, edited by P. ten-Doesschate Chu and D. Ning, 173–89. Los Angeles: Getty Research Institute.

Ko, D. 2019. "Stone, Scissors, Paper: Thinking Through Things in Chinese History." *Journal of Chinese History* 3:191–201.

Konishi, S. 2013. "Discovering the Savage Senses: French and British Explorers' Encounters with Aboriginal People." In *Discovery and Empire: The French in the South Seas*, edited by J. West-Sooby, 99–140. Adelaide: University of Adelaide Press.

Kopytoff, I. 1986. "The Cultural Biography of Things: Commoditization as Process." In *The Social Life of Things: Commodities in Cultural Perspective*, edited by A. Appadurai, 64–94. Cambridge: Cambridge University Press.

Korzybska, H. 2022. "Investir le 'regard' des personnes devenues aveugles. De l'implantation retinienne aux expériences mescaliniennes." In Calapi et al., *Sensibles ethnographies*.

Krmpotich, C., L. Peers, and the Haida Repatriation Committee and staff of the Pitt Rivers Museum and British Museum. 2014. *This Is Our Life: Haida Material Heritage and Changing Museum Practice*. Vancouver: UBC Press.

Kuriyama, S. 1999. *The Expressiveness of the Body and the Divergence of Greek and Chinese Medicine*. Princeton: Princeton University Press.

Laderman, C., and M. Roseman, eds. 1996. *The Performance of Healing*. London: Routledge.

Laforet, A. 2004. "Relationships Between First Nations and the Canadian Museum of Civilization." Paper presented in session on Relationships Between Museums and First Nations, Haida Repatriation Extravaganza, Masset, BC, 22 May.

Lafrance, M. 2018. "Introduction: Skin Studies—Past, Present, and Future." *Body and Society* 24 (1–2): 3–32.

Lahne, J. 2016. "Sensory Science, the Food Industry, and the Objectification of Taste." *Anthropology of Food* 10. http://journals.openedition.org/aof/7956.

Lahne, J., and C. Spackman. 2018. "Introduction to Accounting for Taste." Special issue, *Senses and Society* 13 (1): 1–5.

Lahne, J., and A. Trubek. 2014. "'A Little Information Excites Us': Consumer Sensory Experience of Vermont Artisan Cheese as Active Practice." *Appetite* 78:129–38.

Lahne, J., A. Trubek, and M. L. Pelchat. 2014. "Consumer Sensory Perception of Cheese Depends on Context: A Study Using Comment Analysis and Linear Mixed Models." *Food Quality and Preference* 32:184–97.

Lakoff, G., and M. Johnson. 1980. *Metaphors We Live By*. Chicago: University of Chicago Press.

Lambert, R. 2021. "Le reflet du monde est à l'intérieur de moi: Une ethnographie poétique de l'expérience de l'agoraphobie en Norvège." PhD diss., Concordia University.

Lamrani, M., ed. 2021. "Beyond Revolution: Reshaping Nationhood Through Senses and Affect." Special issue, *Cambridge Journal of Anthropology* 39 (2).

Lange, C. ed. 2022. "The Sensory History of the Islamic World." Special issue, *Senses and Society* 17 (1).

Laplantine, F. (2005) 2015. *The Life of the Senses: Introduction to a Modal Anthropology*. Abingdon: Routledge.

Latour, B. 1987. *Science in Action: How to Follow Scientists and Engineers Through Society*. Cambridge: Harvard University Press.

———. 1993. *We Have Never Been Modern*. Cambridge: Harvard University Press.

Law. L. 2005. "Home Cooking: Filipino Women and Geographies of the Senses in Hong Kong." In Howes, *Empire of the Senses*, 224–44.

Lawrence, S. 2021. "Sonic Intimacies: Performative Erotics and African Feminisms." *Senses and Society* 16 (2): 177–92.

Leavitt, J., and L. Hart. 1990. "Critique de la 'raison' sensorielle. L'élaboration esthétique des sens dans une société himalayenne." *Anthropologie et Sociétés* 14 (2): 77–98.

Le Breton, D. 1990. *Anthropologie du corps et modernité*. Paris: Presses Universitaires de France.

Leenhardt, M. (1947) 1979. *Do Kamo: Person and Myth in the Melanesian World*. Chicago: University of Chicago Press.

Lévi-Strauss, C. 1966. *The Savage Mind*. Chicago: University of Chicago Press.

———. (1969) 1979. *The Raw and the Cooked: Introduction to a Science of Mythology*. Translated by J. Weightman and D. Weightman. Vol. 1. New York: Octagon.

Little, K. 1991. "On Safari: The Visual Politics of a Tourist Representation." In Howes, *Varieties of Sensory Experience*, 148–63.

Locke, J. (1683/1690) 1988. *Two Treatises of Government*. Oxford: Clarendon Press.

———. (1689) 1975. *An Essay Concerning Human Understanding*. Oxford: Clarendon Press.

Lupton, D., and S. Maslen. 2018. "The More-Than-Human Sensorium: Sensory Engagements with Digital Self-Tracking Technologies." *Senses and Society* 13 (2): 190–202.

Lynch, E. 2022. *Locative Tourism Apps: A Sensory Ethnography of the Augmented City*. Abingdon: Routledge.

Lynch, E., D. Howes, and M. French. 2020. "A Touch of Luck and a 'Real Taste of Vegas': A Sensory Ethnography of the

Montreal Casino." *Senses and Society* 15 (2): 192–215.

Macdonald, R. A. 2002. *Lessons of Everyday Law*. Montreal: McGill-Queen's University Press.

Macfarlane, A. 1988. "Anthropology and History." In *The Blackwell Dictionary of Historians*, edited by J. Cannon, 12–14. Oxford: Blackwell.

Macfarlane, I. 1991. *The Origins of English Individualism: The Family, Property, and Social Transition*. Oxford: Wiley-Blackwell.

Macintyre, A. 1988. *Whose Justice? Which Rationality?* Notre Dame: University of Notre Dame Press.

Macpherson, C. B. 1962. *The Political Theory of Possessive Individualism: Hobbes to Locke*. Oxford: Oxford University Press.

Majid, A., and S. Levinson, eds. 2010. "The Senses in Language and Culture." Special issue, *Senses and Society* 6 (1).

Malefyt, T. 2014. "An Anthropology of the Senses: Tracing the Future of Sensory Marketing in Brand Rituals." In *Handbook of Anthropology in Business*, edited by R. Denny and P. Sunderland, 704–21. Walnut Creek, CA: Left Coast Press.

———. 2015. "The Senses in Anthropological and Marketing Research: Investigating a Consumer-Brand Ritual Holistically." *Journal of Business Anthropology* 4 (1): 5–30.

Malinowski, B. 1929. *The Sexual Life of Savages in North Western Melanesia*. New York: Harcourt, Brace and World.

———. 1961. *Argonauts of the Western Pacific*. New York: E. P. Dutton.

Maloney, C. 1976. *The Evil Eye*. New York: Columbia University Press.

Mandrou, R. 1975. *Introduction to Modern France 1500–1640: An Essay in Historical Psychology*. London: Edward Arnold.

Mann, B. A. 2004. "The Greenville Treaty of 1795: Pen-and-Ink Witchcraft in the Struggle for the Old Northwest." In *Enduring Legacies: Native American Treaties and Contemporary Controversies*, edited by B. E. Johansen, 135–202. Westport, CT: Praeger.

Marchand, T. H. J. 2008. "Muscles, Morals and Mind: Craft Apprenticeship and the Formation of Person." *British Journal of Educational Studies* 56 (3): 245–71.

———. 2009. *The Masons of Djenné*. Bloomington: Indiana University Press.

Marchetti, F., and D. Howes. 2020. "A Dialogic Probe on the Atmosphere of Law." *Law and the Senses*, July 15, 2020. http://lawandthesenses.org/probes/dialogic-probe-on-the-atmosphere-of-law-a-conversation-between-florencia-marchetti-and-david-howes.

Marchionni, A.-L. 2022. "Tenter un basculement sensible: Reflexions à partir d'une expérience d'immersion dans le milieu de vie d'une personne autiste." In Calapi et al., *Sensibles ethnographies*.

Marcus, G., and D. Cushman. 1982. "Ethnographies as Text." *Annual Review of Anthropology* 11:25–69.

Marcus, G., and M. Fischer. 1986. *Anthropology as Cultural Critique*. Chicago: University of Chicago Press.

Marks, L. (1975) 2014. *The Unity of the Senses: Interrelations Among the Modalities*. New York: Academic Press.

Marr, D. 1982. *Vision*. New York: W. H. Freeman & Co.

Marryat, J. 1857. *A History of Pottery and Porcelain: Medieval and Modern*. London: John Murray.

Massumi, B. 2002. *Parables for the Virtual: Movement, Affect, Sensation*. Durham: Duke University Press.

Matthews, M. 2016. *Naamiwan's Drum: The Study of a Contested Repatriation of Anishnaabe Artifacts*. Toronto: University of Toronto Press.

Matthews, M., and R. Roulette. 2018. "'Are All Stones Alive?' Anthropological and Anishnaabe Approaches to Personhood." In *Rethinking Relations and Animism: Personhood and Materiality*, edited by M. Astor-Aguilera and G. Harvey, 173–92. London: Routledge.

Matthews, M., J. B. Wilson, and R. Roulette. 2021. "*Meshkwajisewin*: Paradigm Shift." *Religions* 12 (10): 894. https://doi.org/10.3390/rel12100894.

Mauss, M. (1924) 1979. "Real and Practical Relations Between Psychology and Sociology." In *Sociology and Psychology Essays*, translated by B. Brewster, 1–33. London: Routledge and Kegan Paul.

———. (1936) 1979. "Body Techniques." In *Sociology and Psychology Essays*, translated by B. Brewster, 95–123. London: Routledge and Kegan Paul.

———. 1967. *The Gift: Forms and Functions of Exchange in Archaic Societies*. London: Routledge and Kegan Paul.

———. 2007. *Manual of Ethnography*. Oxford: Berghahn Books.

Mazella di Bosco, M. 2022. "Pratique de danse et expériences de soi. Une approche sensible des 'danses libres en conscience.'" In Calapi et al., *Sensibles ethnographies*.

McDougall, W. 1901. "Cutaneous Sensations." In *Reports of the Cambridge Anthropological Expedition to Torres Strait*, edited by Alfred C. Haddon, vol. 2, part 2: 189–95. Cambridge: Cambridge University Press.

McLuhan, M. 1962. *The Gutenberg Galaxy*. Toronto: University of Toronto Press.

Mead, M., and R. Métraux, eds. 1953. *The Study of Culture at a Distance*. Chicago: University of Chicago Press.

Meade, M. S., and M. Emch. 2010. *Medical Geography*. 3rd ed. New York: Guilford Press.

Meilgaard, M., B. T. Carr, and G. V. Civille. 2010. *Sensory Evaluation Techniques*. 3rd ed. Boca Raton, FL: CRC Press.

Merchant, C. 1990. *The Death of Nature: Women, Ecology, and the Scientific Revolution*. New York: HarperCollins.

Merleau-Ponty, M. 1962. *Phenomenology of Perception*. London: Routledge & Kegan Paul.

Métraux, R. 1953. "Resonance in Imagery." In *The Study of Culture at a Distance*, edited by M. Mead and R. Métraux, 343–64. Chicago: University of Chicago Press.

Meyer, B., ed. 2009. *Aesthetic Formations: Media, Religion, and the Senses*. New York: Palgrave Macmillan.

Michaels, A., and C. Wulf, eds. 2014. "Exploring the Senses in Rituals and Performances: An Introduction." In *Exploring the Senses: Asian and European Perspectives on Ritual and Performativity*, edited by A. Michaels and C. Wulf, 1–24. New Delhi: Routledge.

Miller, C., and G. R. Hamell. 1986. "A New Perspective on Indian-White Contact: Cultural Symbols and Colonial Trade." *Journal of American History* 73 (2): 311–28.

Mills, A. 1994. *Eagle Down Is Our Law. Wet'suwet'en Law, Feasts and Land Claims*. Vancouver: UBC Press.

———. 2005. *"Hang Onto These Words": Johnny David's Delgamuukw Evidence*. Toronto: University of Toronto Press.

Mills, A. 2018. "Engaging Aesthetically with Tapa Barkcloth in the Museum." *Senses and Society* 13 (3): 367–74.

Mintz, S. 1986. *Sweetness and Power: The Place of Sugar in Modern History*. New York: Penguin.

Mopas, M. 2019. "Howling Winds: Sound, Sense and the Politics of Noise Regulation." *Canadian Journal of Law and Society* 34 (2): 307–26.

Mopas, M. S., and E. Huybregts. 2020. "Training by Feel: Wearable Fitness-Trackers, Endurance Athletes, and the Sensing of Data." *Senses and Society* 15 (1): 25–40.

Mungello, D. E. 1989. *Curious Land: Jesuit Accommodation and the Origins of Sinology*. Honolulu: University of Hawai'i Press.

Munn, N. 1986. *The Fame of Gawa: A Symbolic Study of Value Transformation in a Massim (Papua New Guinea) Society*. New York: Cambridge University Press.

Myers, C. S. 1901. "Smell." In *Reports of the Cambridge Anthropological Expedition to Torres Strait*, edited by Alfred C. Haddon, vol. 2, part 2, 169–85. Cambridge: Cambridge University Press.

Nedelsky, J. 1997. "Embodied Diversity and the Challenges to Law." *McGill Law Journal* 42:91–117.

Nelson, S. E. 1998/1999. "Picturing Listening: The Sight of Sound in Chinese Painting." *Archives of Asian Art* 51:30–55.

Newhauser, R., ed. 2014. *A Cultural History of the Senses in the Middle Ages, 500–1400*. London: Bloomsbury.

Nudds, M. 2014. "The Senses in Philosophy and Science: From Sensation to Computation." In *A Cultural History of the Senses in the Modern Age, 1920–2000*, edited by D. Howes, 125–48. London: Bloomsbury.

Nylan, M. 2018. *The Chinese Pleasure Book*. Princeton: Princeton University Press/Zone Books.

O'Callaghan, C. 2019. *A Multisensory Philosophy of Perception*. Oxford: Oxford University Press.

Ong, W. J. 1967. *The Presence of the Word: Some Prolegomena for Cultural and Religious History*. New Haven: Yale University Press.

———. 1969. "World as View and World as Event." *American Anthropologist* 71 (4): 634–47.

———. 1991. "The Shifting Sensorium." In Howes, *Varieties of Sensory Experience*, 25–30.

Orleck, A. 2018. "How Migrant Workers Took on Ben & Jerry's." *The Guardian*, 25 February. https://www.theguardian.com/us-news/2018/feb/25/ben-jerrys-migrant-workers-dairy-farms.

Pagani, C. 1995. "Clockmaking in China Under the Kangxi and Qianlong Emperors." *Arts Asiatiques* 50:76–84.

Panagia, D. 2009. *The Political Life of Sensation*. Durham: Duke University Press.

Pangborn, R. M. 1964. "Sensory Evaluation of Food: A Look Forward and Back." *Food Technology* 18:1309–24.

Paterson, M. 2009. "Haptic Geographies: Ethnography, Haptic Knowledges and Sensuous Dispositions." *Progress in Human Geography* 33 (6): 766–88.

Pavsek, C. 2015. "Leviathan and the Experience of Sensory Ethnography." *Visual Anthropology* 31 (1): 4–11.

Paxson, H. 2013. *The Life of Cheese: Crafting Food and Value in America*. Berkeley: University of California Press.

Pearce, N., B. Best, and M. Hu. 2018. "Art Aesthetics in China: Some Observations." *Senses and Society* 13 (3): 282–98.

Pentcheva, B. 2010. *The Sensual Icon: Space, Ritual and the Senses in Byzantium*. Philadelphia: Pennsylvania State University Press.

Peraldi-Mittelette, P. 2022. "Le sens en mots, les sens par les mots." In Calapi et al., *Sensibles ethnographies*.

Peterson, M. 2016. "Sensory Attunements: Working with the Past in the Little Cities of Black Diamonds." *South Atlantic Quarterly* 115 (1): 89–111.

———. 2021. *Atmospheric Noise: The Indefinite Urbanism of Los Angeles*. Durham: Duke University Press.

Piccolino, M., and N. J. Wade. 2013. *Galileo's Visions: Piercing the Spheres of the Heavens by Eye and Mind*. Oxford: Oxford University Press.

Pink, S. 2004. *Home Truths: Gender, Domestic Objects and Everyday Life*. Abingdon: Routledge.

———. 2006. *The Future of Visual Anthropology: Engaging the Senses*. London: Routledge.

———. 2009. *Doing Sensory Ethnography*. London: Sage.

———. 2014. "Digital-Visual-Sensory-Design Anthropology: Ethnography, Imagination and Intervention." *Arts and Humanities in Higher Education* 13 (4): 412–27.

---. 2021. "Sensuous Futures: Re-Thinking the Concept of Trust in Design Anthropology." *Senses and Society* 16 (2): 1–10.

Pink, S., E. Ardèvol, and D. Lanzeni, eds. 2016. *Digital Materialities: Design and Anthropology*. London: Routledge.

Pink, S., and V. Fors. 2017. "Being in a Mediated World: Self-Tracking and the Mind-Body-Environment." *Cultural Geographies* 24 (3): 375–88.

Pink, S., H. Horst, and J. Postill. 2015. *Digital Ethnography: Principles and Practice*. London: Sage.

Piqueras-Fiszman, B., and C. Spence. 2012. "The Influence of the Color of the Cup on Consumers' Perception of a Hot Beverage." *Journal of Sensory Studies* 27 (5): 324–31.

Polanyi, K. 1957. *The Great Transformation: The Political and Economic Origins of Our Time*. Boston: Beacon.

Polli, A. 2017. "Soundwalking, Sonification and Activism." In *The Routledge Companion to Sounding Art*, edited by M. Cobussen, V. Meelberg, and B. Truax, 135–44. London: Routledge.

Pomeranz, K. 2000. *The Great Divergence: China, Europe, and the Making of the Modern World Economy*. Princeton: Princeton University Press.

Porcello, T., L. Meintjes, A. M. Ochoa, and D. Samuels. 2010. "The Reorganization of the Sensory World." *Annual Review of Anthropology* 39:51–66.

Porteous, J. D. 1990. *Landscapes of the Mind: Worlds of Sense and Metaphor*. Toronto: University of Toronto Press.

Poste, L., A. Mackie, G. Butler, and E. Larmond. 1991. *Laboratory Methods for Sensory Analysis of Food*. Ottawa: Agriculture Canada.

Postrel, V. 2003. *The Substance of Style: How the Rise of Aesthetic Value Is Remaking Commerce, Culture, and Consciousness*. New York: HarperCollins.

Provost, R. 2017. "Centaur Jurisprudence: Culture Before the Law." In *Culture in the Domains of Law*, edited by R. Provost, 1–20. Cambridge: Cambridge University Press.

---. 2021. *Rebel Courts: The Administration of Justice by Armed Insurgents*. Oxford: Oxford University Press.

Ramachandran, V. S., E. M. Hubbard, and P. A. Butcher. 2004. "Synesthesia, Cross-Activation, and the Foundations of Neuroepistemology." In *The Handbook of Multisensory Processes*, edited by G. Calvert, C. Spence, and B. E. Stein, 867-83. Cambridge: The MIT Press.

Rapport, N. 2003. *I Am Dynamite: An Alternative Anthropology of Power*. London: Routledge.

Rath, R. C. 2014. "Hearing Wampum: The Senses, Mediation and the Limits of Analogy." In *Colonial Mediascapes: Sensory Worlds of the Early Americas*, edited by M. Cohen and J. Glover, 290–322. Lincoln: University of Nebraska Press.

Raum, M. 2020. "Ben & Jerry's Remove Claim That Ice Cream Comes from 'Happy Cows' amid Lawsuits." *People*, 21

January. https://people.com/food/ben-jerrys-removes-claim-that-their-ice-cream-comes-from-happy-cows-amid-lawsuits.

Rawls, J. 1971. *A Theory of Justice.* Cambridge: Harvard University Press.

Regina v. Marshall. 1999. 3 Supreme Court Reports 456.

Regina v. Van der Peet. (1996). 2 Supreme Court Reports 507.

Reichel, A. E. 2021. *Writing Anthropologists, Sounding Primitives: The Poetry and Scholarship of Edward Sapir, Margaret Mead and Ruth Benedict.* Lincoln: University of Nebraska Press.

Renteln, A. D. 2005. *The Cultural Defense.* Oxford: Oxford University Press.

Rheinberger, H.-J. 1997. *Toward a History of Epistemic Things: Synthesizing Proteins in the Test Tube.* Stanford: Stanford University Press.

Rhys-Taylor, A. 2017. *Food and Multiculture: A Sensory Ethnography of East London.* Abingdon: Routledge.

Rice, T. 2013. *Hearing and the Hospital: Sound, Listening, Knowledge and Experience.* London: Sean Kingston.

Richards, G. 1998. "Getting a Result: The Expedition's Psychological Research, 1898–1913." In *Cambridge and the Torres Strait: Centenary Essays on the 1898 Anthropological Expedition,* edited by A. Herle and S. Rouse, 158–80. Cambridge: Cambridge University Press.

Ricoeur, P. 1970. "The Model of the Text: Meaningful Action Considered as a Text." *Social Research* 38:529–62.

Riedel, F., and J. Torvinen, eds. 2020. *Music as Atmosphere: Collective Feelings and Affective Sounds.* London: Routledge.

Ritchie, I. 1991. "Fusion of the Faculties: A Study of the Language of the Senses in Hausaland." In Howes, *Varieties of Sensory Experience,* 192–202.

Rivers, W. H. R. 1901. "Introduction." In *Reports of the Cambridge Anthropological Expedition to Torres Strait,* edited by Alfred C. Haddon, vol. 2, part 1, 1–7. Cambridge: Cambridge University Press.

———. 1905. "Observations on the Senses of the Todas." *British Journal of Psychology* 1:321–95.

Robben, A. C. G. M., and J. A. Sluka, eds. 2007. *Ethnographic Fieldwork: An Anthropological Reader.* Oxford: Blackwell.

Roberts, L. 2005. "The Death of the Sensuous Chemist: The 'New' Chemistry and the Transformation of Sensuous Technology." In Howes, *Empire of the Senses,* 106–27.

Robins, N. A. 2011. *Mercury, Mining and Empire: The Human and Ecological Cost of Colonial Silver Mining in the Andes.* Bloomington: Indiana University Press.

Robinson, D., and K. Martin. 2016. *Arts of Engagement: Taking Aesthetic Action In and Beyond the Truth and Reconciliation Commission of Canada.* Waterloo: Wilfrid Laurier University Press.

Rodaway, P. 1994. *Sensuous Geographies: Body, Sense and Place*. London: Routledge.

Romanyshyn, R. 1989. *Technology as Symptom and Dream*. New York: Routledge.

Roodenburg, H., ed. 2014. *A Cultural History of the Senses in the Renaissance, 1450–1650*. London: Bloomsbury.

Roseman, M. 1992. *Healing Sounds from the Malaysian Rainforest: Temiar Music and Medicine*. Berkeley: University of California Press.

Rošker, J. S. 2019. "Chinese Theories of Perception and the Structural Approach to Comprehension." In *The Senses and the History of Philosophy*, edited by B. Glenney and J. F. Silva, 21–32. Abingdon: Routledge.

Sacks, O. 2017. *The River of Consciousness*. New York: Vintage.

Salter, C. 2015. *Alien Agency: Experimental Encounters with Art in the Making*. Cambridge: MIT Press.

———. 2018. "Disturbance, Translation, Enculturation: Necessary Research in New Media, Technology, and the Senses." *Visual Anthropology Review* 34 (1): 87–97.

———. 2022. *Sensing Machines: How Sensors Shape Our Everyday Life*. Cambridge: MIT Press.

Santangelo, P. 2005. "Evaluation of Emotions in European and Chinese Traditions: Differences and Analogies." *Monumenta Serica* 53:401–27.

Santos, B. de Sousa. 2018. *The End of the Cognitive Empire: The Coming of Age of Epistemologies of the South*. Durham: Duke University Press.

Sarukkai, S. 2014. "Unity of the Senses in Indian Thought." In *Exploring the Senses: Asian and European Perspectives on Ritual and Performativity*, edited by A. Michaels and C. Wulf, 297–308. New York: Routledge.

Saunders, N. 1999. "Biographies of Brilliance: Pearls, Transformations of Matter and Being, ca AD 1492." *World Archaeology* 31 (2): 243–57.

Saunders, N., and P. Cornish, eds. 2017. *Modern Conflict and the Senses*. London: Routledge, 361–74.

Schafer, R. M. 1977. *The Tuning of the World: Toward a Theory of Soundscape Design*. Toronto: McClelland and Stewart.

Schaffer, S. 1994. *From Physics to Anthropology—And Back Again*. Cambridge: Prickly Pear.

Schneider, A., and C. Wright, eds. 2010. *Between Art and Anthropology: Contemporary Ethnographic Practice*. Oxford: Berg.

Schroer, S. A. 2018. "'A Feeling for Birds': Tuning in to More-Than-Human Atmospheres." In *Studying Atmospheres Ethnographically*, edited by S. A. Schroer and S. B. Schmitt. Abingdon: Routledge.

Schroer, S. A., and Schmitt, S. B. 2018. *Exploring Atmospheres Ethnographically*. London: Routledge.

Schulze, H., ed. 2021. *The Bloomsbury Handbook of the Anthropology of Sound*. London: Bloomsbury.

Schwartzman, S. 2011. *See Yourself Sensing: Redefining Human Perception*. London: Black Dog.

Sears, E. 1993. "Sensory Perception and Its Metaphors in the Time of Richard of Fournival." In *Medicine and the Five Senses*, edited by W. F. Bynum and R. Porter, 17–39. Cambridge: Cambridge University Press.

Seeger, A. 1975. "The Meaning of Body Ornaments: A Suya Example." *Ethnology* 14 (3): 211–24.

———. 1987. *Why Suyá Sing: A Musical Anthropology of an Amazonian People*. Cambridge: Cambridge University Press.

Sekimoto, S., and C. Brown. 2020. *Race and the Senses: The Felt Politics of Racial Embodiment*. Abingdon: Routledge.

Senghor, L. S. 1964. *On African Socialism*. New York: Praeger.

Seth, A. 2021. *Being You: A New Science of Consciousness*. New York: Dutton.

Shapin, S. 2012. "The Sciences of Subjectivity." *Social Studies of Science* 42:170–84.

Sherwin, R. K., and D. Celemajer, eds. 2021. *A Cultural History of Law in the Modern Age*. London: Bloomsbury.

Simmel, G. (1921) 1997. "Sociology of the Senses." In *Simmel on Culture: Selected Writings*, edited by D. Frisby and M. Featherstone, 109–19. London: Sage.

Simpson, A. 2014. *Mohawk Interruptus: Political Life Across the Borders of Settler States*. Durham: Duke University Press.

Skeates, R., and J. Day, eds. 2020. *The Routledge Handbook of Sensory Archaeology*. Abingdon: Routledge.

Skinner, B. F. 1938. *The Behavior of Organisms*. New York: Appleton-Century-Crofts.

Smith, M. M. 2008. *Sensing the Past: Seeing, Hearing, Smelling, Tasting and Touching History*. Berkeley: University of California Press.

Sormani, P., G. Carbone, and P. Gisler, eds. 2018. *Practicing Art/Science: Experiments in an Emerging Field*. London and New York: Routledge.

Spence, C. 2018a. "Crossmodal Correspondences: A Synopsis." In Howes, *Senses and Sensation*, 3:91–125.

———. 2018b. *Gastrophysics: The New Science of Eating*. New York: Viking.

———. 2021. *Sensehacking: How to Use the Power of Your Senses for Happier, Healthier Living*. New York: Viking.

Spence, C., and B. Piqueras-Fiszman. 2014. *The Perfect Meal: The Multisensory Science of Food and Dining*. Oxford: Wiley-Blackwell.

Springer, J. W. 1981. "An Ethnohistoric Study of the Smoking Complex in Eastern North America." *Ethnohistory* 28 (3): 217–35.

Stewart, K. 2011. "Atmospheric Attunements." *Environment and Planning D: Society and Space* 29 (3): 445–53.

———. 2015. *Ordinary Affects*. Durham: Duke University Press.

Stocking, G. W., Jr. 1982. "From Physics to Ethnology." In *Race, Culture and Evolution: Essays in the History of Anthropology*, 133–60. Chicago: University of Chicago Press.

Stoever, J. L. 2016. *The Sonic Color Line: Race and the Cultural Politics of Listening*. New York: New York University Press.

Stoller, P. 1989. *The Taste of Ethnographic Things: The Senses in Anthropology*. Philadelphia: University of Pennsylvania Press.

———. 1997. *Sensuous Scholarship*. Philadelphia: University of Pennsylvania Press.

Stoller, P., and C. Olkes. 1990. "La sauce épaisse: Remarques sur les relations sociales songhaïs." *Anthropologie et Sociétés* 14 (2): 57–76.

Stone, H., R. Bleibaum, and H. Thomas. 2012. *Sensory Evaluation Practices*. 4th ed. San Diego: Academic Press.

Sumartojo, S., and S. Pink. 2019. *Atmospheres and the Experiential World: Theory and Methods*. Abingdon: Routledge.

Sutton, D. 2001. *Remembrance of Repasts: An Anthropology of Food and Memory*. London: Bloomsbury.

———. 2010. "Food and the Senses." *Annual Review of Anthropology* 39:209–23.

Synnott, A. 1991. "Puzzling over the Senses: From Plato to Marx." In Howes, *Varieties of Sensory Experience*, 61–78.

———. 1993. *The Body Social: Symbolism, Self and Society*. London: Routledge.

Tallis, R. 2011. *Aping Mankind: Neuromania, Darwinitis and the Misrepresentation of Humanity*. Durham: Acumen.

Taussig, M. 1993. *Mimesis and Alterity: A Particular History of the Senses*. London: Routledge.

Taylor, K. 2005. *Medicine of Revolution: Chinese Medicine in Early Communist China*. London: Routledge.

Taylor, L. (1994) 2014. *Visualizing Theory: Selected Essays from V.A.R., 1990–1994*. Hoboken: Taylor & Francis.

———. 1996. "Iconophobia: How Anthropology Lost It at the Movies. *Transition*, no. 69: 64–88.

Teil, G. 2019. "Learning to Smell: On the Shifting Modalities of Experience." *Senses and Society* 14 (3): 330–45.

Thibodeau, J., and C. Yolgörmez. 2020. "Open-Source Sentience: The Proof Is in the Performance." Paper presented at ISEA2020. http://www.isea-archives.org/isea2019/isea2020-paperthibodeauyolgormez.

Thom, B. 2001. "Aboriginal Rights and Title in Canada after Delgamuukw, Part One: Oral Tradition and Anthropological Evidence in the Courtroom." *Native Studies Review* 14 (1): 1–26.

Thompson, J. 2015. "Music from the Time of Matteo Ricci." http://www.silkqin.com/01mywk/themes/matteo.htm.

Thompson, M. 2017. *Beyond Unwanted Sound: Noise, Affect and Aesthetic Moralism*. London: Bloomsbury.

Ting, W. Y. V. 2010. "Interpretations: Dancing Pot and Pregnant Jar? On Ceramics, Metaphors and Creative Labels." In *Museum Materialities: Objects, Engagements, Interpretations*, edited by S. Dudley, 189–203. London: Routledge.

Titchener, E. B. 1912. "The Schema of Introspection." *American Journal of Psychology* 23:485–508.

Tomkis, T. 1607. *Lingua, or the Combat of the Tongue, and the Five Senses for Superiority*. Ann Arbor: Early English Books On-Line. http://quod.lib.umich.edu/e/eebo/A62894.0001.001.

Toner, J. P., ed. 2014. *A Cultural History of the Senses in Antiquity, 500 BC–500 AD*. London: Bloomsbury.

Trigger, B. G. 1986. *Natives and Newcomers: Canada's 'Heroic Age' Reconsidered*. Montreal: McGill-Queen's University Press.

Trnka, S., C. Dureau, and J. Park, eds. 2013. *Senses and Citizenships: Embodying Political Life*. London: Routledge.

Trosper, R. 2009. *Resilience, Reciprocity and Ecological Economies: Northwest Coast Sustainability*. Abingdon: Routledge.

Trower, S., ed. 2008. "Vibratory Movements." Special issue, *Senses and Society* 3 (2).

Trubek, A. 2009. *The Taste of Place: A Cultural Journey into Terroir*. Berkeley: University of California Press.

Truth and Reconciliation Commission of Canada. 2015. *Honouring the Truth, Reconciling for the Future*. https://nccdh.ca/resources/entry/honouring-the-truth-reconciling-for-the-future.

Turgeon, L. 1997. "The Tale of the Kettle: Odyssey of an Intercultural Object." *Ethnohistory* 44 (1): 1–29.

Tyler, S. 1984. "The Vision Quest in the West, or What the Mind's Eye Sees." *Journal of Anthropological Research* 40 (1): 23–40.

———. 1986. "Postmodern Ethnography: From Document of the Occult to Occult Document." In *Writing Culture: The Poetics and Politics of Ethnography*, edited by J. Clifford and G. Marcus, 122–40. Berkeley: University of California Press.

Ulloa, A. M. Forthcoming. "Psychophysics of Taste and Smell: From Experimental Science to Commercial Tool." In *Capitalism and the Senses*, edited by R. L. Blaszczyk and D. Suisman. Philadelphia: University of Pennsylvania Press.

Urry, J. 2011. "City Life and the Senses." In *The New Blackwell Companion to the City*, edited by G. Bridge and S. Watson, 347–56. Oxford: Blackwell.

Urry, J., and J. Larsen. 2011. *The Tourist Gaze 3.0*. London: Sage.

Uzwiak, B., and L. Bowles. 2021a. "Epistolary Storytelling: A Feminist Sensory Orientation to Ethnography." *Senses and Society* 16 (2): 203–22.

———, eds. 2021b. "The Ethnographic Palimpsest: Excursions in Paul Stoller's Sensory Poetics." Special issue, *Senses and Society* 16 (2).

Vainker, S. 2004. *Chinese Silk: A Cultural History*. New Brunswick: Rutgers University Press.

Valiquet, P. 2019. "Affordance Theory: A Rejoinder to 'Musical Events and Perceptual Psychologies' by Eric Clarke." *Senses and Society* 14 (3): 346–50.

Van Ginkel, R., and A. Starting, eds. 2007. *Wildness and Sensation: Anthropology of Sinister and*

Sensuous Realms. Apeldoorn, The Netherlands: Spinhuis.

Vannini, P., D. Waskul, and S. Gottschalk. 2012. *The Senses in Self, Society and Culture: A Sociology of the Senses*. New York: Routledge.

Vila, A. C., ed. 2014. *A Cultural History of the Senses in the Age of Enlightenment, 1650–1800*. London: Bloomsbury.

Vinge, L. 1975. *The Five Senses: Studies in a Literary Tradition*. Lund: The Royal Society of the Humanities at Lund.

———. 2009. "The Five Senses in Classical Science and Ethics." In *The Sixth Sense Reader*, edited by D. Howes, 107–18. Abingdon: Routledge.

Voegelin, S. 2018. *The Political Possibility of Sound: Fragments of Listening*. London: Bloomsbury.

Wa, G., and D. Uukw. 1989. *The Spirit in the Land: The Opening Statement of the Gitskan and Wet'suwet'en Hereditary Chiefs in the Supreme Court of British Columbia*. Gabriola, BC: Reflections.

Walzer, M. 1983. *Spheres of Justice: A Defense of Pluralism and Equality*. Boston: Basic Books.

Wang, A. 2000. *Cosmology and Political Order in Early China*. Cambridge: Cambridge University Press.

Weiner, A. 1976. *Women of Value, Men of Renown: New Perspectives in Trobriand Exchange*. Austin: University of Texas Press.

Williams, R. 1976. *Keywords: A Vocabulary of Culture and Society*. London: Fontana.

Wittgenstein, L. 1922. *Tractatus Logico-Philosophicus*. London: Routledge & Kegan Paul.

———. (1953) 2009. *Philosophical Investigations*. 4th ed. Edited and translated by P. M. S. Hacker and J. Schulte. Oxford: Wiley-Blackwell.

———. 1967. "Remarks on Frazer's Golden Bough." *Synthese* 17:233–53.

———. 1977. *Remarks on Colour*. Edited by G. E. M. Anscombe. Oxford: Blackwell.

Wootton, D. 2007. *Bad Medicine: Doctors Doing Harm Since Hippocrates*. Oxford: Oxford University Press.

Yolgörmez, C., and J. Thibodeau. 2022. "Socially Robotic: Making Useless Machines." *AI and Society* 37 (2): 565–78.

Yong, E. 2015. "Why Do So Many Languages Have So Few Words for Smell? And Why do These Two Hunter-Gatherer Groups Have So Many?" *The Atlantic*, 6 November. https://www.theatlantic.com/science/archive/2015/11/the-vocabulary-of-smell/414618.

Zeng, B.-Y., and K. Zhao, eds. 2017. *Neurobiology of Chinese Herb Medicine*. International Review of Neurobiology, vol. 135. New York: Academic Press.

Zika, F. 2018. "Colour and Sound: Transcending the Limits of the Senses." In Howes, *Senses and Sensation*, 2:303–16.

Zubek, J., ed. 1969. *Sensory Deprivation: Fifteen Years of Research*. New York: Appleton-Century-Crofts.

Index

Aagaard, Jesper, 242n2
Amsterdam Centre for Cross-Cultural Emotional and Sensory Studies (ACCESS), 91
acoustemology, 62
acoustic, 9
　astronomy, 111
activity, 15, 17
　brain, 7, 118, 136, 224
　practical, 149–50
　theory, 143
aesth-ethics, 168, 169, 239n13
Aesthetic Formations, 87
aesthetic, 77, 113, 168, 216, 239n13
　action, 84
　industrial complex, 145, 164
aether, 161, 122
affect, 45, 78, 94–95
affective, 37, 45, 68, 94, 96, 165
affordance, 45, 146–47
African, 26, 53, 54
agent, 53, 134, 181, 228
agential, 43, 45, 96
agoraphobia, 98–101
Air, 6, 106, 119, 122, 128, 161
Alien Agency: Experimental Encounters with Art in the Making, 90
Andean, 89, 192, 202, 241n2
Anderson, Ben, 78
Angéras, Anaïs, 90
animals, 11, 24, 141, 167, 171–72, 206, 218
Anishnaabeg, 73–75
Ankersmit, Frank, 239n1
Annales School, 178
anthropological, 4, 49
　method, 3, 48
　research, 11, 30, 78, 81, 156, 180
　linguistics, 85–86
　turn, 180
Anthropologie et Sociétés, 35, 54, 179
anthropologist, 2, 4, 5, 11, 24, 48, 49, 51, 53, 61, 69, 79, 87, 88, 145, 147–48, 151, 172–73, 204, 218, 226–27, 237n1
　post-social, 148, 156
anthropology, 2, 3, 11, 21–22, 32, 36, 48–49, 81, 118, 144, 224, 227, 235n5
　art and, 11, 92, 228
　of the body, 5, 34, 64, 79
　as cultural critique, 118
　history and, 86, 180, 224
　medical, 79, 100, 235n3
　multimodal, 11, 82, 227
　physical, 5, 33
　visual, 4, 11, 48, 82, 101, 227
anthropology of the senses, 4, 5, 9, 12, 16, 17, 21, 47, 48–49, 55, 58–59, 64, 69, 71, 79, 81, 85, 87, 101, 113, 143–46, 149, 153, 162, 167, 173, 177, 181, 204, 227, 233n1, 235n2, 237n2, 240n4
archive, 43, 73
　sensory, 231
　state, 231
Arctic, 21, 29, 112
Arendt, Hannah, 13–16, 223
Aristotelian worldview, 119, 123, 228
Aristotle, 6, 119, 119–21, 123, 124, 128–30, 182–83, 187–88, 236n2
Arnheim, Rudolf, 134
Aroma: The Cultural History of Smell, 169, 170, 240n4

art(s), 9, 10, 11, 23, 41. 57, 73, 77, 92, 110, 151, 199–200, 233n4
  -based practice, 91
  gallery, 10
  separation of the, 189
artisan, 105–8, 170–71
artist, 10, 12, 39, 83–84, 85, 159, 236n5
association, 169–70
  cross-modal 185–86, 188
  extrinsic, 170
  of ideas, 128
  subjective, 165–66, 169
atmosphere, 36–38, 77–79, 84, 103, 111, 169
Atmospheres and the Experiential World, 79
auditory, 25, 29, 33, 53, 62, 197, 201
  culture, 87, 151
Australian, 26, 43, 83
authority, 49, 51, 96, 216, 218

Bach-y-Rita, Paul, 160
Baktaman, 50
Barad, Karen, 143
Barth, Fredrik, 50
Basic Color Terms, 85
Bedouin, 79
behaviorism, 136
Being and Hearing, 64
Benedict, Ruth, 29, 31, 97, 234n2
Bentham, Jeremy, 57
Berlin, Brent and Paul Kay, 85–86
Bertuzzi, Elena, 89
Bille, Mikkel, 78
Birth of the Clinic, The, 57
bitterness, 127, 185, 197, 202, 204, 206
Black, 26, 156, 238n6
blind, 88, 89, 129, 160
Blindness Through the Looking Glass, 64
Boas, Franz, 5, 21–22, 29–33, 36, 47, 156
body, 5, 10, 25, 39–42, 43–45, 59–60, 70, 120, 140, 141, 146, 150, 154, 157–58, 162, 183, 185, 189, 205, 218, 225, 234n7
  anthropology of the, 64–69, 79
  image, 205
  modification, 92
  synergic system of, 142, 162
  techniques, 34–37, 38, 65
Boesoou, 41
Böhme, Gernot, 38, 77–78, 235n4, 239n13
Böhme, Jakob, 127
Book of Touch, The, 240n4
Boring, Edwin, 233n2
Bowles, Laurian, 54–55
Boyle, Robert, 123, 125, 187
Boyle, Sheryl, 105–10
brain, 1–2, 6, 7–8, 22, 23, 59, 118, 133, 136, 138, 141, 157, 160, 183, 224–25
  fetishism, 1
British, 6, 16, 21, 28, 31, 34, 148, 198, 217, 222
Broca, Paul, 5, 21, 23–24, 33, 35, 47
Broglio, Ron, 152
building, 90, 106, 110
Bull, Michael, 86, 182

Calapi, Sisa, 87–89
Calder v. British Columbia, 217, 231
Callow v. Zollinger, 241n3
Cambridge Anthropological Expedition of 1898, 5, 24
Canada, 44, 75, 83, 92, 208, 211, 217, 221, 230–31, 237n3
Canadian, 29, 31, 73, 216, 75, 91, 130, 230–31
  constitution, 230, 237n3, 243n6
  society, 74, 84–85
Canaque (Kanak), 38–42
Cangjie, 184
capital, 132
  accumulation, 132, 211, 237n8
  capitalism, 132, 187
Carpenter, Edmund, 145, 147
Cartesianism, 134, 225
Carver, John, 211–13
Cashinahua, 59
Castaing-Taylor, Lucien, 11, 227

Castel, Louis Bertrand, 160
Cavendish, Margaret, 1, 140–42, 225
Center for the Study of Material and Visual Cultures of Religion (MAVCOR), 91
Centre for Sensory Studies, 90, 102
ceremonial, 62, 70, 74, 210, 215, 218
chemical, 125
    al-, 106, 108, 211
    revolution, 125
chemist, 123, 125
chemistry, 125
    astro-, 111
China, 181–89, 190–207, 230
Chinese, 35, 76, 183–207, 230, 239n3, 240n1
Christianity, 110, 120, 131, 237n8
civilization, 28, 37, 73, 180, 189, 190, 220
    disease of, 234n1
    of the image, 57
Classen, Constance, 48, 72, 88, 120, 127, 140, 142, 145, 187, 233n1, 233n2, 235n2, 240n4, 241n2
Clifford, James, 49, 51
clock, 193–95, 212
cognitive, 42, 66, 118, 132, 134, 150
    revolution, 118, 133
cognitivism, 118, 134
Collins, Genevieve, 110–12, 236n5
colonial, 83, 172, 208–17, 220, 230
colonization, 192, 210–11, 215, 241n1
    de-, 85
Color of Angels: Cosmology, Gender and the Aesthetic Imagination, The, 140
color, 9, 17, 23, 24, 26, 30, 56, 59, 79, 120, 123, 127, 135, 148, 157–60, 164, 185–86, 188, 203
    and sound, 159–60
    terms, 24, 85–86
Columbus, Christopher, 209
Colville, Alex, 236n5
communication, 4, 8, 35, 50, 61, 65, 82, 85, 91, 166, 184, 213–14
computation(al), 134, 137

computer, 6, 45, 134, 137
Confucius, 186
confusion, 9, 186, 200–201
connectionism, 138
consciousness, 8, 39, 41, 72, 136, 138, 139, 167, 225, 227
con-sensus, 4, 17, 84–85, 96, 181, 226, 236n2
consumer, 145, 163, 168, 170–73
contact, 183, 208
    first, 13, 180, 194
context, 24, 25, 48, 72–73, 146, 156, 160, 167, 168, 171, 201, 207, 224
contract, 130, 132, 187
    social, 131
Corbin, Alain, 12, 177–81, 229, 239n1
correspondence, 70, 159. 185, 188
    cross-modal, 62, 158
Cortés, Hernando, 208
cosmos, 6, 41, 59, 117, 122, 126, 127, 131, 186, 187
Cox, Rupert, 63, 233n1
Csordas, Thomas, 65, 69
cuisine, 4, 32, 54
Culhane, Dara, 11, 82, 89
Cultural History of the Senses, 90, 135, 233n2
cultural, 8, 12, 27, 31, 37, 42, 48, 50, 54, 63, 78, 145, 168, 171, 181, 224, 226, 240n1
    cross-, 17, 85, 183, 207, 222, 228, 229, 231, 242n3
    equation, 31
    exchange, 181, 191, 207
    forms, 219
    inter-, 85, 210
    infra-, 147
    intra-, 64, 88
    mediation, 145, 224
    patterning, 31
    practice, 118
    pre-, 156
    relativism, 33
    studies, 9
    values, 2

Culture and the Senses: Bodily Ways of Knowing in an African Community, 8, 10, 66, 149
culture, 8, 9, 13, 31, 32, 37, 49, 50, 51, 55, 61, 65, 71, 73, 81, 86, 87, 91, 118, 146–47, 151–52, 189, 207, 223, 224
   legal, 208
   sensing, 227
   as text, 52
   writing, 49–50, 51, 81, 227

dairy industry, 171–72
dance, 23, 89, 214–17
Daniel, Valentine, 161–62
data, 44–45, 52, 59, 227
   sense, 138
datafication, 43, 227
David, Johnny, 218–19
De Anima, 6, 120
deaf, 27, 63–64
Debaene, Vincent, 36, 37, 234n5
Delgamuukw v. A.G., 217–21
Delgamuukw v. British Columbia, 217, 221, 231
Denney, Peter, 189, 240n4
Deroy, Ophelia, 158
Derrida, Jacques, 58, 89
Desana, 59–60, 83, 237n4
Descartes, René, 120, 133, 134, 140, 225
Description of a New World Called the Blazing World, The, 141–42
description, 48, 52, 125, 179, 203, 204
   scientific, 37
   thick, 50–51, 82
design, 70, 122, 145, 167–68, 197, 199, 215
   anthropology, 55, 167
   sensory, 79, 91, 102
determinism, 24
   racial, 33
device, 112, 195
   digital, 44
   mechanical, 195
   mobile, 42
   optical, 125
   prosthetic, 160
   self-tracking, 226
dialogue, 51–52
Dias, Nélia, 22, 24
difference, 13, 24, 29, 31, 121, 165, 169, 242n3
   just noticeable, 31, 42
   racial, 23, 28
Different Kind of Ethnography, A, 11, 82
disability, 64
disciplinary, 87, 91
   inter-, 83, 91, 113
discourse, 52. 57, 91, 102, 134, 178, 217, 233n5
"Displace," 83
dis-sensus, 4, 17, 226
diversity, 14–15, 88
   sensory, 55, 64, 224
Do Kamo: Person and Myth in the Melanesian World, 39
doctrine, 120, 128, 129, 150, 151, 203
   of direct perception, 151
   psychophysical, 31
   racist, 29
Doerksen, Mark, 92–94
Doing Sensory Ethnography, 10, 101
Douglas, Mary, 35, 65
Downcast Eyes: The Denigration of Vision in Contemporary French Thought, 55, 57
drawing, 11, 40–41, 82, 89
drum, 62, 74, 84–85, 219
Dubois, Danièle, 132–34
Duchamp, Marcel, 57
Dudgeon, John, 202
Dudley, Sandra, 72
Dummett, Michael, 16
Dürer, Albrecht, 57, 140
Durkheim, Emile, 234n4

Eagle Down is Our Law: Wet'suwet'en Law, Feats and Land Claims, 218

ear, 1, 25, 26, 32, 59, 62, 129, 141, 152, 154, 160, 183–84, 200, 214, 241n1
  naked, 152
early modern, 7, 9, 12, 181, 190–92, 194, 195, 205, 211, 230
Earth, 6, 119, 122, 161, 185, 186, 212
Eastern Woodlands, 73, 75, 84, 211, 215
eating, 150, 184, 216
economy, 13
  gift, 211
  market, 211
Egushawa, 215
Elements, the, 6, 78, 119, 122, 123, 125, 128, 131, 132, 161, 182, 185, 202, 228
Elisha, Omri, 238n8
Elliott, Denielle, 11, 82, 89
embodiment, 53, 65, 69
empiricist, 135, 137
emplacement, 69
End of the Cognitive Empire: The Coming of Age of Epistemologies of the South, The, 243n5
energy, 7, 26, 53, 60, 101
English, 27, 34, 86, 134, 139, 148, 198, 211
  language, 86
English-Speaking Justice, 131, 236n5
environment, 33, 38, 69, 78, 93, 110, 112–13, 120, 122, 146–47, 149–53, 160, 164, 167, 168, 172, 192–93, 206
  immersive, 194, 228
  performative sensory, 83–85, 228
epistemic, 106, 107, 139, 233n5
epistemology, 54, 55, 144
  sensuous, 59
equality, 228–29, 230
  complex, 229
equivalents, 151, 157, 158
Essay Concerning Human Understanding, An, 6, 123, 128, 129, 188

essential, 58
  quint-, 122, 172
"ETHER," 111
ethnography, 51–53, 88, 162, 204
  imaginative, 11, 82
  poetic, 97
ethos, 36–37
Europe, 7, 13, 88, 187, 190–207, 196
European, 12, 25, 28, 40, 172, 190–207, 208–14, 230
Evans-Pritchard, E.E., 41, 179
evidence, 29, 124, 220, 231
evolutionary, 23, 24, 29, 30, 41, 85–86
  psychology, 242n2
experiential, 5, 48, 158, 205–6
experimental, 5, 29, 48, 91, 140, 142
  housewife, 142
ExperiSens, 111, 236n5
exploitation, 171, 192, 206
"Explorations in Sensory Design," 79, 102
Exploring Atmospheres Ethnographically, 79
eye, 1, 25, 26, 29, 40, 56, 58, 59, 60, 63, 100, 107, 111, 119, 124, 128, 141, 150, 151–52, 154, 159, 160, 181, 183, 184, 236n4, 241n1
  cat's 194
  evil, 128
  innocent, 152

Far Afield: French Anthropology Between Science and Literature, 36
Farquhar, Judith, 204–206, 239n3
feast, 216, 218–19, 221, 230
Febvre, Lucien, 178, 239n1
feeling(s), 14, 38, 64, 66, 68, 70, 77, 93, 112, 133, 168, 206, 238n12
Feld, Steven, 61–63, 68, 151
feminist, 46, 54, 55, 139–42
fieldwork, 4, 24, 69, 227
Filmer, Robert, 129
Finnegan, Ruth, 5, 8
Fire, 5, 119, 122, 161, 183, 185

flavor, 53, 59, 88, 107, 120, 163, 185, 203
  causation, 204
Fluid Signs: Being a Person the Tamil Way, 161
food, 53–54, 163–64, 167, 205, 236n5
formal, 180, 208, 222, 223, 235n4
Fortune, Reo, 69
Foucault, Michel, 57–58, 178, 204, 233n5
Foul and the Fragrant: Odor and the French Social Imagination, The, 178, 179
"Foundations for an Anthropology of the Senses," 88
France, 22, 33, 35, 130, 178
Frazer, James George, 17
French, 23, 24, 31, 34, 36, 55, 56–58, 132, 133, 177, 190, 211
  anthropology, 21, 36, 87
Fretwell, Erica, 234n3
Friedner, Michele, 63–64

Galileo, 118
gambling casino, 103–4
Garneau, David, 73–74, 84–85
gaze, 54, 57, 102, 140, 235n3, 241n1
Geaney, Jane, 183, 184
Geertz, Clifford, 14–17, 49–50, 235n1, 242n3, 243n4
Gélard, Marie-Luce, 87
Gell, Alfred, 145, 147
gender, 2, 13, 22, 49, 140, 154, 155–56
generic, 155–56
  individual, 156
geography, 70, 171
  gastronomic, 54
  of the senses, 86–87, 88
gesture, 14, 88, 103
Geurts, Kathryn Linn, 5, 8, 10, 66–68, 149, 225–226
Gibson, J.J., 143, 144–47
gift, 211, 213, 216
Gitksan-Wet'suwet'en, 217–21
Glenn, H.P., 241n3
globalization, 13, 181, 206
Goodman, Steve, 64

goods, 49, 145, 173, 209, 210–11, 222, 229, 230
Gottschalk, Simon, 235n7
Graif, Peter, 64
Granet, Marcel, 35
Grant, George, 130–32, 236n5, 237n7, 237n8, 243n4
Greece, 131, 185
Greenberg, Clement, 9
grinder subculture, 92–94
Grontkowski, Christine, 143
Groupe de recherche Cultures sensibles, 91
gustemology, 54

habitus, 12, 69, 179, 204
Haddon, A.C., 21, 24, 25
Hamel, George, 209
Hamilakis, Yannis, 233n5
Hammer, Gili, 64
handling, 75–76
Hannerz, Ulf, 4
Haraway, Donna, 143
Hart, Lynn, 239n1
Hausa, 59
head, 1–2, 6, 14–15, 54, 128, 141, 225, 242n2
Healing Sounds from the Malaysian Rainforest: Temiar Music and Medicine, 60
healing, 60, 74, 203, 235n3
hearing, 6, 22, 23, 27, 56, 63–64, 66, 119–23, 149, 151–52, 154, 157, 158, 161, 184, 189, 216, 217
  not-, 63–64
hearsay, 219
Heart Band, 84–85
heart, 54, 85, 127, 183, 205
  -mind (*xin*), 183–84, 216
heat, 60, 127, 206
  body, 10
Heller-Roazen, Daniel, 121
Helmreich, Stefan, 63–64
Herzfeld, Michael, 48
hierarchy, 4, 23
  sensory, 22, 147, 159, 184

"Histoire et anthropologie sensorielle," 12, 179, 229
historians, 2, 9, 12, 25, 55, 151, 159, 177, 179, 180, 220, 233n2
historical anthropology of the senses and sensations, 12, 177, 180, 181, 229, 239n1
history, 2, 12, 41, 42, 58, 172, 177, 204, 216, 224, 239n1
  anthropology and, 12, 42, 179–80, 224, 228, 229
  anthropological turn, 180
  art, 41, 91, 110, 151
  global, 189
  of law, 233n6
  natural, 25
  oral, 219, 221, 231
  of psychology, 133, 233n2, 233n6
  of the sensible, 12, 178
  as written record, 219
history of the senses, 5, 12, 17, 86, 87, 177, 179, 180, 181, 189, 226, 233n1, 233n2, 240n4
Hobbes, Thomas, 130, 132, 220
Hobsbawm, Eric, 180
Hoffer, Peter Charles, 209, 241n1
Honouring the Truth, Reconciling for the Future, 236n1
Hot and the cold, wet and the dry, 119
Hsu, Elisabeth, 233n1, 240n3
Huizinga, Johan, 239n1
human, 8, 9, 34, 36, 44–46. 73, 113, 123, 130–31, 148, 164, 226
  -machine, 93–97
  object-, 76
  post-, 97
Hume, David, 128
Huron, 211
Huybregts, Ekaterina, 44–45

identity, 15
idiosyncrasy, 2, 14, 157
image, 14, 32, 57, 59, 84, 112, 137, 141, 151–52, 187, 204, 206
  -based inquiry, 10
imagination, 77, 199
immersion, 22, 36–37

implant, 92–93
Impressionism, 56–57
Inca Cosmology and the Human Body, 240n4
Indigenous, 84, 125, 208–212, 222–23, 230
  artifacts, 76
  artists, 83
  peoples, 5, 12, 21, 23, 25, 28, 30, 74, 75, 84, 192, 202, 221, 230
  sovereignty, 230
  wisdom, 84
individual, 2, 37, 39, 43, 88, 118, 130, 146, 148–49, 154, 156, 186–87, 228, 238n7, 238n9, 242n3
  experience, 65, 155
  subject, 118, 154
individualism, 148
  possessive, 2, 129, 132, 187
information, 43, 133
  pick-up, 147, 153
  processing, 6, 7, 44, 133, 138
Ingold, Tim, 143, 144–57, 162, 237n1, 237n2, 237n4, 238n5, 238n7
  interchangeability of the senses hypothesis of, 150–52, 156, 157, 160, 238n5
Inner Touch: Archaeology of a Sensation, The, 121
intellect, 15, 23, 25–26, 95, 110, 183, 234n1
interchangeable, 132, 146–47, 156, 157, 228, 242n3
interpretation, 4, 50, 52, 77, 147, 177
intersensoriality, 63, 64, 162, 226
intersensory, 4, 10, 113, 162, 204, 224
  relations or connections (cooperation, domination, hierarchy, reciprocal, sequencing, threshold, translation), 158–59
introspectionist, 135, 136, 137
Inuit, 21, 29, 231
Iroquois, 214
isolation, 100, 111, 187

Jackson, Michael, 65, 69
Janda, Richard, 241n3

Jay, Martin, 55–57
Jones, Caroline A., 9–10
Jordanova, Ludmilla, 143
Journal of American History, 180
Journal of Sensory Studies, 166
judgment, 14, 36, 129, 165, 223
Jukier, Rosalie, 241n3
justice, 3, 131, 228–29, 243n4
  better part of, 3
  liberal democratic, 131
  multicultural, 223
  and the senses, 13, 17
Jütte, Robert, 233n2

Kaluli, 62
Kandinsky, Wassily, 160
Kangxi, 199, 202
Kant, Immanuel, 77, 133, 235n4
Kapoor, Shivani, 54
Kasirer, Nicholas, 241n3
Keats, John, 128
Keller, Evelyn Fox, 143
kinaesthetic, 10, 32, 33, 89
Kirmayer, Laurence, 65
knowledge, 1, 23, 30, 39, 44, 50, 57, 59, 122, 140–41, 142, 146, 149, 193, 219, 225, 233n5, 235n6
  medical, 142, 191
  objective, 23, 37
  scientific, 140, 157
Korzybska, Helma, 87–89
Kula Ring, 70–71
Kuriyama, Shigehisa, 240n4
Kwoma, 70–71

L'Hirondelle, Cheryl, 83–84
laboratory, 2, 5, 6, 12, 25, 27, 42, 167, 168, 169, 171, 234n6, 236n5
  sensory evaluation research, 144, 167
Laforet, Andrea, 75
Lahne, Jake, 170–72, 235n7, 239n14
Lakoff, George and Mark Johnson, 77
Lambert, Roseline, 97–100, 236n4
Lamer, Antonio, 221
land, 208, 216, 218, 230
  -scape, 56, 152, 153

Lange, Christian, 189, 240n4
language, 4, 14, 15–17, .24, 30, 32, 53, 85–86, 138, 204, 205
  -based inquiry, 10
  written, 220
Laplantine, François, 4, 67, 239n13
Lavoisier, Antoine, 125
Law and the Senses: Sensational Jurisprudence, 234n8
law, 3, 14, 17, 36, 132, 216, 222, 233n6, 241n3
  Aboriginal, 217, 221
  as code, 217
  customary, 208
  common, 221, 241n3
  of evidence, 231
  as feast, 230
  and morality, 36
  natural, 132
  as sensed, 217
Lawrence, Sidra, 54
Le Breton, David, 35
Le Roy Ladurie, Emmanuel, 180
Leavitt, John, 239n1
Leenhardt, Maurice, 5, 38–41, 47, 226
legal, 216–17, 219, 221, 230
  culture, 208, 223
  interaction, 222
  pluralism, 3, 217
  practice, 215, 241n3
  reasoning, 222
  sensori-, 217
  socio-, 234n8
Lévi-Strauss, Claude, 83, 125
Lévy-Bruhl, Lucien, 38, 39, 41
Life of Lines, The, 155, 237n1
Life of the Senses, The, 4
life, 104, 124, 130, 146
  the good, 129
  second, 104
light, 56, 60, 78–79, 84, 98, 100, 101, 127, 129, 135, 152–53, 194, 199
Lingua, or the Combat of the Tongue, and the Five Senses for Superiority, 122, 226
linguistic, 4, 32, 86–86, 236n1
  extra-, 16, 53

listening, 4, 9, 43, 61–62, 63, 67, 76, 154, 155, 162
Locative Tourism Applications: A Sensory Ethnography of the Augmented City, 102
Locke, John, 6, 7, 56, 117–18, 120, 123–32, 135, 187–88, 224, 236n4
Lockean empiricism, 118, 124
Louis XIV, 57
Lupton, Deborah, 43–45, 235n7, 235n8
Lynch, Erin, 101–4

Macdonald, Rod, 241n3
Macfarlane, Alan, 180
Machine Ménagerie, 94–95
machine, 93, 103, 137
   -human interaction, 94–97
   intelligence 95
   mutuality, 96
MacIntyre, Alasdair, 3, 243n5
Majid, Asifa, 85
male, 140, 156
Malinowski, Bronislaw, 69, 70
Maniq, 86
Manouvrier, Léonce, 24
Manual of Ethnography, 35
Marchetti, Florencia, 234n5
Marchionni, Anna-Livia, 88, 89
Marcus, George, 49
Marr, David, 137–38
masculine, 142, 155
   bias, 140
   pronoun, 155–56
   scientific establishment, 141
Maslen, Sarah, 43–45, 235n7, 235n8
Massasoit, 211–13
Massim, 69–71
material, 123, 127, 201, 204
   culture, 189
materiality, 47, 71–72, 151, 198, 240n3
Matthews, Maureen, 75–76
Mauss, Marcel, 5, 33–39, 45, 47, 65, 149, 225, 226, 234n4, 242n1
   triple viewpoint of, 34, 45
Mazzella di Bosco, Marie, 87, 89
McDougall, William, 25, 27–29

McEachern, Allan, 217, 219–21
McLuhan, Marshall, 8
Mead, Margaret, 5, 31–32, 47, 49, 52, 97, 226, 234n2
meaning, 14, 15, 16, 51, 63, 65, 73, 127, 133, 134, 147, 170, 182, 187, 188, 207, 222
   linguification of, 11, 227
measurement, 125, 165, 226
mechanical, 127, 194–95
media, 5, 8, 45, 53, 89, 119, 219, 233n3
mediation, 8–10, 65, 102, 145, 152, 204, 209, 224, 234n8
medium, 8, 48, 53, 65, 78, 84, 152, 161, 213, 219, 221
Meilgaard, Morten, 164
men, 141, 156
   of science, 22–24, 140
Mendeleev, Dmitri, 125–26
mentalities, 41, 178, 230
   "primitive," 41
Merleau-Ponty, Maurice, 57, 64, 143, 145–46, 154–56, 157–58, 162, 226
Mesure des sens, La, 22
Métis, 84–85, 231
Métraux, Rhoda, 32, 52
Meyer, Birgit, 87
Mi'kmaq, 222
microscope, 6, 10, 117, 124, 141, 236n4
migration, 13, 206
Miller, Christopher, 209
Mills, Antonia, 218, 219
mind, 4, 6, 15, 69, 118, 122, 123, 128, 134, 136, 137, 138, 139, 140, 188, 230, 237n2
   -body dualism, 69, 154
   as computer, 5, 137
   enlargement of, 13–14, 16, 222–23
   extended, 225, 242n2
   heart- (*xin*), 183–84
Minsky, Marvin, 137
Mintz, Sidney, 172
Minuit, Peter, 209
missionaries, 26, 38, 41, 190, 195, 196, 199, 202, 213

modern, 7, 10, 29, 120, 123, 125, 127, 131, 151, 154, 172, 181, 193, 199, 202, 203, 205, 207, 224
  postmodern, 52, 54–55, 235n1
Mohawk Interruptus: Political Life Across the Borders of Settler States, 241n1
Monet, Claude, 56
money, 70–71
mood, 38, 103
Mopas, Michael, 44–45
moral, 15, 37, 131, 139, 150, 211
  atmosphere, 37
  reasoning, 14, 15
  tone, 35–36, 38
  value, 149
movement, 89, 127, 137, 146, 154–55, 238n8
MRI machine, 2
multisensoriality, 215
Munch, Edvard, 98
Mungello, David, 191
Munn, Nancy, 69, 71, 153
Museum Materialities, 72
Museum of the Senses, The, 72
museum, 72–76, 83
music, 23, 53, 61, 63–64, 66, 77, 82, 85, 159, 184–85, 187, 199, 200–201
Myers, Charles, 25–29

Natives and Newcomers: Canada's 'Heroic Age' Reconsidered, 211
nature, 73, 117, 127, 140–42, 187
  state of 130, 132
Naytowhow, Joseph, 84
Nedelsky, Jennifer, 14
negotiation, 50–52, 181, 222
network, neuronal, 7, 138
  interrelational, 186
neuromania, 1, 134
neuron, 7, 9, 136–38
neuroscience, 1–2, 118, 134, 224
neurotypical, non-, 88, 89
New Caledonia (Vanuatu), 38, 41
Newton, Isaac, 7, 127, 159
next generation, 80, 87, 90, 227

nineteenth century, 21–22, 26, 56, 178–79, 198, 202, 216
noise, 63, 71, 154
normalization, 3, 181
North American, 34, 98, 205
Norwegian, 99–100
nose, 1, 26, 62, 141, 179, 183
  period, 179
Nudds, Matt, 135–39
number, 43, 104, 121, 123, 125

object, 26, 37, 41, 50, 71–77, 86, 106, 107, 120–21, 129, 137, 140, 152
objectification, 41, 57, 140, 151
objective, 22, 23, 37–38, 58, 140, 160, 171, 204
  inter-, 97
observation, 3–4, 22, 23, 28, 58, 125, 151–52
  participant, 3, 48, 52
ocularcentric, 4, 56, 73–74
  anti-, 57–58
odor, 30, 59, 83, 120, 154, 161, 164, 194
  associations, 170
Oken, Lorenz, 25
Ong, Walter J., 8–9
ontogeny, 147–48
oral, 8, 36, 180, 215, 218, 220, 222, 230
  history, 219, 221, 231
  society, 8
Ordinary Affects, 82
organoleptician, 145, 163
Origin of Forms and Qualities, The, 123

Pacific Northwest Coast, 215
pain, 17, 25, 27–28, 161–62
painting, 9, 23, 56, 73–74, 84, 151–52, 160, 199–200
Panopticon, 57–58
parol evidence rule, 222
pattern, 31, 32, 36, 43, 23, 84, 135, 186, 239n3
  of brain activity, 7, 118, 224
  zheng, 239n3
Peraldi-Mittelette, Pierre, 87, 88

Perception of the Environment, The, 144, 145, 150
perception, 1–2, 14, 21, 23, 29–30, 42, 52, 54, 78, 82, 120–21, 124, 138–39, 146–47, 152, 186, 219, 224
   anthropology, 143, 146, 153, 155–56, 162, 237n1
   archaeology of, 12, 86, 110, 233n5
   auditory, 29–30
   circumference of, 7
   and cognition, 118
   consumer, 170–71, 239n14
   crisis of, 49
   direct, 145, 147, 151
   as information-processing, 44, 133
   mediation of, 152, 224
   as a mode of action, 147
   naturalization of, 138
   normalization of, 3
   philosophy of, 138
   physiology of, 31
   politics of, 13, 154
   primacy of, 57, 143
   recession of, 52, 54
   as representation, 138
   semantics of, 170
   and sensation, 66
   synaesthetic, 157–60
   transformation in, 127
   visual, 21, 147
performance, 26–27, 82, 94–95, 226
Periodic Table of Elements, 6, 125
person, 42, 73, 130, 132, 143, 161, 186, 225, 228
personal, 153, 194, 206
   equation, 23, 31
   perceptual style, 32
perspective, 2, 5, 14, 16, 140, 143, 171, 172, 195, 198, 208, 210, 221–22, 223
   anthropological-historical, 228
   intersensory, 4
   linear, 56, 57, 140, 199, 240n2
   scientific, 123
Peterson, Marina, 63

pharmaceutical, 201–2
Phenomenology of Perception, 143, 157
phenomenology, 5, 40, 65, 139, 143, 144, 155, 162, 173, 238n7
Philosophical Investigations, 17
philosophy, 56, 120, 127, 128, 132, 152, 186, 236n5
   analytic, 16, 140
   Aristotelian, 129
   corpuscular, 123, 187
   feminist, 139
   hermeneutic, 50
   natural, 117, 123, 128, 140
   of perception, 138
   phenomenological, 57, 65, 139, 144
   political, 129, 131
   sensationist, 117, 128
physics, 29, 60, 123, 125
physiology, 23, 25, 31, 34–35, 45, 118, 207
   neuro-, 136
picture, 12, 41, 179, 199–200, 219, 237n2
pilgrimage, 161–62
Pink, Sarah, 5, 10, 55, 101, 233n1
pipe, 213, 214–15
Plato, 56, 120, 140, 182
pollution, 172
polysensoriality, 228
porcelain, 76, 196–99, 207, 230
Porteous, J. Douglas, 152
potlatch, 215–17
practice, 34, 170
   critical, 118
premodern, 6, 122, 140, 154, 188, 193, 202
Presence of the Word, The, 8
presence, 66, 69–71, 78, 89, 147, 209, 219
private, 2, 14, 17, 134
product, 168–73
   aesthetics, 168
   attributes, 166
   development, 163–64
   luxury, 196, 197

properties, 7, 72, 90, 123–24, 125, 135, 138, 163, 170, 202
property, 130
Provost, René, 241n3
psychologist, 2, 42, 120, 133–34, 147, 158
psychology, 1–2, 6, 17, 42, 118, 135, 156, 205, 225, 228, 233n6
  cognitive, 132–33
  and cosmology, 6, 228
  cross-cultural, 228
  ecological, 143, 144, 150
  experimental, 6, 25, 34, 42
  evolutionary, 242n2
  Gestalt, 135–36
  Indian, 161
  of the marketplace, 132
  and philosophy, 138
  and physiology, 34, 45, 242n1
  and psychophysics, 164, 167
  and sociology, 34, 45, 242n1
  Western perceptual, 5, 14, 66, 188, 224, 233n1
psychophysics, 5, 21, 22, 25, 29, 33, 42, 13, 145, 156, 164, 167, 226, 234n3

qualia, 83, 106, 123–24, 134
  quantifying, 134
  qualification of, 134
qualitative, 122, 125
qualities, 123, 124
  gustatory, 198
  olfactory, 198
  sensory, 127
  tactile, 119, 199
  visual, 199

racial(ized), 2, 13, 22, 25, 33, 154, 226
  difference, 23, 28
  taxonomy, 23
Rapport, Nigel, 148
rationality, 3, 56, 65, 209
  and lucidity, 56
Rawls, John, 131, 229, 236n6, 237n7
reality, 51, 65, 132, 138
  augmented, 101, 227
  perceptual, 158
  recession of, 57
reason, 22, 25, 130, 131, 182, 183, 222
  as calculation, 130
  as ratiocination, 130
receptor, 7–8, 118, 128, 134, 135–36, 224
reflexivity, 15, 30, 32, 49, 89, 242n3
Regina v. Marshall, 222
Rentein, Alison Dundes, 242n32
Report on Indian Residential Schools, 84
representation, 22, 43, 50–53, 83, 137, 142, 146, 147, 204
  of the body, 39–41
  collective, 42, 134, 146, 237n3
  crisis of, 49
  of otherness, 83
  perception as, 138
  racist, 26
  tactile, 41
  visual, 41, 193
research-creation, 83, 91–92, 228
retinal, 56–57, 89
revolution, 227
  behaviorist, 133
  chemical, 125
  cognitive, 6, 118, 133
  digital, 134
  psychological, 117
  scientific, 6, 117, 123
  sensorial, 113
  textual, 49, 235n1
Ricci, Matteo, 199, 200
Rice, Tom, 63
Ricoeur, Paul, 50
ritual, 50, 59, 65, 161–62, 185, 214–15
  Christian, 187
Rivers, W.H.R., 5, 21, 25–29, 47
Roberts, Lissa, 125
robot, 94, 137
Romanyshyn, Robert, 56
Rome, 7, 13
Roseman, Marina, 60, 61, 235n3

Routledge Handbook of Sensory Archaeology, The, 86

Sacks, Oliver, 9
Salter, Chris, 83, 91, 236n3
Santos, Boaventura de Sousa, 243n5
Sapir, Edward, 31, 91, 234n2
Sartre, Jean-Paul, 57
Sarukkai, Sundar, 238n11
Schafer, R. Murray, 151
Schulze, Holger, 63
Schwartzman, Madeline, 233n4
science, 61, 119, 123, 139
   between art and, 91
   of the concrete, 125
   as housewifery, 142
   natural, 133, 139
   social, 87, 91, 113
   of subjectivity, 145, 164
scientific, 33
   attitude, 139, 143
   instruments, 164
Sears, Elizabeth, 131
See Yourself Sensing: Redefining Human Perception, 233n4
Seeger, Anthony, 145
self, 41, 49, 56, 121, 154–56, 161, 162, 211
   -contained, 41
   decentring of, 155
   -determination, 230
   -interest, 130–31
   neoliberal, 43
   qualified, 227
   quantified, 22, 42–46, 227
   -serving, 219, 220
   -tracking, 43- 45, 226
Senghor, Léopold Sédar, 225
sensation, 7, 10, 12, 17, 30, 43, 52, 53, 63, 68, 83, 120–21, 126, 133, 137, 146, 153, 161, 170, 188, 196, 199, 201, 206, 226, 234n8, 236n1
   atomic, 136, 137
   categorization of, 134
   and cognition, 1–2, 22, 66
   complex, 121
   electromagnetic, 92
   historical, 239n1
   joint, 158
   measurement of, 22
   medieval, 187
   participant, 4, 44, 48, 77, 98, 103, 168
   and perception, 1–2, 42
   philosophy, 117, 128
   pleasurable, 191
   privatization of, 7
   political life of, 118
   provinces of, 120–21
   quantification of, 165
   relations, 186
   retraction of, 8, 52
   sociality of, 12, 42, 45, 66, 224, 234n7
   subjective, 205
   symphony of, 83
sense, 10, 26, 30, 120–21, 133–34, 153, 169
   -based inquiry, 10, 110
   between the lines, 179, 181, 209, 229
   bounds of, 93, 113
   common, 2, 129, 130, 131, 219, 228
   the common (*sensus communis*), 121, 128–29, 130, 183, 188
   datum theory, 138
   experience, 2, 8, 31, 55, 88, 133, 136, 135, 145
   impressions, 2, 27, 31
   of justice, 3
   -making, 4, 12, 15, 16, 17, 44, 133, 159, 171, 182, 206, 226, 227, 235n8
   of the observer, 24, 179
   organ, 8, 23, 118, 136
   -ratio, 8
   of self, 162
   sixth, 120–22
   uncommon, 2, 17, 228
   universe of, 126

Senses and Sensation: Critical and Primary Sources, 90
Senses and Society, The, 43, 54, 87, 91, 102, 189
senses, the, 2, 4, 6, 8, 16, 17, 24, 32, 45, 48, 56, 58, 76, 77, 92, 120, 122, 128, 129, 130, 131, 134, 135, 147, 159, 167, 169, 182, 184, 187, 224, 228, 241n1
  bewitchments of, 198
  body and, 25, 45
  chemical, 125
  collapse, 161
  confinement of, 6
  and cosmos, 6, 117
  decolonization of, 85
  democratization of, 141
  and the elements, 128, 161, 182–83, 228
  embrace, 133
  five, 5, 6, 83, 119, 120–22, 128, 161, 182–83
  fun for all, 103
  hierarchy of, 22, 25, 150, 184
  justice, 231
  leading with, 133
  measurement of, 5, 21, 22, 42, 164–65
  and moral norms, 150
  nonvisual, 24
  as perceptual systems, 146
  prereflective unity of, 151, 157
  as receptors, 118
  as relationally produced, 2, 17, 58, 226
  separation of. 189
  socialization of, 118
  social life of, 2, 87
  and social values, 201
  techniques of, 118, 226, 235n8
  time of, 231
  subjectification of, 14
  union/unity of, 121, 151, 156–57, 160
  vanquish, 162

sensible, the (*le sensible*), 2, 3, 4, 12, 61, 67, 93, 110, 121, 127, 178
  common, 121, 124
  politics of, 224
  proper, 121, 124
  qualities, 124
  (re)distribution of, 96, 118
Sensibles ethnographies, 87–89
Sensing the Nation's Law, 234n6
sensing, 13, 44–46, 64, 82, 118, 121, 133
  between the lines, 179, 181, 229
  cultures, 227
sensitivism, 118, 134, 239n1
sensor, 7, 44, 85
  society, 235n8
Sensorial Investigations, 2, 17, 224, 229, 234n8
sensorium, 2, 7–9, 13, 17, 29, 42, 59, 62, 77, 78, 86, 120, 143, 162, 223, 226, 230, 242n2
  Anlo-Ewe, 65–66
  being of two, 15, 33, 162
  Cashinahua, 59
  common, 13
  Desana, 59–60, 83
  extended, 225
  five-sense model of, 120, 122, 183
  more-than-human, 45
Sensorium: Embodied Experience, Technology and Contemporary Art, 9–10
"Sensory Entanglements," 83–84
Sensory Ethnography Lab, 11, 91
Sensory Experiences: Exploring Meaning and the Senses, 133
Sensory Experiments: Psychophysics, Race and the Aesthetics of Feeling, 234n3
Sensory Studies Manifesto, The, 17, 236n2
Sensory Worlds in Early America, 209
sensory, 9, 13, 16, 23, 26, 28, 43, 66, 79, 93, 135, 182, 187, 227
  acuity, 5, 25

analysis, 48–49, 164, 167, 239n14
anthropology, 4, 47–49, 55, 58, 69, 87, 101, 144–45, 149, 153, 167, 204, 227, 237n2
archive, 231
capabilities, 23, 25
connection, 76, 159, 161
cosmology, 6, 59–60, 120, 127, 235n2
deprivation, 166
design, 167–68
diversity, 55, 64, 224
ethnography, 10, 11, 46, 55, 67, 87, 89, 97, 102, 167, 172, 206, 227
exchange, 13, 181, 191, 199, 206
experience, 3, 47–48, 152, 171, 193, 204, 224, 226, 239n14
expression, 4, 61, 85
evaluation, 144, 163–67, 169–71, 236n5
history, 12, 86, 179, 233n2, 233n6
imperialism, 241n1
integration, 66
inter-, 113, 204
labour, 160, 235n7
model, 59, 182
modulation, 203
museology, 72–73, 75
multi-, 45, 50, 62, 82, 89, 91, 107, 113, 215
order, 13, 69, 141, 188, 189, 240n4
politics, 54
poly-, 62, 66
practice, 29, 201, 222
processing, 2, 66, 133, 157, 224
professional, 145, 163–66, 169–70
properties, 72, 90, 163, 202
qualities, 127, 138, 163, 166, 171, 181, 191
(re)construction, 105
reflexivity, 32
regime, 3, 88, 18
revolution, 133
science, 145, 166, 167, 172–73
specialization, 149

studies, 17, 64, 80, 86, 87, 102, 118, 233n1, 234n8
turn, 4, 21, 61, 72, 80
values, 88, 182, 191, 208, 223
vocabularies, 27
ways of knowing, 43
work, 44, 235n7
sensuality, 5, 62, 129, 196
Sensuous Scholarship, 2344n8
sentience, 1, 73, 94–96, 183, 242n2
seselelame, 66
settler, 222–23, 230
city skyline, 84
Shapin, Steven, 145, 164
sight, 22–23, 58, 61, 119, 122, 124–25, 149, 151–52, 161, 182, 184, 200
eyesight, 9, 218–19
and hearing, 151, 184
and touch, 197, 215
and water, 119
sign, 14–15, 88, 147, 151, 195, 236n1, 239n3
sign language, 63
signature, 214, 215
Simmel, Georg, 16, 72, 234n7
Simpson, Audra, 241n1
sixteenth century, 178, 191
Skeates, Robin, 233n5
skill, 146, 149
skin, 26, 27, 59, 66, 70
Skinner, B.F., 136
smell, 54, 150, 153, 154, 161–63, 178, 182, 184, 185, 191, 194, 196, 203
Smith, John, 209
Smith, Mark M., 180, 233n2
smoke, 84, 213–14
smoking complex, 84, 213
social, 4, 17, 23, 37, 42, 71–72, 99, 148–49, 154, 167, 171, 182, 216, 229
constructionist, 147
contract, 130–32
force, 76, 154
interaction, 14, 16, 73

social *(continued)*
   order, 187–88, 201
   post-, 148, 156
   practice, 34
   prestige, 196, 198
   relations, 53, 65, 186, 191
   sciences, 34, 87, 91, 113
   and the sensible, 61
   structure, 148, 156
Société d'Anthropologie de Paris, 5, 21–24, 34
society, 130, 148, 182, 187, 228
sociology, 3, 16, 34, 45, 91, 234n6, 242n1
   of the senses, 72, 86, 234n7, 235n7
somatic, modes of attention, 65–66
   work, 235n7
song, 148, 214, 222
Songhay, 53–54, 60
Sonic Color Line, The, 238n6
sound, 8, 11, 14, 30, 53, 61–64, 71, 84, 88, 111–12, 123, 126, 127, 129, 153–54, 158, 159–60, 164, 178, 187, 188, 193–94, 195, 201, 238n6, 238n10
   -scape, 102, 151–52
   studies, 63–64
   -walk, 153, 227
space, 40, 42, 193
   outer, 110–12
   station, 112
Spackman, Christy, 235n7
spectacle, 56, 57, 84
speech, 8, 122, 215, 216, 222
Spence, Charles, 158
Spencerian hypothesis, 25–26, 28
spirit, 41, 127, 133, 210, 213–14, 241n1
spiritual, 162, 184, 201, 213–14
   songs, 218
Spring and Autumn period, 181, 186, 188
Springer, James Warren, 213–14
Sriram, Jayanthan, 239n13
Stafford, Edward, 105

state, 201, 223
   liberal democratic, 129
   of nature, 130, 132
statistics, 29, 36, 165–66
stereotype, 5, 28, 64, 156, 198
Stewart, Kathleen, 82
stimulation, 133, 135, 136
Stocking, George, 31
Stoller, Paul, 5, 8, 47, 53–54, 60–61, 145, 147, 226, 233n3, 234n8
style, 62, 84, 110, 131, 149–50, 152, 180, 199, 200, 201, 237n4
subject, 38, 56, 78, 154
   embodied, 57
   human, 164
   rights-bearing, 132
subjective, 14, 22, 165–66, 204–5
   inter-, 97
Supreme Court of Canada, 221–22, 231
surface, 85, 103, 117, 160, 189, 196, 200
sweetness, 127, 172
symbolic, 4, 50, 169
Synaesthetic Legalities, 234n6
synesthesia, 157–58, 235n3
   color-grapheme, 157
synesthete, 157–58
Synnott, Anthony, 90, 234n7

tactile, 32, 41, 76, 119, 160, 199
   sensitivity, 27–28
Tamil, 161–62
Taoism, 35
Taste of Ethnographic Things, The, 8, 47, 53–54, 233n3
taste, 2, 6, 22–23, 32, 54, 85, 103, 119, 120, 125, 129, 149, 150, 161, 163, 170
   culture, 87
   good, 172
   of place, 171
Taussig, Michael, 1
technique(s), 56, 149
   body, 34–35
   of the senses, 226, 235n8
Technologies of the Picturesque, 152

technology, 10, 44, 45, 134, 193
  audio, 9, 152
  relationship with, 44
telescope, 6, 110, 118, 141
temporal, 56, 78
test, 5, 27–28, 42, 125, 164–66, 169–70, 238n10
testimony, 218–20
text, 49–52
textual, 49, 51
  bias, 55
  -ism, 49
textualization, 52–54
texture, 54, 59, 124, 193, 201
Body Social: Symbolism, Self and Society, The, 234n7
Theory of Justice, A, 131
Thibodeau, Zeph, 94–97
third-person, 143
Thom, Brian, 219
Thomas, Keith, 180
Thompson, E.P., 180
Thornbury Castle, 105–7
thought, 16, 69, 73, 138, 178, 182, 184
three-dimensional, 39–41
Ting, Win Yang Vivian, 76–77
tobacco, 75, 192, 213–14
tongue, 1, 26, 122, 141, 226, 239n3
Torres Strait Islanders, 25–27
touch, 103, 119, 121–22, 148, 161, 182, 200, 215
tourism, 102
Tractatus Logico-Philosophicus, 16, 239n13
trade, 190–201, 209–11
  East-West, 12, 189
training, 28, 43, 62, 112, 149, 169, 200
transposition, 151, 157, 158, 188
treaty, 211, 222
  -making, 209, 211–15, 222
Trigger, Bruce G., 211
Trubek, Amy, 170–72, 239n14
Truth and Reconciliation Commission of Canada, 84, 243n3
Tuareg, 88

TVSS, 160
Two Treatises of Government, 123, 129
two-dimensional, 39–41
Tyler, Stephen, 52, 54, 235n1

universe, 122, 126
Urry, John, 158
Uzwiak, Beth, 54–55

value, 2, 41, 70, 77, 139, 140, 153, 164, 182, 191, 199, 200, 200, 211
  moral, 149
  quali-signs of, 153
  sensory, 88, 182, 191, 208, 223
  social, 201
Vannini, Phillip, 235n7
Varieties of Sensory Experience, The, 8, 47, 55, 145, 149
veil of ignorance, 131, 229
verbocentrism, 4, 16, 50
Vermont, 171–72
Verrips, Jojada, 87
vision, 8, 29, 43, 51, 52, 55, 56–59, 62, 63, 120–21, 124, 128, 134, 147, 150–51, 182, 193–95, 229, 236n4
  computer, 137
  double, 3, 15
  extramission theory, 128
  intromission theory, 128
  linear perspective, 56, 140
Visual Thinking, 134
visual, 4, 8, 21, 28, 29, 32, 55, 63, 76, 87, 102–3, 128, 147, 153, 159, 184, 193, 199–200
  anthropology, 4, 11, 48, 82, 101, 227
  bias, 55, 140
  culture, 87, 151–52
  -ism, 49, 55–56, 152–53, 227, 235n1
  realism, 199
  representation, 41
  tactile-, 160

visuality, 54, 58
visualization, 6, 43, 127

walk(ing), 11, 34, 82, 111, 150, 163, 155, 156, 184, 200, 227
Walzer, Michael, 229, 243n4
Wampanoag, 211–13
wampum, 215
Warring States period, 181, 183, 188
Waskul, Dennis, 235n7
Water, 6, 119, 122, 125, 161, 182, 185
Way of Life: Things, Thought and Action in Chinese Medicine, A, 239n1, 241n4
ways of sensing, 13, 60, 86, 149, 162, 168, 181, 222, 226, 237n1
Ways of Sensing: Understanding the Senses in Society, 233n6, 240n4
Weiner, Annette, 69
Wet'suwet'en, 217–21
white, 10, 26, 28, 70, 106, 124, 156, 167
  man, 216
  paper, 230, 243n6
Whitehead, A.N., 126
Whose Justice? Which Rationality? 243n5
Wildness and Sensation: Anthropology of Sinister and Sensuous Realms, 87
window, 56, 78–79, 98–99, 107, 110
Witchcraft, Oracles and Magic among the Azande, 179
Wittgenstein, Ludwig, 15, 16–17
women, 23, 44–45, 70, 140–42, 154, 155–56, 238n8
women, 44–45, 89, 140, 142, 154, 155

word, 33, 215
  and action, 184
  written, 209
worker, 23, 171, 172, 241n1
World Soundscapes Project, 151
world, 8, 15–16, 32, 40, 41, 50, 52, 54, 56, 63, 102, 117–18, 127, 136, 146, 157, 162, 164, 189, 192, 202, 211, 214, 225
  being-in-the-, 68–69, 71, 96
  blazing, 141–42
  -ing, 11, 82
  life-, 4, 204
  material, 6, 72, 120, 122, 123, 125, 223
  multicultural, 13
  natural, 140
  sensory, 88
  synthetic, 137
  -view, 8, 119, 138, 204, 223, 228, 235n2
Worlds of Sense: Exploring the Senses in History and Across Cultures, 240n4
Writing Culture: The Poetics and Politics of Ethnography, 49, 51, 52
writing, 8, 11, 49, 52, 82, 177, 189, 215, 219, 213, 220, 222, 230, 241n2,
  culture, 50, 81, 227
  history, 180, 239n1

Xichun, Zhang, 203

Yahkâskwan Mîkiwahp, 84–85
Yolgörmez, Ceyda, 95

Zika, Fay, 159–60